Riguito:

que cada d
vida sea gui
y que este libro
ser de utilidad para
encontrar una de
manera su
entender
voluntad.

ONE
YOU
ONE
YEAR

Te amamos
mucho
Tios Amilcar y
Peri y
tus primos
Alex, Isaac y
Eli

365 FOR BOYS

ONE YOU ONE YEAR

ASK. BELIEVE. EXPECT.

CWR

© CWR 2019

Published 2019 by CWR, Waverley Abbey House, Waverley Lane, Farnham, Surrey GU9 8EP, UK. CWR is a Registered Charity – Number 294387 and a Limited Company registered in England – Registration Number 1990308.

For a list of National Distributors, visit cwr.org.uk/distributors

Reading curriculum adapted from various issues of *YP's*, daily Bible reading notes for ages 11 -14, a four-year rolling programme published by CWR.

Scripture references are taken from Holy Bible, New International Version® Anglicised, NIV® Copyright © 1979, 1984, 2011 by Biblica, Inc.® Used by permission. All rights reserved worldwide.

Other versions are marked: *The Message*, Copyright © 1993, 1994, 1995, 1996, 2000, 2001, 2002 by Eugene H. Peterson. *Holy Bible*, New Living Translation, copyright © 1996, 2004, 2015 by Tyndale House Foundation. Used by permission of Tyndale House Publishers, Inc., Carol Stream, Illinois 60188. All rights reserved. The Passion Translation®. Copyright © 2017 by BroadStreet Publishing® Group, LLC. Used by permission. All rights reserved.

Concept development, editing, design and production by CWR.

Cover image: Pixabay/Pexels

Printed in the UK by Linney.

ISBN: 978-1-78259-994-4

CONTENTS

HOW TO USE ONE YOU, ONE YEAR

1 Each day, grab your Bible and your copy of **One You, One Year** and find somewhere where you won't get distracted. Talk to God and ask Him to help you understand what He wants to show you that day.

2 Turn to the right day in **One You, One Year** and find the Bible reference. If it says John 3:16 then go to the book of John (use your Bible contents to help with this), go to chapter 3 (look for a big '3') and finally find verse 16 (shown as a tiny 16).

3 When you've read from the Bible, read everything else on the page in **One You, One Year**. Pay attention to the 'Think' points, which help you consider how what you've read affects your life, and the 'Pray' points, which help you talk with God.

BEFORE WE KICK OFF...

LISTEN UP, LADS!

However you've ended up with this book in your hands, if you're a young guy and you want to explore more of life and faith, you've come to the right place.

There is only One You in the world. Not one person is the same as you – that makes you important! You're an original, so who knows you better than your maker? Try taking this One Year to get to more in-tune with God and see how your life changes as you go through 365 fascinating days.

If you've ever thought that following Jesus is boring, you're in for the shock of your life! We'll be looking at some top themes that we reckon you'll be interested in. The sort of stuff you've got to look forward to includes a guide to being bulletproof, the names of God, Jesus' hero academy, and some big names from the Bible. To mix things up a bit, between the sections you'll find some awesome readings from the Psalms. You *really* don't want to miss this.

There is One You and here is One Year guaranteed to change your life for the better. Are you up for it?

Give it a go!

BRING IT ON

READ: Ephesians 6:10–20

> **KEY VERSE:** 'Put on the full armour of God, so that you can take your stand against the devil's schemes.' (v11)

Did you know that we're in a battle? It's not a physical battle though. We are fighting the 'spiritual forces of evil'. Following Jesus makes Satan absolutely furious and he *will* pick fights against you to try and stop you living for Jesus. You'll be tempted to do things that God doesn't approve of. But, as Paul reminds us, we can 'be strong in the Lord and in his mighty power' (v1). We can be kitted out from head to toe in heaven-made armour and come out on top. Pretty cool, right?

The 'flaming arrows of the evil one' don't always appear on our radars. Our enemy fights dirty, and can be very, very sneaky. But Paul didn't expect us to go down, or give in. He tells us to stand against these forces, stand our ground, and stand strong – and over the next few days we'll see what armour we've got to help us with this. Bring it on!

PRAY Lord, thank You for providing me with spiritual armour to wear through life. Help me to remember there is nothing in the world that You can't defeat. Amen.

 **BULLETPROOF**

HEADS UP

READ: Isaiah 59:12–20

KEY VERSE: 'and the helmet of salvation on his head' (v17)

So, the first piece of armour that Paul lists in Ephesians: a helmet.

Have you ever heard of the idea that our minds can be like battlefields? Negative thoughts can sometimes seem to pop into our heads out of nowhere. And our thoughts affect us. They can creep into what we believe, and then how we behave.

How will a helmet of salvation sort this out? Well, our 'salvation' means that Jesus has saved us! He has saved us from sin; He has saved us from death! Although Satan tries to get it into our heads that God doesn't care about us or that we're not good enough for Him, if we're wearing that protective headgear, there's no way he'll get through. If we protect our minds by understanding that God has forgiven us, the way we see things can totally change. And if we fill our heads with the truth of how Jesus has saved us, it will spill out into the way we live our lives.

THINK Do you want this helmet? Do you want others to have it? It's free to anyone who believes that Jesus is Lord and asks for His forgiveness! We can't earn it, we just need to receive it.

CHOOSE YOUR ATTITUDE

READ: Philippians 2:1–11

KEY VERSE: 'have the same mindset as Christ Jesus' (v5)

Attitude is so important when taking on the opposition. If you go out there thinking it'll be easy, you could be in for a shock. If you go out there thinking you can do it on your own, you'll most likely be proved wrong.

The helmet of salvation helps us with more than just negative thinking. Some parts of our lives need extra protection. Our attitudes come under constant attack. Moodiness, stubbornness and arrogance are a constant threat that can damage our relationships with God and others. Going into action when we're feeling mean, self-centred and moody is the surest way to invite more trouble. It's not the way Jesus went into battle to save us.

Jesus' attitude was not 'me first' but 'God first'. He didn't arrive offering selfies with the crowds, He didn't come to be served but to serve others. His attitudes were controlled by love.

When we put on the helmet of salvation, Paul tells us we are to 'have the same mindset as Christ Jesus' (v5). That's a pretty big challenge! But let's adopt Jesus' way when we're with our friends – and with our enemies.

PRAY
Lord, I'm sorry for when my attitude is out of line. Help me to see things the way You do. Amen.

BULLETPROOF

THE HEART OF THE MATTER

READ: Romans 13:8–14

KEY VERSE: 'So let us put aside the deeds of darkness and put on the armour of light.' (v12)

Paul tells us to put on the 'breastplate of righteousness'. Righteousness is being 'right' with God, which is what we are when we accept Jesus. And where does the breastplate go? Right over the heart. And boy, do we need to protect our hearts out there!

Today's reading introduces us to three of Satan's tactics that can knock us to the ground if we're not prepared. He wants us to:

1. Be out of control. People do this in all sorts of ways, and sure – it might look like great fun. But we're not fit for battle if we're behaving stupidly and not engaging our brain cells!

2. Have wrong desires. The Bible is really clear on how we should behave romantically. When guys and girls start using each other and ignoring God's way for relationships, they're in the danger zone.

3. Be jealous. This can ruin relationships, and rust away your armour – leaving you exposed.

So how do we 'wear' our righteousness? Right across the heart. By getting right with God – every day.

PRAY Father God, thank You for saving me. Please protect me from the things that would distract me from following You. Amen.

TOWER ABOVE IT

READ: Proverbs 18:10

KEY VERSE: 'The name of the LORD is a fortified tower; the righteous run to it and are safe.' (v10)

Once again, that word 'righteous' has cropped up — what we are when we're right with God. It's wise guy King Solomon who wrote today's proverb, and he has some advice for us when our minds and hearts feel under attack.

So, why a 'tower'? Cities back then were protected by strong walls (sometimes four metres thick). The city entrances were the weak points, so they built tall towers either side of the gates to fire at the enemy from. The towers that Solomon built contained guard rooms and were a kind of fortress in themselves. If the city was taken, those in the towers could still fight on.

We all have weaknesses that need special protection. Our virtual 'tower' is the name of the Lord Jesus Christ. Jesus towers over the enemy. He is greater and more powerful than anybody and anything.

It is in the name of the Lord Jesus that we are saved, can speak directly to God and ask for help, win our struggles against evil, and receive strength for the spiritual battle.

THINK Is God your first or last thought when you're in trouble? Remember that the name of the Lord is your tower of strength. Get close to Him.

BULLETPROOF

WHAT HOLDS IT ALL TOGETHER

READ: Ephesians 4:20–32

KEY VERSE: 'put off falsehood and speak truthfully to your neighbour' (v25)

There's a reason that Paul links the belt with the truth: it holds the entire outfit together.

Roman soldiers didn't risk laying into the enemy with their breastplates and cloaks flapping around in the breeze. They tucked their cloak and tunic into a belt so they didn't trip up. This belt was like a leather apron that protected the lower body and provided a place to put the sword. So, when Paul talks about the 'belt of truth' in the armour of God (Eph. 6:14), we can see it's a pretty important part.

God is truth. Completely genuine and 100% trustworthy. So, what does that make us as children of God? Children of truth, of course! Putting on the belt of truth is more than just knowing the truth, it's living truthfully. Truthful people want to be honest (v28) and put things right in their relationships (v26). They encourage people rather than gossip about them. They forgive rather than stir up trouble (vv29–32). We live in a pretty dishonest world, but people are always looking for the truth. How important is it to you?

PRAY God, thank You that I can trust You completely. Help me to value the truth as You do. Amen.

NO WORD OF A LIE

READ: Isaiah 45:17–19

KEY VERSE: 'I, the LORD, speak the truth; I declare what is right. (v19)

Why is God so powerful? Why is it that God knows best? Why is it that God can be trusted? The answer is that God *is* truth. He never has and never will lie to us.

Our enemy, however, hates truth. The Bible calls Satan the 'father of all lies'. His tactics are to get us to go way off track on the sly without anyone knowing – and if we're not careful, we can begin to believe the lies that he's feeding us: 'No one loves you.' 'You're weird-looking.' 'You're useless.'

But when we put on the belt of truth, we are choosing to believe God when He says, 'You are mine... you are important... I love you' (Isa. 43:1,4). Knowing who we are in God's eyes is essential. So here's a battle tactic: remind yourself of God's truth.

Know who He is: 'Know therefore that the LORD your God is God: he is the faithful God' (Deut. 7:9).

And know who you are: 'I am fearfully and wonderfully made' (Psa. 139:14). That's the truth!

THINK What lies do you believe about yourself? That you're stupid? Unloved? Ask God to show you how He sees you. The creator of the universe made you, and He doesn't make mistakes!

BULLETPROOF

NEW SHOES

READ: Isaiah 26:1–8

KEY VERSE: 'You will keep in perfect peace those whose minds are steadfast' (v3)

What do you think of when it comes to the word 'peace'? Peace and quiet? Your sister leaving you alone? World peace? Hippies?

Paul tells us that we need to get our 'feet fitted with the readiness that comes from the gospel of peace' (Eph. 6:15). You might be wondering, why *peace*? And why *shoes*?

Firstly, God's 'perfect peace' doesn't depend on how we're feeling – we can experience it even in the worst situations. Peace is what we feel when we put our trust totally in God to handle whatever it is we're going through.

A Roman soldier wouldn't have gone on duty in his slippers. Soldiers wore chunky, studded sandals with the thickest soles, complete with shin pads. So, what does God's peace do as footwear? It can keep us standing steady. It takes us where we need to go – down the path God has for us. And it crushes the devil's dirty tactics. If there's anything in your life that's destroying your peace, give it to God. He can handle it!

PRAY Lord Jesus, thank You for Your perfect peace. I trust in You to guide me down the right path, and I give You the situations in my life that are destroying my peace. Amen.

LET IT GO

READ: Philippians 4:1–9

KEY VERSE: 'And the peace of God, which transcends all understanding, will guard your hearts and your minds in Christ Jesus.' (v7)

Euodia and Syntyche were two women in the church at Philippi, and when they fell out it caused problems for the church. We've all been in silly arguments that get out of control. When this happens, we need to ask God to fix our relationships with His peace.

Paul told the two of them to stop fighting each other and team up to carry on telling others about Jesus (v2). Notice that God hadn't stormed off during their disagreements – He was nearby waiting to help them to sort things out (v5).

But what about the other things in life that stress us out and bring us down? It's right here, crystal clear in verse 6: 'Do not be anxious about anything.' Wow! Instead of getting worried or wound up, God wants us to offload our concerns onto Him. He can deal with our negative thoughts and help us live at peace with Him, ourselves and others.

So, just as you wouldn't go out of the house without your shoes on, don't go out without putting on God's peace.

THINK **Do you walk into arguments that can be avoided? How could you make peace instead?**

BULLETPROOF

FLAMING ARROWS

READ: Mark 4:35–41

KEY VERSE: 'Why are you so afraid? Do you still have no faith?' (v40)

Have you ever felt like your faith was under attack? Things go wrong, people insult your beliefs, or you just have doubts? Well, you're not alone.

Paul knew about this and he encouraged Christians to 'take up the shield of faith, with which you can extinguish all the flaming arrows of the evil one' (Eph. 6:16).

Roman shields were state-of the-art. The enemy would often dip their arrows in tar and set them on fire so the Romans needed protection that would be up to scratch. Their shields were made with wood, leather and either bronze or iron. That's pretty solid!

Our faith in Jesus is always under attack. When the disciples were shaken up by the sudden storm, they were afraid and panicking. But Jesus stepped in. He then had a word with them about their lack of faith. They had seen the problem and convinced themselves they couldn't handle it, while all along Jesus had been there to help them. God's power is way bigger than the things we fear, and our faith in Him is a shield to us.

PRAY

Lord God, I have faith that You are in control. Whatever comes at me, help me to remember that You will protect me. Amen.

STAY AWAKE!

READ: 1 Peter 5:5–11

KEY VERSE: 'Resist him, standing firm in the faith' (v9)

We are warned that Satan lurks around looking for our weak points. And let's face it, we all have weak points.

In today's verses we have three top tips for how to use our shields of faith:

Stay humble! We can't do this all on our own. We need God, and we need each other. 'Humble yourselves, therefore, under God's mighty hand' (v6).

Be alert! Satan tries to distract our attention so he can get round us. He 'prowls around... looking for someone to devour' (v8). Stay sharp!

Resist attacks! We all face pressure and temptation, but we have a 'family of believers' (v9) to help us with this. The Roman army designed their shields so that they could be held together, forming a shell that would protect them on every side, knowing that the enemy would find it difficult to force their way through them. This is what God wants for us as His Church!

We all need a strong defence. Use these tips to get behind your shield of faith today!

THINK **Do you share your weaknesses and struggles with others, or keep them to yourself? Try to find a trusted Christian friend who can support you.**

BULLETPROOF

ALIVE AND ACTIVE

READ: Hebrews 4:12–16

KEY VERSE: 'For the word of God is alive and active. Sharper than any double–edged sword' (v12)

Attack can sometimes be the best form of defence. And now that we've got our armour on, God has given us the most powerful weapon EVER! What is this weapon? It's this: 'the sword of the Spirit, which is the word of God' (Eph. 6:17).

A sword? We're told to use... a sword? Well, not a literal sword – so don't go getting any funny ideas!

The sword is used to describe the Word of God (the Bible). A double-edged sword was a short sword with a metal blade sharpened on both edges. These weapons were used by the Roman army and could do some serious damage. They were seriously dangerous.

So what does it mean that the Bible is even sharper than that?

We're certainly not meant to use the Bible to do damage, but the Bible is powerful stuff. It can be used to help us in any spiritual battle than might come our way. We're also told that the Bible is alive and active – it's real! Even though it was written a long time ago, it's full of great stuff.

It's relevant, it's real, it's powerful.

PRAY Father, thank You for speaking to me through the Bible. Please help me to love hearing from it. Amen.

WHEN YOU'VE READ THE BOOK...

READ: Matthew 4:1–11

KEY VERSE: 'Jesus answered, "It is written"' (v4)

Do you know the feeling of thinking up a really good come-back after the conversation has ended? Well, the Bible is FULL of come-backs!

Today's reading backs up the fact that the Bible is our weapon, 'sharper than any double-edged sword'. When we are tempted with negative thoughts or a selfish attitude, the Bible helps us to fight back.

When Satan tried to get the better of Jesus, the Son of God answered back to each temptation with the Word of God. Jesus was starving and exhausted, and the devil took the opportunity to try and tempt Him, but Jesus would not fall for that! He used the Bible to respond to all of Satan's tricks. Knowing our Bible really well is important, as people will often try to twist what it says. In verse 6, Satan misquoted the Bible to try to trick Jesus – but Jesus knew He was being lied to and answered back with the words of Deuteronomy 6:16. Satan is powerless against the Bible.

Get to grips with it, memorise verses and spend time in it.

THINK Is there anything you do that you know you shouldn't? Next time you're tempted, look up what the Bible says about it.

BULLETPROOF

TAKE IT TO THE CHORUS

READ: 2 Chronicles 20:14–30

KEY VERSE: 'Jehoshaphat appointed men to sing to the LORD and to praise him... as they went out at the head of the army' (v21)

This is probably a first in military strategy: sending in a choir to lead the army into battle. Yep – singing. Psalm 149 tells us to go on the attack with the 'praise of God' and a 'double-edged sword' in our hands. God's Word is powerful whether it is read, spoken or sung.

God's people were about to face off against the combined strength of the Moabites, Ammonites and Meunites. They were totally outnumbered. Wisely, Jehoshaphat asked God to help them. The result wasn't down to them – it was up to God. A secret weapon was unveiled – but not of the stabby or exploding variety. The attack would be led by men singing the praises of God! Madness? Actually, no. From the moment they belted out praise about the greatness of God's holiness, the enemy was diving for cover and left in bits. The battleground was renamed the 'valley of praise'.

When we praise God, He works in our favour. It doesn't matter if we're tone-deaf – it's what's in our hearts.

PRAY Jesus, You are worthy of all my praise. When times are tough, help me to praise You even more. Amen.

PRAY ON

READ: James 5:13–18

KEY VERSE: 'Is anyone among you in trouble? Let them pray.' (v13)

It's one thing to have all you need to complete a task, but it's another to complete the task well. When Paul wrote about the armour of God, he also gave us the key that would allow us to use it to its full potential: 'pray in the Spirit on all occasions with all kinds of prayers and requests' (Eph. 6:18).

Prayer is simply talking with and listening to God. We might pray for a miracle, for an opportunity, for forgiveness or for a change – and the results can be awesome!

Today's verses give us an idea of how, when and why we should pray. When we're facing difficulties we can talk to God. But not just then. It can also simply be when we're happy! We can talk to God all the time. Why should we pray? Because it works, and it helps us get closer to God. We get to know Him more, and so we can understand ourselves and life more. The question really is, why shouldn't we pray?!

PRAY Father God, thank You for hearing my prayers. It's incredible that I can talk to You about anything. I want to know You better through prayer. Amen.

SUITED AND BOOTED

READ: Ephesians 6:13–17

KEY VERSE: 'put on the full armour of God' (v13)

As we wrap up on the armour of God, let's recap what we've found out so far:

- With the *belt of truth* we resist the devil's lies and replace them with God's truth.
- With the *breastplate of righteousness* we protect the belief in our hearts that we are made right with God through Jesus.
- With the *shoes of peace* we are kept in God's perfect peace no matter our situation.
- With the *shield of faith* we protect ourselves from doubt and attack, so that we can completely trust in God's promises.
- With the *helmet of salvation* we protect our minds from negative thinking, knowing we are saved by Jesus.
- With the *sword of the Spirit (the Word of God)* we can fight back against the devil, knowing we have Jesus on our side.

Want one last bit of advice? Well, notice how today's reading starts with 'put on'. It's no use to us if our armour's left in the wardrobe – we have to *put it on*! The armour of God is available to you – so get dressed!

PRAY Lord, thank You for the armour You give me. Help me to choose to wear it daily. Amen.

WHO'S THE KING?

READ: Psalm 97:1–12

KEY VERSE: 'he guards the lives of his faithful ones and delivers them from the hand of the wicked' (v10)

When you've been put into teams for an activity – perhaps a game or even some work – have you ever been really glad that you've had a certain person on your side? Having someone on our team who is really good at what they do is the biggest confidence boost.

Throughout everything, we've got God on our side. And He's really good at what He does. Whatever challenges we face, we do so with the King who is totally in charge. Just look at how powerful this psalm says He is! He has a red carpet of fire, He has a light-switch for lightning, and He's even stronger than the mountains. If there's anyone we know we're safe with, it's Him.

But sometimes it's hard to believe that God is really the King. When people in school give you a hard time for being a Christian, it's easy to feel like God's losing. Although we can't always see it with our eyes, this psalm gives us a picture of just how powerful God really is.

THINK
We're on God's team but we also have other team members – other Christians. Do you meet up with your team regularly?

PSALM

CHEST X-RAY

READ: 1 Samuel 16:1,4–13

> **KEY VERSE:** 'People look at the outward appearance, but the LORD looks at the heart.' (v7)

Today we meet singer-songwriter, David. God had a few things to teach this guy, and they apply to us too. David was the youngest of eight brothers – last in the pecking order. His life was set up to be a shepherd and nothing more. And when God sent Samuel to choose one of the brothers as the next king of Israel, David wasn't even called in for an audition.

Samuel thought David's oldest brother, Eliab, would have been good for the job. He had everything going for him: strong, confident and handsome – he seemed like the ideal person. But God doesn't judge people by how they look. He knows how they think and behave. David's brothers didn't have the qualities that God wanted. So, eventually, David was called for an interview... and God gave him the job!

Do you ever feel not good enough compared to others? Well, you don't need to feel like that! Why? Because God thinks you are important. He has actually chosen you to be in His family (Eph. 1:4). You can't get more important than that!

PRAY Father, thank You for always seeing me as important. Please help me to not judge others by what they look like. Amen.

KING DAVID

A GIANT PROBLEM

READ: 1 Samuel 17:20–30

KEY VERSE: 'Why have you come down here? And with whom did you leave those few sheep in the wilderness?' (v28)

Ever faced a giant problem? Not just a bit of hassle, but a difficult situation of King Kong size? How did you cope? When Goliath appeared on the scene, David and his other brothers had a choice – fight or flight?

We begin to see why God chose David as king and not his brother Eliab. When faced with a nine foot chunk of muscle named Goliath, Eliab ran away (along with the rest of the Israelite army). David, on a visit to the camp, knew *he* couldn't defeat the Philistine hulk – but God could.

Eliab's other weaknesses were shown when he was under pressure. When he heard David talking tough, pointing out the disgrace of running away and not trusting God, he was angry and jealous. His baby brother should be at home looking after the sheep, not showing him up! Eliab accused David of being big-headed. But David wasn't boasting about his own power, only God's. He was ready to face the giant, armed with only God's strength.

PRAY Father God, help me to remember how strong You are, and to be brave and trust in that every day. Amen.

NO CONTEST

READ: 1 Samuel 17:32–40,47–50

KEY VERSE: 'for the battle is the LORD's, and he will give all of you into our hands' (v47)

It was one of the most uneven contests of all time. Goliath was the undefeated super-heavyweight champion of the world. David had fought off a lion and a bear, but no one gave the shepherd boy a chance to win in this fight...

Ding ding: round one. Goliath stomps out of his corner and leads with a jab to David's ear. He follows it with a left-right combination about David being made into bird food. David ignores it and leads with a jab that God will shrink Goliath.

Another jab from David, saying that the Lord will be the winner. Goliath tries to go for him... the youngster slings a shot to Goliath's head – the champion is down!

David didn't worry about the situation. He trusted God and went forward one step at a time. If you are faced with a giant problem, try not to worry about it. If you are part of God's family you have a Father in heaven who will help you sort it. You are never alone.

THINK Think about some times when God has helped you out in the past. Did you expect Him to do what He did?

FRIENDS FOR LIFE

READ: 1 Samuel 18:1–5

KEY VERSE: 'he loved him as himself' (v1)

After the giant clash, David was invited to stay at the palace with King Saul and his son, Jonathan. This was surely about to get messy! David and Jonathan were both in line to be next king of Israel. Jonathan had been the rightful heir to the throne. However, because his father, King Saul, had been disobedient, God intended to take the throne from Saul's family. David had already been chosen by God to be the next king. Would the two lads become enemies?

Surprisingly, in between David's harp playing, they became best friends! They even promised to be loyal to each other for the rest of their lives. This was a true friendship. Jonathan was prepared to let God have His way and acknowledged David as a prince. What would you have done in Jonathan's shoes?

Real friendship happens when we care about others like we care about ourselves. One way that we can do this is by praying for our friends. The more we pray for them, the more we will care for them.

PRAY Lord Jesus, thank You for my friends. Please help them with anything going on in their lives right now, and help me to be a good friend to them. Amen.

KING DAVID

A WINNING ANTHEM

READ: 1 Samuel 18:6–14

KEY VERSE: 'David continued to succeed in everything he did, for the LORD was with him.' (v14, NLT)

King Saul was swamped by hundreds of women as he returned from battle – and he loved every minute of it! That is, until he realised that most of them were members of David's new fan club. The catchy song they sang then got on his nerves. The song meant that David was more popular than him. And to make it worse, it had now become the number one hit.

David's bravery in battle had made him everyone's hero and jealous Saul had just about had enough. He decided that he did want David to hang out around him more – he wanted him hung out dead. It was the first of many attempts that Saul made to kill David. So, David had to rely on God to protect him from Saul and the Philistines. And God never let him down. He gave the young leader success in all he did, and the song remained at number one – much to Saul's hatred.

THINK Following God's plan for our lives isn't always easy, but we can always know that God is with us. Have you ever had no choice but to rely on God? What happened?

THE FUGITIVE

READ: 1 Samuel 22:1–5

KEY VERSE: 'he became their commander' (v2)

From palace harpist and Israel's favourite, to on the run and hiding in caves from Saul and his men... what a crazy time! But David wasn't alone for long. His family knew their lives would be threatened and came to join him. Overall, about 400 men – many who hated Saul, some who were criminals – joined up with David.

The land was rocky, dry and dusty – full of hidden dangers. There was almost no food or water. But despite his own problems, David was concerned about how his parents were doing and did everything he could to make sure they were looked after properly. This was also a big test for David's leadership skills, and he was shown to be a natural! Each person had arrived with a history of fear and failure, but David helped them to put the past in the past and work together to carry out God's plans for their lives.

When our lives are shaken up by sudden changes, we need to let God teach us new things through our experiences. And even in the worst times it's good to care for the people around us.

THINK David was turning into an amazing leader. What leaders do you know? What skills and qualities do they have that you most respect about them?

KING DAVID

TEMPER, TEMPER

READ: 1 Samuel 25:2–19,32–33

KEY VERSE: 'Praise be to the LORD... who has sent you today to meet me.' (v32)

David had treated Nabal's men and animals well. But when Nabal refused to return the favour, David threw a hot-headed wobbly. He really threw his toys out the pram. Nobody treats a harpist like that and gets away with it!

Anger spells danger. David, in a fit of rage, wanted revenge at any cost after Nabal disrespected him.

If God hadn't sent Nabal's wife Abigail to intervene, a bloody battle would have started – all over some food! Abigail's arrival with a takeaway brought David back to his senses. He realised what a fool he had been and how close he had come to murder.

Letting anger take over is never a good idea and never leads to good decisions. God wants you to have a warm heart, not a hot head. So if you tend to get wound up about things and lose your temper, take a deep breath and go to God first. He understands and will help you go about things the right way.

PRAY Father, help me to keep calm and talk to You about what is going on when I get wound up. Show me how I should respond – what I should say and what I should do. Amen.

JUSTICE

READ: 1 Samuel 25:25,36–42

KEY VERSE: 'He has kept his servant from doing wrong' (v39)

When we are treated unfairly, it's tempting to take matters into our own hands. But is that the best way to deal with it?

Nabal was not a nice guy, there's no question about it. He was a fool by name and nature (v25). The drunken farmer had no idea that his wife, Abigail, had saved his life by getting a takeaway meal to David – he was too busy going crazy at a wild party. In the morning, as he recovered from a crazy night, his wife explained what she had done. It was all too much for Nabal – he had a heart attack and died ten days later. David was thankful that he had not gone ahead and taken the law into his own hands. God had stopped him and handled the situation Himself.

We often want justice done immediately, and if someone appears to be getting away with doing something that we know is wrong, we can get pretty annoyed. But God wants us to let Him deal with these situations. He knows about all the horrible things happening in the world and won't let them slide.

THINK Are you going through something that feels totally unfair? Give it to God and trust Him to sort it in His own time.

KING DAVID

DOING THINGS GOD'S WAY

READ: 1 Samuel 26:1–11

KEY VERSE: 'the LORD forbid that I should lay a hand on the LORD's anointed' (v11)

David's big test to practise what he'd learnt from the incident with Nabal came soon after, when he was given a golden opportunity to get rid of Saul and become king.

Saul had now tried to kill David twice. But this time, it was David who had the opportunity to pin Saul to the ground. With one plunge, he could get rid of the man who was hunting him down and become king of Israel. After all, God had told David he would become king, hadn't He?

But David's row with Nabal had taught him not to react without thinking. Yes, God wanted David to be king of Israel, but not by murdering Saul. To kill Saul would be totally out of order (and not a great start to being king!). David had to wait patiently for God to deal with Saul and give him the crown.

We should never go about making something right happen in the wrong way. Our motives *and* actions need to be right. It's always best to go with God's plan and timing.

PRAY Lord, help me to not only get the right thing done, but also to get it done in the right way. I want to always please You. Amen.

WHEN THE GOING GETS TOUGH

READ: 1 Samuel 30:1–8,17–19

KEY VERSE: 'David found strength in the LORD his God.' (v6)

David and his men were absolutely gutted. While they had been away, the Amalekites had raided their base at Ziklag and kidnapped their wives and children. The men wept till they dropped. David was distraught. And to make matters worse, his men were turning their anger on him. What was David to do? Wisely, he took the matter to God who promised him success if he stormed after the kidnappers.

David set off with his best troops and gate-crashed the Amalekite party. The kidnappers were put out of action and all the hostages were released. It was a highly successful rescue mission – thanks to God.

Some events in life can be so devastating that even the toughest of people find it difficult to cope. David knew he did not have the strength to deal with the situation and wisely turned to God for advice and help. Trusting God in times of trouble can be hard but as we do, He can use our faith to encourage others as well as us.

THINK Do you ever panic when you face something really bad that you don't know what to do about? The first and best thing to do is talk to God and ask for His help.

KING DAVID

GOOD THINGS COME TO THOSE WHO WAIT

READ: 2 Samuel 2:1–7; 5:1–5

KEY VERSE: '[David] reigned over all Israel and Judah' (5:5)

Saul is killed in battle. David is crowned king. It should be a time to get up and boogie, but David still sings the blues...

Saul and Jonathan had both died defending Israel at war, but the amazing thing is that David not only grieved over Jonathan's death, but also over Saul's! Although Saul had been a complete nightmare, David still recognised that he had been God's chosen leader, and was saddened by his death.

David was first made king of Judah, and then the whole of Israel. The shepherd boy was now God's 'shepherd', caring for the nation of Israel. David knew he was going to become king but it took a while for this promise of God to happen. He didn't try to make it happen himself but waited for God to bring it about. Waiting is tough – especially when we have asked God for something we feel sure is right. But remember, God uses the waiting time to get us ready for the things that lie ahead. And the great thing about God is the wait is always worth it.

PRAY

Father God, whenever I'm waiting for You to do something, please help me be patient and become more like You. Amen.

STAYING CLOSE

READ: 2 Samuel 5:6–12

KEY VERSE: 'And he became more and more powerful, because the LORD God Almighty was with him.' (v10)

David's palace was in Hebron. But he needed a more central location for a capital city – somewhere that was easier to defend. So his eyes turned to Jebus (now Jerusalem). But there was one problem: the Jebusites. They were everywhere and made the city seem impossible to capture.

The Jebusites were so confident no one could break through their sturdy protection that they mocked David and his men. But they had underestimated David. He led his men up the secret water tunnel, used by the Jebusites to bring water to the city when they were being attacked. David caught the enemy by surprise and made the city the capital of the Israelites. Jerusalem is still known as the City of David today.

In verse 10, David shares the secret of his success – he became more and more powerful because the Lord was with him. If we want the Lord to be with us, we have to want to follow Him.

THINK Have a chat with your Christian friends about what they find tough about being a Christian, and talk about how you feel too. Then share some things you have learnt from your study of David so far.

KING DAVID

PLANNING PERMISSION

READ: 2 Samuel 7:1–21

KEY VERSE: 'Here I am, living in a house of cedar, while the ark of God remains in a tent.' (v2)

David was building his dream palace when he realised something. He was living in luxury while the Ark of the Covenant (which symbolised God being with His people) was being kept in a tent. David had an idea...

It turned out that God wanted a temple, but He didn't want David to build it. God had already decided that the temple would be built by the next king, David's son. This was a shock to David but he was thrilled that God was going to keep the throne in his family, and that the Temple would be built – even if he would not be around to see it.

It's not easy to give up our plans, dreams or ambitions when God shows He has other plans for us. Neither is it easy to hand over a project that was your idea to someone else (and see them get the credit). The lesson to be learnt is that we need to share all our ideas and plans with God before we start them.

PRAY Lord God, thank You that I can trust You and Your plans for my life. Help me to not argue when You remind me that You know best. Amen.

PULL UP A CHAIR

READ: 2 Samuel 9:1–9

KEY VERSE: 'you will always eat at my table' (v7)

It was tradition for a new king to wipe out the last remaining relatives of the last king and anyone else with a claim to the throne. Saul had one remaining relative: Jonathan's disabled son, Mephibosheth. Would David order his execution?

Mephibosheth had broken his legs when he was young and they had not healed properly. He was on the run with a disability and low self-esteem. He even described himself as a 'dead dog' (v8). Mephibosheth expected the worst, but he got the best! Not only did David spare his life, but Mephibosheth was treated as a prince. He was given land, servants and the honour of eating at the king's table. Why? Because David had promised Jonathan that he would always treat his family well, and he kept that promise.

This is a brilliant picture of what God has done for us. Even though we turned away from God, he doesn't treat us badly. Instead, He loves us, forgives us and welcomes us into His family. Do you sometimes come to God expecting the worst? God loves you and promises to look after you.

PRAY Lord Jesus, I'm sorry for thinking that You'll reject me when actually You really want to be my friend. I love and worship You. Amen.

KING DAVID

THE STATE OF AFFAIRS

READ: 2 Samuel 11:2–5,8–13

KEY VERSE: 'The woman was very beautiful' (v2)

David knew it was completely out of order to have an affair with another man's wife. But after eyeing Bathsheba up from a distance, he got carried away. One thing led to another and… the casual one-night stand was disastrous. Bathsheba became pregnant and the affair could not be hidden. David was prepared to do anything to prevent a royal scandal, but Bathsheba's husband, Uriah, was a good man.

David came up with a plan to trick Uriah into thinking he was the father of the baby. But Uriah was not prepared to spend a romantic night in with his wife while his fellow troops were living rough on the battlefield. So David's trick wouldn't be believable anyway. And now, David didn't know what to do. He could imagine what chaos might start if people found out. Would the scandal bring down his government? He hatched another desperate cover-up plan (as we'll find out tomorrow).

THINK Sometimes we think we can get away with doing wrong. We think we can handle it, but we just end up making a big mess. Do you ever feel like that? Talk to God about any messes you've got into.

FROM BAD TO WORSE

READ: 2 Samuel 11:14–21,26–27

KEY VERSE: 'But the thing David had done displeased the LORD.' (v27)

David's hit rock-bottom. Again, he has the chance to admit what he's done. But instead he covers it up – and the result is serious.

David planned to put an end to Uriah by ordering him to the front line. It worked. David finally gets what he wants. But at what cost? This 'man after [God's] own heart' (Acts 13:22) has allowed his sin and guilt to come between himself and God. Now he can't seem to write any more worship psalms and his harp sounds way out of tune. Is there any hope for him?

When we cover our tracks to hide something we've done, we might think we've got away with it. That's never true though. Everything we do affects others in some way, good or bad. Worst of all, breaking God's rules separates us from Him. David stopped writing psalms at this time because his close relationship with God was damaged. We all mess up, but don't try to hide anything from God – He wants us to be open with Him.

PRAY Father God, I'm sorry for when I mess things up. Please show me what I should do to sort things out. Amen.

KING DAVID

WHEN THE TRUTH COMES OUT

READ: 2 Samuel 12:1–9,13–23

KEY VERSE: 'I have sinned against the LORD.' (v13)

God sent the prophet Nathan to David to tell him he needed to turn away from what he had done, stop lying, and ask for forgiveness. Thanks to a helpful story involving a little lamb, David realised what he'd done and fell apart with regret. He owned up to everything and faced the sad consequences of his actions. But that's not all – the baby born from the affair did not survive.

When we read things like this happening in the Bible, it can be really hard for us to understand. Being sorry doesn't always mean that everything turns out OK, but it's the best thing to do. God forgave David and their relationship was back on track, but forgiveness doesn't always get rid of the consequences. The main thing to always remember is that God is a God of love – He is love even when we don't understand Him. However He decides to deal with sin is His business, and we can always trust Him.

The most important thing to know is that nothing is too bad for His forgiveness.

THINK **Are you feeling guilty about something at the moment? Take the chance now to give it over to God now and receive His forgiveness and freedom.**

BELOVED BY THE LORD

READ: 2 Samuel 12:24–25

> **KEY VERSE:** 'and because the LORD loved him, he sent word... to name him Jedidiah' (v25)

David discovered that God was prepared to forgive him, despite the bad things he had done. Yes, there were awful consequences, but his relationship with God was back on track. David and Bathsheba had a second child. The boy was named Solomon which means 'peace'.

Kings often had two names – one official, and a second 'family' name. Nathan turned up again, this time not with a story about a lamb, but a message from heaven: God wanted the child's family name to be 'Jedidiah', meaning 'beloved by the Lord'. David and Bathsheba were over the moon. There was no doubt they had been forgiven.

Sometimes we really need to learn from our mistakes. But God doesn't hold grudges when we ask for forgiveness, and He always wants us in His family. David and Bathsheba now knew this for sure.

PRAY Lord, thank You so much for never holding grudges. I'm so glad that You always forgive me for whatever I've done when I ask. You deserve all the praise and glory – You are amazing! Amen.

KING DAVID

A FAMILY SAGA

READ: 2 Samuel 15:1–14

KEY VERSE: 'and so [Absalom] stole the hearts of the people of Israel' (v6)

David is forgiven and knows it, but God had warned that difficulties would come to his family. Here it comes in the shape of Absalom, one of David's sons, who wanted to overthrow his dad as king.

Absalom is very crafty in how he goes about this. He goes around trying to turn people against his father. Then, when he thinks he's got everyone convinced, he declares that he is king. David hears of this and flees. And then civil war breaks out. Later in the story we find out that against David's wishes, Absalom is assassinated in the battle. David remains king but mourns the death of his son.

Absalom's rebellion shows us what happens if we let jealousy eat away at us. It's very easy to look at other people and wish we had what they have. But this type of thinking can lead us to make some bad decisions that end up causing us trouble. God doesn't want us to be jealous of others, He wants us to know that we are valuable as we are.

PRAY Father God, help me not to be jealous of other people and what they have. I want to be happy with who You have made me to be. Amen.

DAVID'S GREATEST HITS

READ: Psalm 27:1–14

KEY VERSE: 'Wait for the LORD; be strong and take heart and wait for the LORD.' (v14)

As far as songs of the Bible are concerned, David probably has the most hits to his name (73 psalms!), and that's not to mention all the modern worship songs that have used parts of his psalms in the lyrics!

David and his harp went through a lot together. He wrote psalms when he was being hunted down, when he'd messed up, and when God had saved him. With a pretty eventful life, you'd think David would have been spending his time doing other things, not writing songs!

But David was a man who relied on God. Look at how he says to 'wait for the LORD' (v14). He knew that the best way of dealing with anything in life was to talk to God about it. David was in constant communication with God. That's a great lesson for us to learn from his life – to go to God with absolutely everything. The good, the bad and the ugly.

THINK Why not try writing your own worship song, rap or poem? Tell God how you feel and what's going on in your life right now. You can be totally honest with Him.

PSALM

ON THE GUEST LIST

READ: Psalm 98:1–9

KEY VERSE: 'Shout for joy to the LORD, all the earth' (v4)

Have you ever not been invited to something and been really upset about it? Today's worship psalm is about the whole earth being invited to something and saying, 'Yes'. It's about the whole of creation having a party, and it's not going to be a nice little polite tea-and-biscuits thing – it's going to be a MASSIVE celebration praising God.

The people who sang this song were God's people from the titchy little nation of Israel. He is their God and you might think they wouldn't want anyone else to know about Him. But here they are telling the whole world to praise God and saying that all nations are going to know Him.

Do you ever feel like Christianity is just for a few people? Maybe the people you get on with? Well, we can all feel like that sometimes, but it's a good job for us that God doesn't feel that way! He wants *everyone* to come to Him. He is preparing a party and the whole world is invited.

PRAY Lord Jesus, thank You that anyone can be a part of Your party. Please be close to my friends, and give me a chance to tell them about You. Amen.

CONFIDENT

READ: Psalm 2:1–12

KEY VERSE: 'You are my son; today I have become your father.' (v7)

Imagine the most unfit guy you know lining up for a race against all the super-athletes at your school's sports day. He wouldn't stand a chance! Now imagine if he started saying that he was the champion! It would look stupid, wouldn't it? Well, Psalm 2 is a bit like that. Weedy little Israel and their king are singing a cocky song to the huge nations around them.

Of course, this song isn't stupid because it's true – God had chosen Israel to carry out His plan. He was saving the world through them. That's why they were so important. Just look at the confidence they had, knowing that God was there for them!

This psalm became more and more important as years went by. Israel fell apart and the kings fizzled out BUT God's promise could never fizzle out. Because of that, this song gave people hope that God would bring a perfect king to finally carry out His plans. We now know that this happened and that the great king is Jesus. He has made a way for the world to be brought back to God!

THINK
The people of Israel were brave because they knew God was backing them. He's backing you too! So ask Him for the courage you need.

PSALM

MAKER OF ALL THINGS

READ: Genesis 1:1–13,31; 2:1

KEY VERSE: 'In the beginning God created the heavens and the earth.' (1:1)

Some of us have a name that seems like a really good fit; for others of us, our name is nothing like our character. For example, someone called Joy might be a right misery! But God is always true to His names – and He has lots of them! Let's take a closer look at the very first one...

Just four words into the Bible, we are introduced to God for the first time as 'El' (the singular of God) or 'Elohim' (the plural for God – as in God the Father, Son and Holy Spirit). 'Elohim' means 'creator'. God is the mighty powerhouse of *all* life and matter. He made the universe and everything in it – it didn't exist before He got to work on it. He is the ultimate power. No one can destroy Him. By nature, God is a stunningly brilliant creator. From a show-stopping sunset to a fantastic forest, we can see God's creativity all around us.

THINK **Think about how much God has created. The world, the solar system, the entire universe – everything! When you recognise God as the world's creator, does that make you think differently about looking after it?**

NAMES OF GOD

ACTIVELY INVOLVED

READ: Genesis 2:1–7,18–22; 3:8–9

KEY VERSE: 'But the LORD God called to the man, "Where are you?"' (3:9)

When God created humans He introduced Himself as 'the LORD God'. When you see 'Lord' all in capitals, it is translated from the Hebrew word 'Yahweh' or 'Jehovah', which means 'active presence' or 'life-giving one'.

God wants to create, to give life, and to be actively involved in the lives of the people He has created. The Lord spent time with Adam showing him His creation. Can you imagine the fun they had?

Unfortunately Adam's rebellion brought death into God's creation and destroyed his close relationship with God. But the Lord doesn't change – even when humans messed up, Jesus gave up His own life so that we could live and be in relationship with Him once again. The Lord is our 'Yahweh' – the 'life-giving one'.

God is not far away; He wants to be involved in our lives. But like Adam, sometimes we can push Him away. To know God's presence in our lives, we need to make Him Lord of our lives.

PRAY Lord, thank You for wanting to be close to me and give me life. I am sorry for when I've ignored You. Thank you for sending Jesus to die for me, so that I could have a relationship with You. Amen.

COMPLETELY CAPABLE

READ: Genesis 17:1–22

KEY VERSE: 'I am God Almighty' (v1)

Why is a 99-year-old man rolling on the ground with laughter? Well, God told him what he'll get for his 100th birthday. And it's not a letter from the Queen. This is going to be interesting...

Meet Abraham and Sarah. Sarah had never been able to get pregnant, and Abraham was dealing with the embarrassment and confusion of being called the 'father of many nations' when not one person was calling him 'Dad'. Then, when they're at what we now would see as 'grandparent' age, they get told a baby will be coming their way soon. Abraham might not have laughed so hard if he had listened carefully to the way God introduced Himself (v1). He says He's 'El Shaddai' meaning 'God – the Enough'. One year later it's Sarah who gets the giggles (Gen. 21:6–7) when she gives birth to the son God had promised them.

God is enough for the impossible to happen. God is enough for any situation. Nothing is too difficult for Him to handle. He has no limits, and He loves doing the unexpected!

THINK Do you ever doubt that God can do something? Are there things that you haven't talked to Him about because you think He can't help with them?

EVERLASTING ARMS

READ: Deuteronomy 33:26–27

KEY VERSE: 'The eternal God is your refuge, and underneath are the everlasting arms.' (v27)

Life is full of changes, whether it's change with friends, family, school or even just the weather. Everything around us can be constantly shifting, but God is the same yesterday, today and forever.

Here God is introduced as our 'Eternal God'. (For you Bible heads, the Hebrew words for Eternal God are 'El Olam'.) It's amazing to know that God will always be around and will always be the same. Our Eternal God is pictured with 'everlasting arms'. Why? Well, God knows we need support and so He scoops us up in His loving arms.

So when God promises to forgive us and look after us, it's not just for today. It's FOREVER, because He is the 'Forever God' – it's in His nature! If you have any doubts that God loves you or cares for you, talk with Him about your fears. Let God show you that He is your Eternal God. Our moods, feelings and situations might change, but God remains the same.

PRAY Father God, thank You for always being the same. I'm so glad that You'll always be with me and never change. Help me to know how much You love me. Amen.

NAMES OF GOD

EVERYTHING WE NEED

READ: Genesis 22:1–14

KEY VERSE: 'So Abraham called that place The LORD Will Provide.' (v14)

Remember Abraham, the 99-year-old laughing man we met two days ago? Well, he's not laughing this time. Because, after all that, God has now told him to sacrifice his son, Isaac.

God tested Abraham's faith in a very strange way, but He never intended that Isaac should actually be barbecued. God's not like that, and Abraham knew this. God had even promised Abraham that Isaac's family line would become a great nation. Abraham knew from experience that God always kept His promises, no matter how impossible they seemed. So he knew that God could be trusted.

When Isaac pointed out that they had brought the barbecue set but not the meat, Abraham replied that the Lord would provide. It was at the last moment that God provided a different sacrifice, sparing Isaac's life. 'Jehovah Jireh' means 'God who provides'. Abraham knew that God could be trusted to live up to His name. While God doesn't ask us to do anything like what He asked Abraham, He still provides for us in every way we need, even providing His own Son, Jesus, as our Saviour.

THINK
Think about how much God has provided for you. Why not try to write a list and then praise Him for all those things?

PERFECT HEALER

READ: Exodus 15:22–27

KEY VERSE: 'for I am the LORD, who heals you.' (v26)

Have you ever noticed that God doesn't usually give us all the details of His plan at once? That He tends to take us one step at a time? Moses and the Israelites knew all about that.

Moses has led the Israelites out of slavery; he's guided them across the Red Sea (which God parts just as the entire Egyptian army is about to reach them); and now they have been travelling for three days without finding drinkable water, and are about to collapse from thirst. Interestingly, thirst was the first plague God brought on the Egyptians, turning their water source – the Nile – into blood. For the Israelites, He does the opposite, turning the bitter spring into drinkable water.

He uses the moment to introduce Himself as the Lord who heals ('Jehovah Rophe' in the original Hebrew), and says that if the Israelites listen to Him and obey Him, He will not bring on them the diseases He brought on the Egyptians. He quenches their thirst, and now wants to heal their diseases. God has power over sickness!

PRAY Father, You are the great healer. I bring before You anyone that I know who is sick and ask for You to heal them and show Yourself to them. Amen.

NAMES OF GOD

COMMANDER-IN-CHIEF

READ: Exodus 17:8–16

KEY VERSE: 'Moses built an altar and called it The LORD is my Banner.' (v15)

Armies in ancient times carried a banner into battle, and during the battle the banner served as a rallying point for the troops.

Moses' staff symbolised the authority of God. It was used to bring plagues to Egypt and open a path through the Red Sea. So, when the Amalekites launched their desert attack on the Israelites in the wilderness, Moses reached for his staff. Using his staff as a banner, Moses held it high on a hilltop while the battle raged. While he held the banner high, the Israelites pushed back their enemies; as soon as he dropped his hands, the Israelites were the ones being pushed back.

Because of this, a new name for God is introduced: 'Jehovah Nissi' – the Lord is my banner. God is our base. When we lift God up in our lives we walk in His power and are winners. When we try to do life without God, not only do we become tired and weak, we miss out on all the great stuff He has planned for us!

THINK
What parts of your life would you say that God is in? And what parts would you say that He is out of? How can you change this so that He is in all parts?

HE'S GOT YOU COVERED

READ: Jeremiah 23:1–8

KEY VERSE: 'This is the name by which he will be called: The LORD Our Righteous Saviour.' (v6)

Have you ever had a big problem that you just could not fix on your own? Maybe it was something you'd done wrong, something someone else had done to you, or just a really tricky situation that you needed help with.

In Jeremiah's time, God's people were in BIG trouble. They had become as bad as you can get. Into this mess steps God, announcing Himself by a surprising new name, 'Jehovah Tsidkenu' – the Lord Our Righteousness.

God sees that people are destroying themselves and each other, and He knows that they need His help – He alone has the power to save them from their evil ways. So God tells Jeremiah that He's sending a holy King to earth (Jesus) who would trade all our 'wrongness' for His complete 'rightness'. 'Being right' – as in a God-kind-of-right, completely right and good – is something that no person in the history of the world has ever been able to be, except Jesus. Amazingly, He loved us anyway – in all our mess – and chose to give up everything so that we could gain everything.

PRAY Lord Jesus, thank You for making me right. I praise You for the amazing gift that You have given me. Amen.

NAMES OF GOD

KEEP CALM AND TRUST GOD

READ: Judges 6:1,11–14,19–24

KEY VERSE: 'So Gideon built an altar to the LORD there and called it The LORD Is Peace.' (v24)

Feeling confused, frightened or frustrated? Gideon was. His life was going in circles. Like lots of people, he kept disobeying God, then asking forgiveness, then returning to his old habits again. To add to his troubles, the Midianites raided after every harvest, stealing crops and setting fields on fire. Like the rest of the Israelites, Gideon was hungry and hassled.

It was into this situation of chaos that God revealed His name 'Jehovah Shalom' – the Lord is Peace. Now Shalom-peace is not a nice little 'I feel relaxed' kind of peace. This kind of peace is packed with power! Shalom means completeness, safety, wellbeing, and peace. Now that's what Gideon needed. But he wasn't sure that God could deliver it. It took a staff, meat, bread and fire (work that one out! vv20–22) to convince him. But God didn't just convince Gideon who He was – 'Jehovah Shalom'. He also showed Gideon his own God-given identity – 'mighty warrior' (v12). Having peace in life is all about knowing God, and knowing who we are in Him.

THINK
What are some things that you are confused or frightened about? Do you want God to give you His 'shalom' in these situations? Ask Him!

COMPLETE CARE PACKAGE

READ: Psalm 23:1–6

KEY VERSE: 'The LORD is my shepherd' (v1)

In Bible times sheep were easy prey for wild animals and thieves. Shepherds could fight off attackers or do a runner. The good shepherds were those who protected their flocks at all costs. David spent his early years as a shepherd – caring for his sheep, even getting into combat with lions and bears to protect them. So when God introduced Himself as his shepherd, David was over the moon.

What more could he want? If the Lord was caring for him, he had everything he needed. Just as he had searched for good fields for his sheep, so God would look after his needs. David knew how freaked out sheep get by rushing water, and was relieved to know that God would lead him by still water and bring peace to his life.

David had used his staff to reach out for stray sheep and keep others away from danger. So it must have been comforting to know that God would keep him on the right paths and rescue him from danger. When the Lord is your shepherd, you have everything you need.

PRAY Father, thank You for being my shepherd and always looking to do what is best for me. That's just amazing and I am so thankful to have You in my life! Amen.

NAMES OF GOD

LORD OF ALL

READ: Isaiah 6:1–8

KEY VERSE: 'I saw the Lord... seated on a throne' (v1)

At the time when God gave Isaiah this vision, there was a growing crisis in Israel. The people were worshipping false gods, and eventually this would bring disaster to the nation. The bloodthirsty Assyrian army were a constant threat, and God warned Isaiah that the people were about to become slaves of the Babylonians. The future looked grim.

It's right here that we find another name for God. The word 'Lord' in verses 1 and 8 comes from the Hebrew word 'Adonai', meaning Lord and master – the one who rules all things with royal majesty and power. God's encouragement to Isaiah was that while kingdoms come and go, His government is strong and everlasting.

Isaiah was completely gobsmacked by his vision of God. As he took in the awesome holy power of God, he realised how unholy he was in comparison. God used this revelation not to scare Isaiah silly, but to help Isaiah recognise his own sinfulness, to forgive him and get him ready to serve his Lord and master.

THINK Sometimes we can take God's kindness for granted and forget that He is actually Lord and master. We need to respect Him as well as be friends with Him.

UNSHAKABLE

READ: Psalm 18:1–3

KEY VERSE: 'The LORD is my rock, my fortress and my deliverer' (v2)

Have you ever heard the expression 'rock solid'? It's used to describe someone or something strong, dependable and secure. That's quite a good way to describe God, don't you think?

God is our eternal rock – unshakable, unmovable, reliable and secure. No one can take Him by surprise or conquer Him by force.

In Old Testament times, a city or fortress built on a high rock was easy to defend. And in the New Testament, we hear how a man who built his house on rocky foundations instead of on sand was safe when the floods came.

David, the psalm writer, described God as his rock, and he wasn't the only one that saw God that way. Joseph knew God as his rock – who kept him strong and steady through many trials. The prophets Samuel, Isaiah and Habakkuk all spoke of God as the rock of His people. And Christ is described as the rock that our spiritual water comes from.

God wants to let us know that He's our rock! It's clearly very important to Him that you know you can depend on Him.

PRAY Lord, thank You for being strong, secure and dependable. I want to base my life on You, my rock. Amen.

INTO HIS IMAGE

READ: Leviticus 20:6–8,22–26

KEY VERSE: 'I am the LORD, who makes you holy' (v8)

A few days ago, we looked at how Jesus makes us right with God, but what do we do with that? Once you're made right, should you just live as you like with a few 'forgive me' prayers thrown in? No way! God wants His people to lead lives that are amazing because they are holy – lives that show people what He is like.

'Holy' simply means 'set apart for God'. It's our way of saying, 'Lord, I want to spend my life thanking You, living for You and serving You.' It's choosing to live God's way, not our way. But again, we can't do that by ourselves. God's ways are just too wonderful for us to achieve. But don't despair! Right after giving the Jews His long list of instructions on 'how to be holy', God introduced Himself as 'Jehovah M'Kaddesh' – 'the Lord who makes you holy'. So not only did God make a way for us to be forgiven, He's now able to make us holy!

THINK **Is there something that you keep going back to God to ask for forgiveness for? It's no fun messing up in the same way, over and over. But God can help you leave that behind – talk with Him about it.**

STUCK ON YOU

READ: Ezekiel 48:35; Revelation 21:1–4

KEY VERSE: 'THE LORD IS THERE' (Ezek. 48:35)

Have you ever seen somebody really upset? It's hard to know what to say when a person is feeling that way, but most of the time they just value someone being there for them.

God gave both Ezekiel and John glimpses of His future plans for us. And He introduced Himself by a new name, 'Jehovah Shammah' – the Lord is there. What a difference God makes to a place when He is there! John literally fell to the floor when he saw a vision of the future place God has prepared for His followers – it was beyond incredible! There was genuine, over-the-top joy – no sadness or pain, no sickness or frustration, no death. Why? Because God is there, and God's presence makes all the difference. One psalmist wrote: 'Better is one day in your courts than a thousand elsewhere' (Psa. 84:10).

The most amazing thing? God is with us, all the time! From the moment we ask Jesus to be in our lives as Lord, He never leaves us. He is always with us, protecting us, guiding us and pouring out His love-filled blessings and power upon us.

PRAY Lord, thank You for always being there for me in every situation I have ever faced, and any I ever will. Amen.

NAMES OF GOD

WHAT A NAME

READ: Matthew 1:18–21; Philippians 2:10

KEY VERSE: 'give him the name Jesus, because he will save his people from their sins' (Matt. 1:21)

God's names are very special, each one describing what He is like. So when He introduces His Son, it's with the most precious name of all. Jesus means 'Jehovah saves'. God came to earth to save us from the separation humans caused when we first ignored Him, way back in the Garden of Eden.

We've been ignoring Him, living by our own rules ever since. But Jesus willingly chose to sacrifice Himself to rescue us, so that we could come back to our loving God and spend eternity with Him. 'Jesus' is the most powerful name in existence. It's a name you can count on – a name you can call on, and you will be saved. How incredible! No other world religion worships a Saviour like Jesus. If there's one characteristic about Him that stands out for you, let it be this: He has saved you. You've done nothing to deserve it, but He loves You that much. What an amazing God He is!

THINK
Have you ever thought about what your friends believe about Jesus? Why not ask them what they think about Him? It could be a chance to tell them what He's really like.

LIGHT IT UP

READ: John 8:12

KEY VERSE: 'Jesus... said, "I am the light of the world."' (v12)

Yes, only one verse to read today, but it's worth reading several times. When God spoke to Moses He called Himself 'I AM' – the one who has always existed and always will exist. So when Jesus came to earth it should be no surprise to hear that He introduced Himself as 'I AM...'

The New Testament was written in Greek, and the Greek word for light is 'phos'. The word 'phos' is where we get words such as photograph (meaning writing with light), and phosphorous (meaning glowing in the dark) from. Have you ever seen phosphorous glowing? Maybe one day you could talk your science teacher into setting some alight. But get your goggles on – this stuff gives off such a fierce, intense light that you will probably need to shield your eyes. Jesus' light is even stronger than this.

Jesus called Himself 'I AM' because He *is* God. He described Himself as the light of the world because He is holy. His holiness is like a fierce, intense light that overpowers the darkness of our unholy world.

PRAY
Lord Jesus, empty me of all darkness, cleanse me with Your forgiveness, fill me with Your Holy Spirit and help me live like a bright light for You. Amen.

NAMES OF GOD

THE ONLY WAY

READ: John 10:1–10

KEY VERSE: 'I am the gate; whoever enters through me will be saved.' (v9)

Jesus often referred to Himself as the good shepherd to us beloved sheep who are often making baa-d choices. Now He explains just what a good shepherd does and introduces Himself by a new name – our gate.

In ye good olde Bible days, shepherds herded their flocks to pastures during the day and back to a sheepfold at night. The sheepfold had strong stone walls covered with thorns to defend it from those wanting to sneak over to grab a cheap leg of lamb for their Sunday roast. It also had one entrance. But the gate was not a big iron one with padlocks – the shepherd was the gate. He would lie across the entrance to keep the sheep in and the thieves out.

Jesus introduced Himself as our gateway to safety and security for eternity. He is the one entrance by which we can know God. It's only through faith in Jesus, His death and His resurrection that we can be with God both now and forever. And Jesus the good shepherd knows us by name, cares for us and protects us.

THINK The Bible tells us that once we've entered through the gate, nothing can steal us away from God. Do you know that you belong to God?

HE REIGNS SUPREME

READ: Psalm 8:1–9

KEY VERSE: 'LORD, our Lord, how majestic is your name in all the earth!' (v1)

As we have seen, one word cannot begin to cover the awesomeness of who God is, what He is like and what He has done. When David says 'majestic' in this psalm it can also mean glorious, magnificent, mighty, powerful – words are not enough!

As David looked up at the night sky he was overwhelmed with the power and majesty of God. The universe that God made was so big! And David felt so small compared to it. That someone as big as God who flung the stars into space should do so much for someone as small as him really impressed David. He was star-struck by the awesome greatness and love of God.

David the king had to take his crown off to God the King of kings. The brilliance and majesty of the universe made his royal title seem rather small in comparison. In absolute awe, the king praised the Lord and told Him He was majestic. Beyond-the-universe majestic! How can we respond to the glory and power and majesty of God? By PRAISING Him!

PRAY Lord, You are awesome and absolutely incredible. I'm so impressed with all that You've made! Thank You for also choosing to make me. Amen.

NAMES OF GOD

NO MISTAKE

READ: Psalm 8:1–9

KEY VERSE: 'what is mankind that you are mindful of them, human beings that you care for them?' (v4)

We're carrying on with the same psalm as yesterday for today's reading. Why? Because this psalm tells us *loads* about how important we are to God!

We are a very special part of God's creation. In the middle of all the fantastic things in creation, like the moon and the stars, God chose to 'crown' humans with 'glory and honour' (v5). Amazing! We are so tiny compared to the moon and the stars, but who is it that God has a big place in His heart for? Us. And who is it He does the most for? Us! That's how much He values us.

Lots of people live their lives wondering what they are worth and if they are loved. Well here's the truth: the creator of the universe, the same one who put the sun in the sky, loves you more than words can say. He cares so much about us that He watched His own Son, Jesus, suffer on a cross so that we could be set free.

THINK God cares for us, so let's care for each other. Is there anyone you know who could do with being made to feel cared about today? Think of something you could do for this person!

TAKING CARE

READ: Psalm 104:10–30

KEY VERSE: 'All creatures look to you to give them their food at the proper time.' (v27)

Do you have any pets? If so, how good are you at looking after them? Does God look after the world in a similar way to how we look after our pets?

The people of God understood that He had not only created the universe but that He is fully alive and at work in it all the time. That is why we are able to see God all around us in the world. He's holding the whole thing together and making it work.

It's good to know this. It means that God is very, very close to us. When we pray for a miracle, we're not asking God to step into the world from way out in space somewhere – He's already here! When we see that God is at work in everything, it's easier to believe that He can do anything! He's doing a lot of behind the scenes work that keeps this world running. The psalm tells us some of the things that God has done and still does. He is brilliant at taking care of us and this world.

PRAY Lord, I believe that You do care about me and about this world. When I feel like You don't care, please help me to remember the truth. Amen.

PSALM

FAMILY PORTRAIT

READ: Luke 1:1–7

KEY VERSE: 'Both of them were righteous in the sight of God' (v6)

Over the next few weeks, we'll be looking at the life of John the Baptist. John was a man with a mission: to prepare the way for Jesus. John was also a man with a message: 'Turn back to God!'

John's dad was one of the 20,000 priests in Israel. The priests were divided into 24 groups. John's dad's group was the eighth group. Each group would take turns in being on duty at the Temple in Jerusalem. Both John's mum and dad were great-great-(lots of greats)-grandchildren of the first high priest, Aaron. And it was probably expected that their son would become a priest as well.

But for a long time John's parents weren't able to have a baby – which made his mum feel like a bit of a failure. But then John came along and his parents encouraged him to love and obey God, just like they did. They were very old when John was a teenager, but he loved and respected them.

John's relative, Mary, lived in Nazareth with her husband Joseph. She had her baby, Jesus, when John had just been born.

THINK Do you look or act like members of your family? Whatever they're like, God wants us to be like Jesus.

HIGHWAY TO HEAVEN

BIRTH ANNOUNCEMENTS

READ: Luke 1:8–17

KEY VERSE: 'Do not be afraid, Zechariah; your prayer has been heard' (v13)

When a member of a royal family has a baby, there is usually an official announcement. John had two very unusual birth announcements...

One was written by the prophet Malachi – 400 years before John was born. The second was made by an angel – nine months before John was born. So all around, not your everyday announcements.

The first announcement went something like this:

'God is pleased to announce that another great prophet, like Elijah, will be born. This person will prepare people for the Saviour of the world.' (Based on Malachi 4:1–6.)

The second, something like this:

'God is pleased to announce that Zechariah and Elizabeth are to have a baby boy, John. This very special baby will be filled with the Holy Spirit, grow up and get people ready for the arrival of the Saviour of the world.'

Zechariah was on duty at the Temple when he saw an angel by the altar. You can imagine how thrilled he was to find out he would be a dad (especially when he and Elizabeth were thought to be too old to have a baby)!

PRAY Thank You, God, for men and women like John who tell people about You. Please help me to do that as well. Amen.

LIFESTYLE CHOICES

READ: Luke 1:14–17; Matthew 3:4

KEY VERSE: 'he will go on before the Lord, in the spirit and power of Elijah' (Luke 1:17)

John was going to be God's representative announcing the arrival of King Jesus. Did he set up his headquarters in Jerusalem for maximum impact? Did he dress to impress? Did he enjoy the finest food? Let's find out...

Dress: John wears a rough cut camel skin coat with matching wide leather belt. This style was modelled by Elijah (2 Kings 1:8) and is out of date by 600 years. The rough, hairy material is extremely uncomfortable to wear and looks cheap.

Food: John's favourite dish is locusts and fresh honey. Ideal for those on a gluten-free diet.

Home: John lives in the hot, dusty wilderness around the Dead Sea. It's famous for being one of the worst areas to live in. Ideal for a single person who likes sand, salt water and hill climbing.

God was impressed with John. He had chosen a man full of the Holy Spirit – a man of power. John was tough but not cocky. He wasn't fussed about being seen. His whole focus was to point people to Jesus.

THINK Do you want to be seen or do you want to point people to Jesus? Which do you think is better in the long run?

IMPOSSIBLE!

READ: Luke 1:18–25

KEY VERSE: 'How can I be sure of this?' (v18)

Have you ever doubted that God would answer your prayers or do something amazing in your life? Zechariah could not believe that God was going to give him a son. He and his wife were far too old.

What a dramatic scene in the Temple! A speechless Zechariah was trying to communicate with the crowd via sign language. Now we all love a game of charades, but can you imagine what they were thinking? Maybe they thought he'd lost his marbles. After all, here was a well-respected man in the community playing word games with them – in the Temple! Something must have happened.

Zechariah had lost his speech because he doubted the angel's promise. We can hardly blame him for finding it hard to believe. He and Elizabeth were far too old to have children – weren't they? Sometimes we don't really believe that God can help. It's good to remind ourselves that nothing is too hard for God, who created the universe – and us. After all, our heavenly Father wants to give good things to those who ask Him (Matt. 7:11).

PRAY Creator God, who made the universe, help me to really believe and understand that nothing is too difficult for You. Amen.

WHAT'S IN A NAME?

READ: Luke 1:57–67,76–77

KEY VERSE: 'No! He is to be called John.' (v60)

It didn't take long for the news to spread all around Judea. 'Have you heard? I wonder what it means? Who is this child going to be?'

Zechariah had been unable to express how excited he was to become a father. And after his awkward game of charades, he could only communicate in writing. Eight days after the birth came the ceremony for the child to be dedicated to God. Traditionally, a child would be named after a close relative, but Zechariah confirmed (in writing) that their son was to be called John – the name God had chosen. Immediately, he could speak again, and he burst into a song! The lyrics spoke of John being a prophet who would prepare the way for the Lord.

Names were very important to Jewish people, and nearly always had a special meaning. John means the 'grace of God'. The Old Testament was based on law. But John was to announce God's New Testament (or agreement) with people – based on grace (God's love). We cannot keep God's laws perfectly and so God's grace is needed to save us when we mess up.

PRAY Heavenly Father, thank You for the Bible, which teaches me so many good things. I want to always be open to learn from You. Amen.

THE WILDERNESS YEARS

READ: Luke 1:80; 4:1–2

KEY VERSE: 'the child grew and became strong in spirit; and he lived in the wilderness' (1:80)

So, where did John train for his special assignment from God? Bible College? The Temple? University? Actually, he headed for the place where many of God's great leaders trained – the wilderness.

PROPHET TRAINING COURSE
Venue: The wilderness around Jericho.
Cost: Everything.
Accommodation: None. Students do not have belongings or any sort of comfort to distract them from their studies.
Core subjects: Prayer. Learning the Scriptures. Listening to God. Singing psalms. Meditating on God.
Extracurricular activities: Survival training.
Meals: Locusts and honey.

No one enjoys going through a difficult time. But we can be strengthened by these times. John's training was not comfortable at all, but it did teach Him to rely on God. Remember that God is a great teacher who knows what we are going through and wants to strengthen our trust in Him.

THINK Have you ever been through a difficult time in your life that has made you stronger? What did you learn from this?

HIGHWAY TO HEAVEN

WAIT... WAIT... GO!

READ: Luke 3:1–3

> **KEY VERSE:** 'He went into all the country around the Jordan, preaching a baptism of repentance for the forgiveness of sins.' (v3)

John spent a long time in the wilderness – probably until he was nearly 30 years old. Was he wasting his energy in this dry place? What was he waiting for?

The answer is clear: God has a right time for everything and John was prepared to wait for that time. The moment God gave the green light, John was in the fast lane, accelerating into action. He went where God told him to go and said what God told him to say. Sometimes we may be raring to go off and do something but God says 'No' or 'Wait'. It can be tempting to just go for it anyway, but that can get us into all kinds of trouble. Maybe God hasn't given the OK because we're not ready yet.

At other times God wants to accelerate into action but it doesn't suit our timing. We feel that right now isn't the best time to go along with God's plan, so we stay put and cause a jam. John was prepared and willing to obey God in everything.

PRAY Father, I want to do what You want me to. Please show me what this is and help me to trust You. Amen.

ROADWORKS AHEAD

READ: Luke 3:4–6

KEY VERSE: 'Every valley shall be filled in, every mountain and hill made low.' (v5)

A king riding in a chariot would have men go ahead and remove any rocks in his path. The Romans forced thousands of slaves to flatten hills and fill valleys so they could make straight, even roads.

700 years before John started preaching, Isaiah predicted John's work (Isa. 40:3–5). He described John as someone moving ahead of a king preparing a clear, straight, level route. And who was coming along that route after John? None other than Jesus, who would die to save us and restore our relationship with God.

We have habits that need to be taken away for King Jesus. These are things that block off areas of our lives from His control. Ask God to show you some things that shouldn't be in your life. (Read Galatians 5:19–20.)

We also have valleys, parts of our lives that are not full and where something is missing. Ask God to show you what good things, like peace and joy, He would like you to have more of. (Look at Galatians 5:22–23.)

PRAY Holy Spirit, please show me the areas of my life that need some work and are in the way of my journey with You. Amen.

HIGHWAY TO HEAVEN

U-TURN!

READ: Luke 3:7–9

KEY VERSE: 'Produce fruit in keeping with repentance.' (v8)

Most of the books in the New Testament were originally written in the Greek language, and the Greek word for 'to turn around' also means 'to repent'.

John's preaching came as a shock to the people listening. They had wanted God to send someone to deliver them from the Romans who occupied their land, and here was someone calling them a 'brood of vipers'! But they quickly realised that they had been going the wrong way and asked John what they should do.

John told them that they needed the wrong things that they had done, and were still doing, to be taken out of their lives. And God was sending someone to do just that – Jesus!

John told them to turn away from the wrong things they were doing and turn to God instead. That's what repentance means. But it wasn't just about saying a quick 'sorry' prayer: how they acted from then on would show how much they had really changed – because actions speak louder than words.

THINK **Is there anything you need to turn away from? Ask God for forgiveness and help with this, then think about ways to try and stop yourself from turning back again.**

CAUTION!

READ: Matthew 7:15–20

KEY VERSE: 'by their fruit you will recognise them' (v20)

John was a prophet who pointed people to Jesus, but there were other prophets who were fake: false prophets with wrong motives, thoughts, ideas and words.

Jesus warned the people not to be fooled by false prophets. At first they might seem harmless, like sheep, but underneath they were dangerous, like wolves – causing serious damage by telling big lies.

A simple test was to see what kind of character they were. Did they display 'good fruit' as listed in Galatians 5:22–23 such as love, joy, peace, kindness, gentleness and self-control? If they didn't show any of these qualities then John said they were like bad trees bearing bad fruits. And bad trees are pretty useless – only to be used as firewood on a fire.

John's motivation in life was to point people to the only hope we have. He was definitely a 'good tree' showing 'good fruit'. Let's aim to be the same – showing 'good fruit' in order to do good things.

THINK **What sort of fruit can be seen in your life? If we want to see God do good things through us, we need to ask Him to help us to develop good qualities, like those in Galatians 5:22–33.**

HIGHWAY TO HEAVEN

BRANCHING OUT

READ: Luke 3:10–14

KEY VERSE: 'What should we do then?' (v10)

John was very practical. He didn't set his listeners impossible goals but pointed them to the next step. When people asked, 'What should we do then?' he didn't reply by suggesting general things like, 'Be loving' or 'Be kind', but he said things like 'Share your food'. He didn't tell tax-collectors and soldiers to go and become pastors, but to do their current jobs in the right way.

God can do the same for you. He can show you areas where you can be challenged to do something good for others. He can also show you areas that need changing in order to show 'good fruit' – the good stuff that comes from following Him.

Let's look at some examples of 'good fruit' in everyday life that might be a good starting point:

- Treating everyone as we want to be treated
- Telling the truth
- Trusting God

Now let's look at the 'bad fruit':

- Being rude to people
- Telling lies
- Ignoring what God says

PRAY Dear God, please show me how to display 'good fruit'. I want to go about my everyday life in Your way. Amen.

HOLY WATER AHEAD

READ: Matthew 3:11–17

KEY VERSE: 'He will baptise you with the Holy Spirit and fire.' (v11)

Why was John called John the Baptist? Well, because he baptised people who had turned to God! But why did he baptise them?

When non-Jews wanted to follow the Jewish faith, they would be baptised. These new Jews would be dipped under water to show that they had left their old way of living. They would then rise out of the water to show that they had started living in a new way.

John baptised those who wanted to show their decision to live for God. But John announced that a more powerful person was coming who would baptise with the Holy Spirit. That person was Jesus. To John's surprise, Jesus came to see *him* and asked to be baptised! Why?

Jesus didn't need to turn away from sin and start a new way of life, because He did not sin. But He wanted to be one of us in every way if He was going to die for our sin. And God responded to this by saying how pleased He was with His Son.

THINK Baptism is about showing the world that we are turning away from sin, and turning to Jesus instead. Have you been baptised? Is it something you would like to know more about?

MERGING ON TO MAIN ROAD

READ: Luke 3:15–18; John 3:25–34

KEY VERSE: 'He must become greater; I must become less.' (John 3:30)

Crowds were flocking into the desert to hear John speak. Some even thought that John was the person God had sent to save the world. What did John do with his new-found fame?

He gave the fame to Jesus. When he spoke, he spoke about Jesus – telling of how amazing and powerful He is. And when it came to comparing himself and Jesus, it was no contest. Jesus was way, way ahead. John didn't even feel jealous when his disciples left him to follow Jesus. In fact, he wanted them to! It was all part of God's plan for his life. John wanted himself to shrink in people's minds, while Jesus took centre stage.

God has plans for all of our lives, really great ones! But that doesn't mean that we're going to be the centre of attention. The plan God had for John was amazing, but it was all about showing people Jesus. Let's try to be people who want Jesus to be the centre of attention.

PRAY Lord Jesus, I only want You to be the centre of attention. Please help me to use my life to make that happen in the world around me. Amen.

ROAD BLOCK

READ: Luke 3:19–20

KEY VERSE: 'Herod... locked John up in prison' (v20)

Scandal! Roman ruler to file for divorce and then marry his brother's wife! The magazines would have had a field day. But they of course didn't exist back in those days and, even if they did, anyone who criticised Herod faced the chopping block. The religious leaders turned a blind eye, and no one was brave enough to say the whole thing was wrong. No one, that is, except...

John's 'Turn to God' protest came to an end when he was arrested. John had spoken against Herod of Antipas, who was the ruler of Galilee, for lying and cheating. His recent comments, describing Herod's affair as 'evil', had got him locked up without any hope of release. Herod's new wife, Herodias, whose father was responsible for murdering babies in Bethlehem 30 years ago (in an attempt to kill Jesus), really had it out for John. So much so that she wanted the death sentence for him.

To John, wrong was never right, no matter who was doing it. He spoke against it, even if it meant Herod would be after him.

THINK **Do you speak out when you see something happening that is clearly wrong? When we are close to God, the things that upset Him start to upset us.**

EXPECT LONG DELAYS

READ: Matthew 11:2–6

KEY VERSE: 'Go back and report to John what you hear and see' (v4)

John had really looked forward to the arrival of God's Son, and here he was stuck in prison! What was happening? What was Jesus doing? John had to know.

Jesus let His actions speak louder than His words and told John's messengers to tell him everything they had seen Jesus do. All of the great miracles. And Jesus also had a special message for John in prison: 'Happy is the man who trusts me and doesn't stop believing.'

Can you imagine how annoying it must have been for John to be out of the action he had been preparing for? It would have been like spending ages setting up and organising a game and never playing it. But John played his part in God's plans. We can also play our part. We may not be there to see our prayers for others being answered, or see people who we talk to about Jesus receiving Him, so it is important that we keep trusting God and don't get down about these things.

PRAY Lord God, help me to be patient and know that You will always finish the work that You start. I leave it all in Your trustworthy hands. Amen.

END OF THE ROAD

READ: Mark 6:17–29

KEY VERSE: 'So he immediately sent an executioner with orders to bring John's head.' (v27)

Have you ever wondered why God allows good people to get hurt? Life doesn't seem to be fair sometimes. John's treatment by Herod is a classic example. It's awful when a 'good and holy man', which is how Herod described John, could be killed because of a wife's grudge. See how Herod went from sin to sin in the way he handled his affair – eventually killing John at the request of his wife's daughter.

We live in a world that does not want God, and all kinds of unfair things happen as a result. Where is God when all this evil is happening? The answer is: right in the middle of it – as Jesus, nailed to a cross. But God raised Jesus from the dead! Evil may have its way for a while, but God will win in the end.

Herod made a serious mistake when he got carried away with drinking and dancing. Remember, we have an enemy who likes to catch us out. Let's be alert so that we can see his tactics coming, and take a stand against him.

THINK
Have you ever felt unfairly treated? Whenever that happens, talk to Jesus about it. He knows what it is like because He's been through it Himself.

HIGHWAY TO HEAVEN

LASTING IMPRESSION

READ: Matthew 21:23–27

KEY VERSE: 'for they all hold that John was a prophet' (v26)

What do you think of John the Baptist? We're now going to take a look at what an impact his life made on those around him.

Most of the ordinary people around Jerusalem were poor and not very educated, but they were good judges of character. Lots of them had little time for the arrogant, well-dressed, hypocritical religious leaders, many of whom had ripped off the poor. But they liked John. He was honest, straight-talking and practised what he preached. He was the real deal. There was something special about him. When he spoke, his words hit the spot. There was no doubt about it, he spoke with power – God's power.

The Temple was full of clever teachers, but none of them could preach like John. Crowds came from the Judean hills and travelled for days out into the wilderness to listen to John's sermons. The religious leaders looked down their noses at him, but the ordinary people were convinced that what John was saying was from God. As Christians, let's try to be aware of the impact we make through the way we live.

PRAY Lord Jesus, You are the perfect example of how to act and speak. Help me to make a good impression on others. Amen.

BOLD IMPRESSION

READ: Mark 6:20

KEY VERSE: 'When Herod heard John, he was greatly puzzled; yet he liked to listen to him.' (v20)

OK, so John was liked by most Jews. But what impression did Herod have of him? The two had eyeball to eyeball meetings while John was in prison.

John wasn't just doing God's work in front of crowds. Here we see Him having a conversation with Herod in private about God. God's words are (in Bible speak) sharper than the sharpest sword, cutting deep into our thoughts, and showing who we really are (see Heb. 4:12, NLT). No wonder Herod felt uncomfortable!

It can be too easy to hide away from saying the things that God wants us to say because we are afraid of upsetting our friends, or losing them as friends altogether. It's time to be brave and realise that God will help us to say the right thing at the right time, in the right way.

Did you notice that Herod liked John's talks, even though he found them disturbing? John was different. He didn't smooth-talk Herod to try and get out of prison. He simply explained things from God's viewpoint. And God wants us to do the same!

THINK **Next time an opportunity comes to tell others about Jesus, why not go for it? Don't be afraid of not knowing what to say — God will help you.**

HIGHWAY TO HEAVEN

GENUINE IMPRESSION

READ: Luke 7:24–25

KEY VERSE: 'What did you go out into the wilderness to see?' (v24)

John never knew what Jesus said about him. But we do... Before Jesus told the crowds what kind of person John was, He told them what John wasn't.

John was not:

- Someone who changed his opinions to impress people. He didn't say one thing to one person and another to someone else. John gave the same message to everyone – turn away from wrong living and turn to God.
- The type of guy to live an easy life or want to impress people with a title, his clothes, belongings or anything else. Expensive chariots and designer robes weren't his thing – he lived for something, or rather someone, better than these.

It's not just about what we are that makes an impression on others. It's about what we are not. If we are not two-faced or big-headed, people are more likely to listen to us. If we're not like everyone else, we show that we stand for something. Let's ask God to help us to make a good impression on those around us.

PRAY Father God, I want to follow You whatever situation I find myself in, not the crowd. I want to live for You. Amen.

GLOWING IMPRESSION

READ: Luke 7:26–30

KEY VERSE: 'A prophet? Yes, I tell you, and more than a prophet.' (v26)

What else did Jesus say about John? Having told the people what John wasn't, Jesus announced who he was.

John was more than a prophet – he was the person God told the prophet Malachi about 400 years ago. A special messenger to prepare people for God's Son, the Saviour of the world.

And how did the people react to this statement from Jesus? (Look at verses 29 and 30.) The religious leaders who had not been baptised by John rejected what Jesus was saying. They thought their way was best and did not want to submit to God's way. But those who had been baptised by John, even the worst of them all – the tax-collectors – listened to Jesus and accepted His teaching. God's way was best and He had a purpose for them! They began to understand this.

How you live your life can help people to be open to listening to Jesus and following Him. The best thing we can ever do for someone is point towards Jesus.

THINK Some people will ignore what we say about Jesus, but it's still worth talking about Him throughout our whole lives, even if just one person listens and starts thinking about Him. Do you agree?

GREAT IMPRESSION

READ: Luke 7:28

KEY VERSE: 'among those born of women there is no one greater than John' (v28)

John did not think of himself as great. He did not even think of himself as worthy enough to carry Jesus' sandals (Matt. 3:11). He turned the spotlight away from himself so that people would see Jesus. You see, it's when you are humble that God makes you a champion. And the less focused you are on making yourself look good, the greater you are in God's eyes.

Wait for this mother of all compliments from none other than Jesus: 'John, you are the greatest man who has ever lived!' So that also makes him the humblest man who ever lived.

Wait, though. Did you catch the last part of the verse? The least person in the kingdom of heaven – that's you and me – is greater than John. How? Not because of anything we have done: but because through the death and resurrection of Jesus, we have become God's children. And as God's children, we receive blessings – because we are part of God's family.

PRAY

Lord, show me how to listen to others and put their needs before my own. Give me a helpful attitude so that I will be happy to do jobs that others don't want to, and to help me be humble. Amen.

POWERFUL IMPRESSION

READ: Acts 19:1–6

KEY VERSE: 'On hearing this, they were baptised in the name of the Lord Jesus.' (v5)

What happened to those who turned to God and were baptised by John? Some took John's advice and followed Jesus straight away; others didn't follow Jesus so quickly. But God had not forgotten them.

These men had attended John's 'Turn to God' protest and had been baptised to show the world they meant business. Many years later they were in Greece. No, they weren't on an all-inclusive holiday. They were respected citizens of Ephesus who worshipped God – but they did not know about Jesus and the Holy Spirit. Paul was able to tell them about Jesus and what He had done for them. He was able to explain that Jesus had returned to heaven but had sent the Holy Spirit to live in Jesus' followers.

The penny finally dropped! Hadn't John said that God was sending someone to baptise with the Holy Spirit? It was all making sense. The men couldn't wait to show the world that they wanted to follow Jesus – and the Holy Spirit gave them the power to live and serve the God they loved.

PRAY Father God, thank You that nothing is wasted with You. I love that something I say or do now could impact someone's life in years to come, all because of You! Amen.

HIGHWAY TO HEAVEN

SHAKE THE EARTH

READ: Psalm 114:1–8

KEY VERSE: 'Tremble, earth, at the presence of the Lord' (v7)

At any big sports event, there are a lot of people feeling very strongly about something — whether their team is the best or the other team is the worst! And they don't hold back; they scream and shout about it! But it's all just a load of noise until each team joins together and sings the same song. Then it becomes very powerful. Well, when we sing to God together, it is even more powerful than that! Why? Because of *who* we're worshipping!

In the New Testament, Paul writes about a time he spent in prison. Even though he and his friend Silas were facing a really terrible situation, they started praising God. Do you know what happened? 'Suddenly there was such a violent earthquake that the foundations of the prison were shaken' (Acts 16:26). That's the power of worshipping God together; that's the power of God!

The psalms turn the feelings of people who are excited about God into songs that worship Him. And there's a lot to sing about, considering all He's done for us! He's powerful and that's why worship is too.

THINK Do you find praising God to be powerful? Try really putting your heart into what you're singing next time and see what happens!

NUMBER ONE FAN

READ: Psalm 139:1–18,23–24

KEY VERSE: 'you know me' (v1)

Who do you like hanging out with best? Probably people you can relax with – people who know you well and accept you for who you are. Well this song is about how great it is to be on God's team because He knows *everything* about us!

God knows us even better than we know ourselves. He made us unique! He knows our good side, our bad side, our interesting, boring, fun, dull, strong, weak, nasty and kind sides – and He still wants to be close to us. He knows absolutely everything about us and He still loves us. Now that's something worth singing about!

The way that the psalm ends is important too. The songwriter knows he's not perfect, and he asks God to give him a check over. God is totally for us, not against us. He wants to help us improve in any and every way we can – so that we can be more like His Son, Jesus. He's not like a mean or uncaring teacher – He's more like our number one fan! Always there and ready to boost us up!

PRAY Father, it's amazing that You see every part of me and are still my number one fan. Please help me to become more like Jesus in the ways that I need to. Amen.

PSALM

OBEDIENT TO GOD

READ: Genesis 11:27–32; Hebrews 11:8

KEY VERSE: 'By faith Abraham, when called to go to a place he would later receive as his inheritance, obeyed and went, even though he did not know where he was going.' (Heb. 11:8)

When you just can't wait for something to happen, having to hang around for it can be really tough. We live in a world of next-day delivery – we hate the wait! The story of Abraham and Sarah tells us of some amazing promises that God made. But the promise they wanted God to keep the most was the one thing they had to wait for.

Let's start at the beginning: before God changed his name to Abraham, our main guy was called Abram. He and his family lived in a rich town called Ur, but what made them leave?

Even though it hadn't been long since God sent the huge flood, the people had once again turned away from Noah's God. Even Abram's dad worshipped idols. Yet Abram realised the God of Noah was real and for him. So Abram, Sarai (his wife – soon to be known as Sarah), Terah (his dad) and Lot (his nephew) left Ur and headed towards Canaan.

THINK
Change can be really hard, but God is there to talk to about it. Are you finding it hard to adjust to changes in your life?

PROMISES

GOD OF PROMISES

READ: Genesis 12:1–9

KEY VERSE: 'I will make you into a great nation, and I will bless you; I will make your name great, and you will be a blessing.' (v2)

While Abram was at Harran, God made some promises to him. These were not your everyday 'I promise I'll tidy my room' type of promises, they were *big* promises. Four thousand years later, let's see if God kept them.

Did Abram's descendants become a great nation?
The great nation is Israel. Attempts to destroy the Jews have failed. They are still in the land promised to Abram.

Was Abram blessed?
Yep! Abram had wealth and power. However, his biggest blessing was being able to talk with God about anything.

Has Abram's name become great?
It's not only Jews and Christians who respect him, but Muslims too.

Has everyone been blessed through Abram's descendants – the Jews?
Jesus was born as a Jew. Through Jesus, anyone in the world can become friends with God. So yes, we've all been blessed.

THINK God is trustworthy and keeps His promises. Can you think of any promises He's made to you?

GOD OF TRUTH

READ: Genesis 12:10–20

KEY VERSE: '"What have you done to me?" [Pharaoh] said. "Why didn't you tell me she was your wife?"' (v18)

Abram was settled in the Promised Land when the land dried up and there was no food. With these problems, did he wonder if he and Sarai had been right to leave Ur?

Abram and Sarai headed south into Egypt in search of food. News that there was a beautiful woman in town reached Pharaoh, who wanted to add her to his collection. At this point, Abram bottled out of trusting God. He was afraid to say that Sarai was his wife in case Pharaoh had him killed in order to marry her. So he pretended Sarai was his sister. God, however, was having none of it. He had plans for Sarai to be the mother of a great nation. So Pharaoh was taken out of action with a serious illness until the truth came out.

Abram got himself into a big mess by telling lies. But although he let God down, God made sure Abram and Sarai were allowed to return to the Promised Land with all the food they needed.

PRAY Lord, thank You that You love to help me and are always there. Please help me to live my life relying on You, not lies. Amen.

GOD KNOWS

READ: Genesis 13:1–13

KEY VERSE: 'Abram called on the name of the LORD.' (v4)

After a lot of bother in Egypt, Abram hit the road, returned to Bethel and sorted things out with God. But the problems didn't stop there.

The issue was that Abram and his nephew, Lot, had so many sheep and cattle that they couldn't all fit on the fields in that area. Abram had the right to first choice on the land. After all, God had promised it to him, not Lot. But he offered Lot first choice instead, and Lot got greedy. He decided to take the fertile Jordan valley, leaving the dried up mountains to Abram. Abram knew he was getting a rubbish deal but didn't complain. He wanted to part ways on good terms.

But was it such a bad deal? Lot had not talked with God about the decision. Had he done so, God would have pointed out the dangers of going to live near Sodom and Gomorrah. The people there were bad news. Lot's decision gave him fat cattle but brought him and his family a lot of sadness.

THINK God knows things that we don't know. Do you talk to Him about decisions you have to make? It makes sense to because He always knows what's best.

PROMISES

GOD FIRST

READ: Genesis 13:14–18

KEY VERSE: 'Go, walk through the length and breadth of the land, for I am giving it to you.' (v17)

Ever felt like you've become worse off for doing the right thing? Lot had made his choice; did that mean Abram was left with second best? Lot rushed off to claim his land, a 25-mile stretch of the Jordan valley. Abram remained on the hilltop with land that was wild and rocky. How would his sheep survive?

God always works for the good of those who put Him first. There was no way Abram would come out of this second best – not with God in charge. God told Abram to look up, then look around. He could see for miles and miles in every direction, right out to the coast, along the Jordan valley, and over the hills. God promised that all this land would be his – including Lot's patch.

So how did Abram celebrate? He built an altar and worshipped God!

Going God's way might not always make us popular at the time, but you can guarantee this: if you put God first, you'll come out on top. Who or what comes first in your life?

PRAY Dear God, I know that You want the best for me and I am deciding to put You first in my life. I trust You. Amen.

ABRAM TO THE RESCUE

READ: Genesis 14:8–16

KEY VERSE: 'He recovered all the goods and brought back his relative Lot and his possessions, together with the women and the other people.' (v16)

Lot found that things were far from easy in the land he'd chosen. His get-rich-quick plans took a setback when Kedorlaomer, a tough-nut outlaw, forced the local businessmen to cough up protection money. They paid him off for 13 years before deciding to gang together and refuse to pay anymore.

Lot's gang came off badly in the mob fighting that followed, and he and his family were captured.

How did Abram react to the news? Did he laugh and say, 'Serves him right'? Lot had been really selfish in grabbing the best land for himself, so he had it coming, didn't he?

Nope, Abram got a gang of 318 men ready to go on a search and rescue mission. In a daring night raid Abram, with God's help, chased the mob out and rescued Lot, his family and all their belongings! Abram risked his life to save his selfish nephew. That sounds a lot like what someone else we know did – Jesus!

THINK
Jesus gave up His life to set us free from sin and death. As He doesn't hold grudges, even when we've messed up, are there any grudges you need to let go of?

PROMISES

PRIEST-KING

READ: Genesis 14:17–24

KEY VERSE: 'praise be to God Most High, who delivered your enemies into your hand' (v20)

Abram returned as a hero, and Melchizedek, the king of Jerusalem, congratulated him. Melchizedek wasn't only the king, but a priest of the most high God. He gave credit where it was due – to God.

At a time when most people worshipped the sun or man-made idols, Melchizedek knew better. He didn't congratulate Abram for winning the battle. He congratulated him for having God on his side. He didn't praise Abram for being successful – he praised God. Melchizedek, the first recorded priest-king of Jerusalem, believed that God who created everything could do anything. He praised God for simply being the best.

Abram showed his thanks to God by giving 10% of the goods he had captured to Melchizedek. He returned the rest to its rightful owners in Sodom, refusing to keep any for himself. He had already promised God he wouldn't accept any gifts from the dodgy characters in Sodom. He didn't need their help, which probably wouldn't be very helpful, or money – he had God on his side!

PRAY
Lord Jesus, I also think You are the best. I praise You for all the things You do in the world and in my life, both big and small. Amen.

COUNT ON IT

READ: Genesis 15:1–6

KEY VERSE: 'Do not be afraid, Abram. I am your shield, your very great reward.' (v1)

As soon as Abram turned down the king of Sodom's offer, God arrived on the scene as Abram's 'very great reward'.

Abram opened his heart to Him. He shared with God the things that were really bothering Him. He and Sarai had tried to have children but hadn't been successful. And let's face it, all God's promises about Abram becoming the father of a great nation were depending on him having children. If God didn't make him a dad soon, all would be lost. If he had no heir, one of his servants would inherit everything from him.

But God knew what He was going to do. He asked Abram to look up and open his eyes. As Abram star-gazed he took in God's promise. He would have a son! Impossible as it might seem, he would finally be a real father with so many descendants that there would be too many of them to count! God said so, and Abram trusted that He would make it happen – somehow.

THINK Do you ever wonder if God really cares about the things that bother you? Here's something to remember: if it's bothering you, He's bothered.

PROMISES

SAFE

READ: Genesis 15:7–21

KEY VERSE: 'I am the LORD, who brought you out of Ur of the Chaldeans to give you this land to take possession of it.' (v7)

God promised childless Abram that his family would grow into a great nation – and with that promise was a guarantee that they would have their own land. God's promise was huge. How about Abram's faith?

Abram knew that the land God promised was full of tough-talking tribes who wouldn't want him marching in and settling down. He just couldn't work out how his family would ever be strong enough to take them all on. After making sacrifices to God, he fell into a deep sleep. But what God told him as he slept scared him. He learnt that although he would enjoy a long and peaceful life, his descendants would spend 400 years as slaves in a foreign land.

But then God threw a light on the situation, and suddenly the future looked far, far brighter. God promised to rescue the Israelites and help them claim their land from those troublesome tribes. Abram's family *would* live where God had promised.

PRAY Heavenly Father, when the future scares me, please remind me of how far You've already brought me and of how safe I am in Your hands. Amen.

THE WRONG PLAN

READ: Genesis 16:1–6

> **KEY VERSE:** '[Sarai] said to Abram, "The LORD has kept me from having children. Go, sleep with my slave; perhaps I can build a family through her."' (v2)

Ten years after arriving in Canaan, Abram, now 86, and Sarai still had no children. They had waited for God to give them a son but nothing had happened. What now?

God's plan – Plan A – was that Abram and Sarai would have a son. And Abram believed God would work to that plan. But after years of waiting, the couple came up with Plan B. The result would be the same – a son – but via their servant Hagar, not Sarai.

Abram and Sarai didn't speak to God. They just put Plan B into action and Hagar became pregnant. But they hadn't read the small print for Plan B: family problems were guaranteed. There was trouble from day one. Jealous Sarai treated Hagar badly and eventually the young, pregnant servant ran away from home.

God hadn't forgotten about Plan A, He just had it on hold. Abram made the big mistake of rushing ahead of God. Instead of trusting Him, Abram put his own plan into action.

THINK Do you sometimes want to do things your way without speaking to God? Next time you're tempted to rush into something, try talking and praying with a Christian friend first.

PROMISES

SPOT ON

READ: Genesis 16:7–16

KEY VERSE: 'She gave this name to the LORD who spoke to her: "You are the God who sees me"' (v13)

Abram and Sarai's Plan B was a disaster that left Hagar on the run and alone. What did God make of it all? He sent an angel to find Hagar. God still cared about her and her baby. He wasn't going to leave her to fend for herself in the desert. The angel asked Hagar to talk about what happened and what she planned to do. God knows it's important that we have someone to talk to.

The young girl needed a lot of support and love, and the best place for her to be was at home. But there would have to be changes. Hagar should begin by working things out with Sarai and helping her. But she was understandably worried about the future and what would happen to her baby, so God let her in on a secret. She was expecting a boy – a son who would grow up to have many descendants.

When we are going through a hard time, God sees us. He wants us to talk to Him about how we feel. We can trust Him.

PRAY Thank You, God, that You will always see and care for me. Please remind me to always talk to You in hard times. Amen.

FULL STOP

READ: Genesis 17:1–8,15–22

KEY VERSE: 'Yes, but your wife Sarah will bear you a son, and you will call him Isaac.' (v19)

Remember this? Abram is 99 years old. Sarai is 90. God now explains that time is right for them to have a son. Abram just laughs. Well, what would you have done? Looked it up in a science textbook?

There was no way it was humanly possible for this retired couple to have children. Abram struggled to get his head around it. He didn't tell God about his doubts but God knew about all of them.

God had to put in a 'Yes, but...'; Yes, but you WILL have a son and you WILL call him Isaac. There were no doubts as far as God was concerned. He went into detail about Isaac's future and even gave the couple an arrival date.

God had a new name for Abram – Abraham, meaning 'special dad to loads of children'. He also had a new name for Sarai – Sarah, meaning 'princess'. With all their faults and failings, God still loved this couple.

THINK **Sometimes we have a hard time believing that God cares for us when things don't work out in the way we had hoped. How can you help yourself to trust in God's care in future?**

PROMISES

NO LIMIT

READ: Genesis 18:1–15

KEY VERSE: 'Is anything too hard for the LORD?' (v14)

There are some people who let whatever you say to them go in one ear and out the other. It's like talking to a brick wall! No matter how many times God promised Abraham and Sarah, the doubts were still lingering.

When three strangers turned up, Abraham invited them in for a bite to eat. Little did he know he was entertaining the Lord.

As Sarah eavesdropped on the mealtime conversation, she heard one of their guests say she would give birth to a son in a year's time – and she had a quiet chuckle. 'No chance,' she thought. Sarah believed she was way past her sell-by date as a mother. But the Lord didn't lay into her for her lack of faith. Instead He asked them a question: 'Why did Sarah laugh? Is *anything* too hard for the Lord?'

Rather than answering the question, Sarah lied about her sniggering: 'I didn't.'

'Yes, you did,' The Lord replied. He knows everything.

God had answered His own question by saying, 'I WILL return next year... and Sarah WILL have a son.' He has no limits. He can do anything He wants!

PRAY Lord, when life gets tricky, thank You that there's no limit to what You can do. No problem is too hard for You. Amen.

REAL

READ: Genesis 18:16–21

> **KEY VERSE:** 'I have chosen him, so that he will direct his children and his household after him to keep the way of the LORD.' (v19)

As Abraham walked his guests out, he got some good news and some bad news.

The good news was that Abraham really would become father to a powerful nation. God also told him the secret of being the best dad – teaching your children to love and follow God. God wanted Abraham's family to set an example to all other families by doing things His way.

The bad news was that Lot and his family, living in Sodom, were about to be burnt to a crisp. Sodom and Gomorrah had become cities full of evil. God wasn't going to tolerate the people's behaviour any longer. Lot and his family hadn't joined in with the wild partying, but they hadn't walked away from it. They lived a double life – one to please the bad guys and another to please God. It didn't work. God wants us to be real and for Him all the time.

PRAY Father, I'm sorry for times when I care more about what other people think of me than about what You think of me. Please help me to be loyal to You. Amen.

GOD OF FORGIVENESS

READ: Genesis 18:22–33

KEY VERSE: 'For the sake of ten, I will not destroy it.' (v32)

God is about to detonate the dynamite — His judgment on the 'sin cities'. Abraham knew God was serious about dealing with the wickedness in Sodom and Gomorrah.

God's still against sin today. So the Bible warns us to get right with Him while we have the chance. God hates the wrong things we do and wants to save us from them because He loves us. We can work this out for ourselves as we read what Abraham asked the Lord: would those who obeyed God get the same deal as those who didn't? Even if there were only 50 of them — or fewer? Not at all.

God is tough on sin but He's also kind. He gives people time to think through the way they live, and escape. That's why two angels were on their way to Sodom — to help Lot and his family get out.

God sent Jesus into our world to give us a way out of danger too. When we trust Jesus, we're safe.

THINK Is there anything that you need to ask God to forgive you for? It can be difficult to own up to sin, but it's easier when we realise that God loves us and wants us to go to Him.

DON'T LOOK BACK

READ: Genesis 19:12–29

KEY VERSE: 'But Lot's wife looked back' (v26)

It was make-your-mind-up time for Lot and his family. How seriously would they take God's warning to leave their homes as He was about to destroy the city? At first, Lot seemed in no doubt that God would do as He said. He rushed round to his future sons-in-law and told them to pack their things. Sadly, they treated Lot's words as a big joke. They didn't care about obeying God.

Perhaps this affected Lot's own opinion. Suddenly he didn't seem so keen to get out either. God's angels had to practically drag him, his wife and two daughters away. Even then Lot argued over where they were told to go to be safe!

As for Lot's wife, she went along with God to start with, but didn't really want to leave her life in Sodom. Her heart was still in the city and so she became a pillar of salt.

Despite Lot's hesitation, he and his daughters reached safety because they'd finally done as God had asked them to.

PRAY

Heavenly Father, I want to give You control of my life today – not just part of it, all for it. Thank You for sending Jesus to let me escape from sin. I am so grateful! Amen.

PROMISES

FAITHFUL FRIEND

READ: Genesis 20:1–17

KEY VERSE: 'he is a prophet' (v7)

Some people have a hard time learning their lesson. Remember how Abraham lied to Pharaoh to save his own skin? Remember the trouble that caused? Well, surely he wouldn't pull the same trick again to Abimelek?

Believe it or not, Abraham did. He said he was Sarah's brother to keep himself safe (again!), and let her be taken off to the palace. All God's promises were forgotten as Abraham pushed God out and looked after number one.

But once again, God came to the rescue. God couldn't let Abimelek ruin His plans to start a great nation, so He warned the king. Abimelek was horrified and returned Sarah home immediately.

Was God's friendship with Abraham spoilt by Abraham's lies and lack of faith? Not at all. God told Abimelek that Abraham was a prophet (v7). You see, He still had big plans for His friend and nothing would change that. God even came up with a way to deal with the aftermath. He told Abimelek to ask Abraham to pray for him, and Abraham's prayers brought good results not just for Abimelek, but for Abraham too.

THINK
God knows we let Him down but He doesn't write us off. We are still His children even when we get it wrong, and He loves us just the same.

GOD OF LAUGHTER

READ: Genesis 21:1–7

KEY VERSE: 'the LORD did for Sarah what he had promised' (v1)

At last Abraham really is going to be a dad. He's 100 years old and Sarah is expecting their child – just *as* God promised and just *when* God promised.

Only a year before, when God had told Abraham he'd be a father, Abraham had laughed. God had fed him this line for over 20 years, and the joke was starting to wear thin. When Sarah heard that God planned to make her a mother, she'd laughed too. At her age she thought there was no chance.

And now both Abraham and Sarah were laughing again because God had kept His promise. But this was a different type of laughter. It didn't come from their doubts, it came from God Himself. Sarah said as much: 'God has brought me laughter!' Finally, they had a son. God had exchanged their zimmer frames for a pram!

So – is anything too hard for God? Not a chance! God had already named the baby, and Abraham didn't object to the choice. His son was called Isaac – which in Hebrew means 'He laughs'.

PRAY Holy Spirit, please change me so that I learn to trust You in all situations. Let Your goodness be seen by others through my life. Amen.

PROMISES

NO FAVOURITES

READ: Genesis 21:8–21

KEY VERSE: 'God heard the boy crying, and the angel of God called to Hagar from heaven and said to her, "... Do not be afraid"' (v17)

Forget Everton v Liverpool – Sarah v Hagar was a rivalry like no other.

God had promised that Abraham's heir would be the father of a great nation – a nation into which He would send the Saviour of the world. Would this special nation come from Hagar's son, Ishmael, or Sarah's son, Isaac? Ishmael was the eldest, but God had always said His promises to Abraham would be fulfilled through Sarah.

Abraham was upset over the family squabbling. He loved both his sons – so did God. And God had the answer. Isaac's children would become the special nation God had chosen to show His ways to the world – the Jews. Ishmael's children would become a great nation too – the Arabs.

God didn't love Isaac more than Ishmael. He proved it by looking after Hagar and Ishmael in the desert all those years ago. God has different plans for all of our lives, but that doesn't mean He loves us any more or less than others.

THINK Do you ever think that God seems to have favourites? He has no favourites, He just chooses to use people in different ways.

PEACEMAKER

READ: Genesis 21:22–34

> **KEY VERSE:** 'Abraham planted a tamarisk tree in Beersheba, and there he called on the name of the LORD, the Eternal God.' (v33)

Remember King Abimelek, the second person Abraham fooled into thinking that Sarah was his sister? (A weird habit of Abraham's!) Some of his men had hijacked a well that Abraham had dug.

Both Abraham and Abimelek had vowed to not fight each other, and the hijacking of the well was the first test of their agreement. Would Abraham keep his promise or would he use force to take back the well?

Abraham wisely decided to talk the matter through with Abimelek. He discovered that the king knew nothing of the hijacking, nor did he approve of it. Abraham's attitude as he went into the talks was important too. He didn't storm in all guns blazing. Instead he brought gifts. Abimelek, completely shocked, accepted the gifts and confirmed that the well was Abraham's. The situation was resolved.

When a friend appears to be doing something against you, it's best to calmly talk to them – most of the time this is enough to sort the situation out.

PRAY Lord, when I get caught up in an argument, help me to remain calm and be a peacemaker so that the situation can be worked out. Amen.

PROMISES

THE TEST

READ: Genesis 22:1–8

> **KEY VERSE:** 'God himself will provide the lamb for the burnt offering, my son.' (v8)

We're back at this story again. Having waited so long for a son, Abraham had his faith tested to the limit. God asked him to sacrifice Isaac... *What?* This didn't make sense. First, although some people in Canaan did make human sacrifices, God *hated* this. Second, all God's promises to Abraham depended on Isaac being alive and having children of his own.

Clearly, God had no intention of any harm coming to Isaac. However, he wanted to test Abraham's faith in a dramatic way. He had an incredible lesson to teach him that would explain how God can rescue us from death. Even the place God chose was significant — Mount Moriah. Years later the Jews would sacrifice animals here to avoid the death penalty for their sin.

So what did Abraham make of God's request? Incredibly, he decided to trust God, and took Isaac up the mountain. There was no way God would break His promises. It had taken Abraham 100 years to believe God that much, but now he did.

THINK Are you having a tough time at the moment? God always keeps His promise to be with you. Keep talking to Him and to other Christians.

GOD'S GREATEST BLESSING

READ: Genesis 22:9–19

KEY VERSE: 'through your offspring all nations on earth will be blessed, because you have obeyed me' (v18)

Abraham's faith was being stretched to the limit. God had asked him to sacrifice his only beloved son, Isaac.

All Abraham could do was trust in God's unchanging character and His unchanging promises through Isaac. Abraham even believed God could raise him from the dead (Heb. 11:18). And his faith was rewarded! The moment the knife was drawn, God moved in to spare Isaac's life. 'Do not lay a hand on the boy,' said the angel of the Lord.

God then showed Abraham an alternative sacrifice: a ram trapped in a bush by its horns. God hadn't changed, nor had His plans; Isaac would live to have millions of descendants. Abraham had trusted the Lord and the Lord hadn't let him down.

God told Abraham that everyone on earth would be blessed because Abraham had obeyed Him (v18). That includes us today. How? Because Abraham's greatest descendant, God's own Son, Jesus, was born a Jew. Just like the ram died instead of Isaac, Jesus died so that we can live. He is the Lamb of God who takes away our sin.

PRAY Lord Jesus, I thank You with all my heart for giving up Your life so that I can spend mine with God forever. Amen.

PROMISES

BEST WIFE

READ: Genesis 24:1–9

KEY VERSE: 'The LORD, the God of heaven... will send his angel before you so that you can get a wife for my son' (v7)

Abraham had a problem. Isaac needed a wife... but who? Abraham didn't want Isaac to marry any of the local girls. He knew they had no time for God. They worshipped false gods and lived only to please themselves. He feared that if Isaac married a Canaanite, his son would drift away from God and begin worshipping idols. God had told Abraham to teach his children right from wrong, and that included in their love lives.

Abraham wanted his son to marry a girl who loved God. That narrowed down the field a bit. Abraham knew the right girl for Isaac would be God's choice. He wanted God to play matchmaker because he trusted that God always has our best interests at heart. God's choice would be the best person in the world for Isaac. So Abraham sent his servant out with the task of bringing back God's choice of wife for his son.

THINK
Is there someone you've got your eye on? Take a minute to think about the effect that getting involved with that person would have on your relationship with God.

PRAYER FIRST

READ: Genesis 24:10–27

KEY VERSE: 'LORD, God of my master Abraham, make me successful today, and show kindness to my master Abraham.' (v12)

We all face choices. What should I have for breakfast? Who should I hang out with today? What subjects should I pick at school? Abraham's servant travelled up north on his quest for God's choice of wife for Isaac. He headed straight to the local spot that was popular with the girls – the well. When he was almost there, to make sure he wouldn't get confused, the servant said to God, 'When I ask a young woman for a drink, if she gives me a drink and waters the camels too – let that mean she's the girl You've chosen for Isaac.' (See verse 14.)

Now when Rebekah appeared, that's exactly what happened. And Rebekah was not only beautiful, but kind and caring too. As God made His choice, the servant couldn't help but worship Him.

The reason the servant's quest was successful was because he prayed before doing anything else. He asked God to be in charge. Then he waited patiently for God to lead him to the right person.

PRAY Dear Lord, You know what decisions I have to make right now. Please show me the right way to go, and give me the patience and understanding I need. Amen.

PROMISES

FROM GOD

READ: Genesis 24:28–52

KEY VERSE: 'Laban and Bethuel answered, "This is from the Lord; we can say nothing to you one way or the other."' (v50)

Abraham's servant was certain he'd met the perfect bride for Isaac. He'd even given her a ring – a nose ring, but still a ring! Now what would her family make of this? When Rebekah came home showing off her new piercing, big brother Laban rushed out to see the man Abraham had sent.

No, he wasn't in overprotective big brother mode – he welcomed him with open arms. Laban knew straight away that Abraham's servant was a man who loved God. And in the discussions about the marriage proposal, the servant name-dropped the Lord multiple times. He couldn't stop talking about all that God had done.

When Rebekah's family had listened to the whole story, it was learn there was nothing at all to argue about. God had clearly planned all of this out. All they could do was agree with Abraham's servant and say, 'This is from the Lord.'

THINK When you look back, can you see times when God was clearly working in your life? If you're waiting for Him to make something clear at the moment, be patient and keep talking with Him.

HAPPY ENDING

READ: Genesis 24:53–67

> **KEY VERSE:** 'Isaac… married Rebekah. So she became his wife, and he loved her' (v67)

So, between the servant and the family, the marriage was agreed. But Rebekah and Isaac had never met each other. This could have been very, very awkward! Would they be as happy about the match as Abraham's servant was?

Rebekah was keen to marry someone who loved God, which she knew Isaac did. Even so, how did she feel about marrying an unknown man and moving far away from her home? That was a lot of change. But, given the choice of another ten days at home or catching the next camel to meet Isaac right away – she was on the next camel!

As for Isaac, when the camel arrived at the platform, he was spending time with God in a field (one way to make a good impression!). He saw Rebekah and rushed to meet her. When he learnt how God had brought them together, he was over the moon. The couple married and the Bible simply tells us that Isaac loved his wife (v67). A happy ending all round.

PRAY

God, when I can just see a small piece, You see the whole puzzle. Help me to trust You more with the big decisions in my life. Amen.

PROMISES

PROMISES KEPT

READ: Genesis 25:1–11

KEY VERSE: 'His sons Isaac and Ishmael buried him in the cave of Machpelah near Mamre' (v9)

Sarah had passed away, and Abraham had remarried and had six more sons. And with these, six smaller nations were born. However, Isaac was still Abraham's heir and the father of the special nation God had promised.

God said Abraham would have a long and peaceful life, and He was right – as always. Abraham lived to be 175 years old – and that is *old*! After he died, both Ishmael and Isaac were at their father's funeral. Family fights had caused the two boys to live apart but they were reunited by Abraham's death. And there is no record of any argument between them over Abraham leaving everything to Isaac. The sons worked together to make the funeral arrangements.

Isaac's descendants are still living in the land God promised them all those thousands of years ago.

But God's promise to bring freedom to all families in the world (Gen. 12:3) is what it's all about. God has kept His promise in Jesus, Abraham's greatest descendant. If there's one thing that can never be argued about, it's this – God keeps His promises.

PRAY Lord, thank You that because of Jesus, You accept me as Your child and I can know You are my Father. It's amazing! Amen!

I HATE YOU!

READ: Psalm 109:1–15

KEY VERSE: 'They repay me evil for good, and hatred for my friendship.' (v5)

Today's psalm is a seriously angry one! 'Argggh! I hate you!' is the feeling behind this psalm. The songwriter has an enemy and, boy, does he wish bad things would happen to him! Do you ever feel like this? Has someone got you really, really angry? It can be so tempting to repay their wrong with another wrong, can't it?

Well, in the New Testament, Jesus explained that God wants us to forgive our enemies, because, after all, we have been forgiven by God. Jesus taught us how to love those who are mean or rude to us. Even on the cross, He asked God to forgive those who had so hatefully put Him in that awful place.

It's by no means easy. Everything within us may want to lash out. But let's think about why we should forgive. God is patient, forgiving and kind. And with the Holy Spirit living in us, we can be these things too. When we forgive others, we show them what God is like.

THINK If you need some help dealing with your anger towards someone, instead of blowing your top, talk to God about it. Let Him help you stop hating and start forgiving.

PSALM

THIRSTY?

READ: Psalm 42:1–11

KEY VERSE: 'My soul thirsts for God, for the living God.' (v2)

Today's psalm writer was probably writing this psalm as a refugee. A terrible war had destroyed Israel and the people had been dragged off as slaves to foreign countries. The Temple had been vandalised and smashed up. That was very, very serious. The Temple was more than just a building; it meant that God was with His people. So what did it mean if the Temple was a pile of rubble? Had God deserted His people?

The singer feels a long way from God's presence. He is sad and very low. But in the middle of all his sadness, all he knows is that he is desperate for God. He chooses to believe that God loves him and that He will come to His people again, even though it seems impossible.

Being 'thirsty' means that you really want something that you haven't got just yet. Jesus said that He is looking for people who really want to be close to God but know that they haven't got there just yet (Matt. 5:6).

PRAY Lord, please come and be with me. If I'm thirsty, show me more of You. If I don't feel that thirst, give me a taste of just how amazing You are so that I will be! Amen.

PSALM

JESUS

READ: Matthew 1:18–25

KEY VERSE: 'give him the name Jesus, because he will save his people from their sins' (v21)

Joseph and Mary didn't have to Google baby names when they found out Mary was pregnant. They knew the baby was a boy and they had been given the name for Him already! In Jewish tradition, the father would name the child. And here we get a clue why Joseph didn't name the baby. He wasn't the father – God was. So it was God who named His Son, and what a great name He chose – Jesus!

Everyone knew what that name meant. It was a popular name already. Jesus meant 'Saviour'. More than that, God spelt out what His Son had come to save people from – sin!

Jesus wasn't the only name God came up with in heaven. He also chose the name Immanuel. Six hundred years before Jesus was born, God let Isaiah in on His big plan (Isa. 7:14). Immanuel means 'God with us'. God's Son had come to live with us!

Jesus is God with you – yes, you! He promises that He will always be with you (Matt. 28:20). You are never alone.

THINK Jesus is with you in your neighbourhood, your school, your home, your life! What sort of welcome do you think He deserves?

HIS NAME IS...

MAN

READ: 1 Timothy 2:1–6

KEY VERSE: 'the man Christ Jesus' (v5)

Jesus is called many names and each one tells us something new about Him. Let's look at some of them over the next few weeks.

Jesus restricted Himself to living in a human body for just over 30 years. He experienced growing up and being a young person, with all the stresses that come with it. So when you face hard times in your teenage years, know that you can talk to Him about it because He's been there too! Then, as a man, Jesus experienced hunger, thirst, tiredness and stress. Also, famously, He faced temptation and was victorious over it! Jesus went through a lot of same stuff we go through, and He gives us a great example to follow in dealing with these things.

In 1 Timothy 2:5, Jesus is described as 'the man' – not just a man but *the* man. The greatest, gentlest and most awesome man ever. That makes Him the best role-model, but also the best friend that we could ever want.

PRAY

Lord Jesus, I am so thankful that You came to earth. Help me to always try and be like You and remember that You understand what life is like. Amen.

LIGHT

READ: John 8:12–19

KEY VERSE: 'I am the light of the world.' (v12)

Light is a five-letter word you could use instead of the word 'Jesus', which shows us what He's like and what He's done for us. It's used 33 times in John's Gospel alone!

In the days of Moses, God lit up the way to the Promised Land with a pillar of fire. This was celebrated at the Feast of Tabernacles when four large bowls in the Temple courtyard were filled with oil and the priest's uniform from the last year, and then were lit for everyone in Jerusalem to see. Light was also associated with freedom. It was in this culture that Jesus announced He was the light of the world. He was the pillar of fire leading people of all backgrounds to God.

To celebrate their victory over Antiochus IV (a Syrian dictator who tried to stop them worshipping God), the Jews held an annual festival of lights. Candles and torches were lit in every home and kept burning for eight days. In the evenings they sang and danced to music. Jesus, our light, came to win our freedom from the darkness of living without God.

PRAY **Thank You, Jesus, for lighting up my life, showing me the way and giving me freedom. Help me to always choose to follow Your light. Amen.**

HIS NAME IS...

THE WAY

READ: John 14:1–9

KEY VERSE: 'I am the way' (v6)

In Moses' day God used a cloud by day and a fire at night to show the Israelites 'the way' (Deut. 1:33). From then on people spoke about following God's 'way'. Psalmists sang songs asking God to show them His 'way'. And then Jesus arrived, giving Himself another title...

Sat-navs can show us different routes to get to the destination we have entered, but in Jesus' day there was only one safe route between places – 'the way'. So when Jesus called Himself 'the way' He was stating that it's only through Him that we can be saved.

There was also another meaning to this name. Jesus often referred to the first five books of the Bible, the law, as 'the way' because it told them the way to live their lives. So in saying that He was 'the way', Jesus was announcing that the old way of becoming right with God through sacrifices was over. Instead, He was about to become the sacrifice to open up a new way.

THINK Some people live their lives not knowing what God thinks of them and if He accepts them. When we trust in Jesus, no matter what we've done, we are saved and forgiven! Do you believe that?

FIRST AND LAST

READ: Revelation 1:8–18

KEY VERSE: 'I am the Alpha and the Omega' (v8)

Before sat-navs, most people used an 'A-Z' map book to find their way around. When John was shown a vision of heaven, he saw an A *and* Z. No, not a guidebook of heaven, but the most awesome person.

The New Testament was written in the Greek language and while our alphabet starts with 'A' and ends with 'Z', the Greek alphabet starts with 'Alpha' and ends with 'Omega'. Jesus used this to show that He is the first and the last.

He is the first because He was there at the beginning of everything, creating our world and everything in it. He is the last because He is in control of all events in the future and will reign with God the Father over a new heaven and earth (Rev. 21–22).

He is our 'A' because Jesus is with us from the beginning of our lives, knowing us before we were born (Psa. 139:14–16). He is our 'Z' because, if we believe in Him, when we die we'll be with Him forever.

THINK **With Jesus as our A-Z, we never need to feel lost, because He can show us the right way ahead. Got a situation where you need someone to point you in the right direction? Ask Jesus.**

HIS NAME IS...

THE TRUTH

READ: John 14:6; 18:33–38

KEY VERSE: 'I am... the truth' (14:6)

When people exaggerate we ask them to 'get real'. People who are honest and tell it like it is are 'real' with themselves and others. Was Jesus real with people?

Pilate asked Jesus an interesting question: 'What is truth?' Truth means nothing hidden. It is possible to say something that is true without telling the truth – you can reveal some facts but not others to mislead people. This is why in a court of law you are required to tell 'the truth, the whole truth and nothing but the truth'.

When Jesus said, 'I am the truth', He could equally have said, 'I am real'. Jesus didn't tell lies or try to con people. He didn't make Himself out to be anything He wasn't. He could easily have denied being a king to Pilate and avoided crucifixion, but Jesus was real. Jesus didn't just tell the truth, He IS the truth. It is not in His character to mislead, deceive or lie. He is 100% genuine, trustworthy and reliable – a friend who cannot and will not let you down.

PRAY Jesus, thank You for being so trustworthy and for being my friend. I want to be true and real – please help me with this! Amen.

GATE

READ: John 10:1–9

KEY VERSE: 'Very truly I tell you, I am the gate for the sheep.' (v7)

Many of those who listened to Jesus owned sheep or were hired to look after flocks. So, Jesus used an example based on their experience to help them understand who He is.

There was one way in or out of sheepfold. A shepherd stood by the gate to count his sheep in the fold. Sick or wounded sheep would be singled out for treatment, and those not belonging to him, turned away.

We've mentioned before about how shepherds slept across the entrance, acting as a 'living door' to protect their sheep. Jesus didn't say He was one of many ways to God, but 'the gate'. The only entrance to the kingdom of heaven. You cannot be forgiven and enter the security of God's family without meeting Him first! It is Jesus who opens up our access to the Father.

Also, once we've entered through the gate (been saved by Jesus) we don't need to only be with Christians. The sheep could go in and out, and we can get to know all sorts of people too!

THINK Do you have friends who love Jesus, as well as friends who don't? It's great to have a mix of both!

HIS NAME IS...

RESURRECTION

READ: John 11:17–27,38–44

KEY VERSE: 'I am the resurrection' (v25)

One of Jesus' best friends was dead. To make matters worse, Jesus had arrived late for the funeral. The dead man's relatives were distraught. Was this the best time for Jesus to announce a new name? It was, as it happens. Jesus' sense of timing is always perfect.

Poor Martha was overcome with grief when her brother Lazarus died. When Jesus arrived He introduced Himself as 'the resurrection and the life'. Resurrection means 'to stand up again'. Was Jesus claiming He could bring Lazarus to life and up on his legs again? Yes! Jesus has power over death. And he demonstrated it by commanding Lazarus to walk out of the tomb. Lazarus, his feet still wrapped together with burial cloths, came out like a bandaged pogo stick!

Jesus' promise is that all who believe in Him will live even though they die. In other words, when Christians die, that is not the end. Jesus is there to see us 'standing up again' in heaven with a new body and eternal life!

PRAY
Lord Jesus, thank You for having power over death and promising that everyone who trusts You will be with You forever. I trust You and want to live for You. Amen.

BREAD OF LIFE

READ: John 6:30–51

KEY VERSE: 'I am the bread of life.' (v35)

After providing bread for the 5,000+ people, Jesus announced that He was the 'bread of life'. He expected those listening to be able to work out what He meant.

Back in the time of Moses, six days a week for 40 years, God delivered 'bread from heaven' – wafers that tasted like honey. This 'bread', called manna, gave hundreds of thousands of Jews the protein, vitamins and energy they needed to survive in the desert. Seven times as He was speaking, Jesus said He came down from heaven (vv33-58) – not to fill stomachs but to fill out lives. Jesus was the new manna God had sent to bring new life to the world.

But what does that mean? Well, Jesus provides us with what we need in life. He is where we can draw our energy from. More than that, He is able to satisfy us. Lots of us can feel 'spiritually hungry' without realising it. Some people describe this as having a 'God-shaped hole'. Jesus fills us so that we don't feel that hunger anymore – He is what we've been craving.

THINK Do you value the 'bread of life' in this way? Do you thank God for Jesus? Tell Jesus how much you appreciate Him, and tell others as well!

HIS NAME IS...

VINE

READ: John 15:1–8

KEY VERSE: 'I am the true vine' (v1)

In the Old Testament, the Jews were pictured as a grape vine that God had planted. And vines were carved on the outside of synagogues to remind people that God cared for them. Jesus' announcement that He was the true vine was a bit of a shell-shocker. God was still the gardener, but Jesus was the vine and those who believe in Him were the branches.

If a grape is removed from the life supply of the vine, it dries up. If we remove ourselves from Jesus, we shrivel up too! But if we stay close to Him, we grow. To take this further, a vine branch can produce lots of grapes or it can grow wild, with all wood and little fruit. We can also show spiritual fruit, or become a tangled mess. Pruning (getting rid of the unwanted bits) is what makes the difference.

The Greek word for 'prune' also means 'to clean'. God wants to clean up our lives. The result, the spiritual fruit – a big, awesome mix of love, joy, peace, patience, kindness, goodness, faithfulness, gentleness and self-control in our lives.

PRAY Father, thank You for being my provider and for cleaning up my life. Help me to stay connected to You so that I can continue to grow and produce good fruit. Amen.

GOOD SHEPHERD

READ: John 10:1–29

KEY VERSE: 'I am the good shepherd.' (v11)

In the Old Testament, God described Himself as a good shepherd caring for His flock, the flock was not of the woolly four-legged variety, but the two-legged species – His people. Jesus introduced Himself to the world as the shepherd – the good shepherd with the emphasis on *good*.

Let's look at the difference between a regular old shepherd and Jesus...

A HIRED SHEPHERD: Doesn't own the sheep. He doesn't bother to remember their names. If thieves or wild animals arrive on the scene he shouts, 'Abandon sheep!' and runs for his life. The sheep are captured, killed or scattered.

THE GOOD SHEPHERD: He knows each of His sheep by name. His sheep recognise His voice and follow Him when He calls to them. They are absolutely safe – 100% secure. He protects them at all costs – even to the ultimate cost of dying for them.

With Jesus as your good shepherd there is nothing to be scared of. He always cares for you. Nothing you do can ever remove you from God's family.

THINK **Do you find it easy or difficult to see Jesus as your protector when you can't physically see Him?**

HIS NAME IS...

FOUNDATION

READ: 1 Corinthians 3:10–23

KEY VERSE: 'For no one can lay any foundation other than the one already laid, which is Jesus Christ.' (v11)

What do you base your life upon? What makes you do the things you do?

Jesus once told a story about two builders. One was foolish and built on sand. The other was a wise guy who built on rock-solid ground. The building on sandy foundations collapsed in the first storm. The one with solid foundations didn't rock. Paul continues the theme of this story by asking about the foundations of our lives. Some people build their lives on their future hopes, desires and dreams. Others build their lives around people or belongings. Paul learnt that Jesus is the only foundation worth building your life on. He is totally secure, reliable and strong.

You see, while having dreams is great, what happens if the dream doesn't work out? It's not safe to build our lives on things that can crumble. Jesus is the only foundation that won't ever let us down. So let's base our lives on Him!

PRAY **Lord Jesus, I am so thankful that You are strong and invite me to base my life upon You. Help me to always see You as my foundation, not anything or anyone else. Amen.**

CHRIST

READ: John 1:35–42

KEY VERSE: "We have found the Messiah" (that is, the Christ).' (v41)

Andrew introduced Jesus to his brother as 'the Christ'. To most of us, Christ is simply another name for the Lord Jesus. But to Andrew, Peter and the people of that day, the word 'Christ' was heavily loaded with meaning. Christ meant 'the anointed one'. People chosen to be kings or priests were anointed.

From the earliest times, God promised to choose, anoint and send someone to save the world. His choice was His Son, Jesus. When Andrew met Jesus, he realised he hadn't been speaking to an ordinary man, or even a special man – but God's 'anointed one'. That's why he was so keen for Peter to meet Jesus.

Some time later, Jesus asked His disciples who they thought He was. Peter answered, 'You are the Messiah [Christ], the Son of the living God' (Matt. 16:16). It wasn't a lucky guess. God had let Peter in on His secret – Jesus is the one anointed by God to be our Saviour.

THINK
We belong to the one and only anointed Saviour; we belong to the King of kings. What might some privileges of this be?

HIS NAME IS...

BAPTIST

READ: Luke 3:1–17

KEY VERSE: 'He will baptise you with the Holy Spirit and fire.' (v16)

Remember John, the relative of Jesus? A while back, we looked at His life and what He went around doing. He preached that people should do a U-turn away from wrong and follow God. Many turned to God and were baptised in water by John. It wasn't long till he was nicknamed 'John the Baptist'. But did you know that Jesus also baptised?

John the Baptist prepared people for the arrival of Jesus. He made a point of telling his disciples that Jesus would do more for them than he could. John baptised people in water to show they had turned to God for forgiveness. But Jesus would baptise people with the Holy Spirit – God living in them! The English word 'baptise' comes from the Greek word *baptizo*. It means to soak, drench or sink. So Jesus would send the Holy Spirit to live within them and it wouldn't just be a trickle, but a complete drenching so that they could show the world their new life in Jesus.

PRAY
Holy Spirit, I want to see more of You in my life – not just a little bit, but a complete drenching! Please show Your mighty power in my life. Amen.

PEACE

READ: Isaiah 9:6; John 14:27–31; 16:33

KEY VERSE: 'Prince of Peace' (Isa. 9:6)

Are you feeling stressed as if everywhere you go seems to be filled with noise, distractions and confusion? Well, take time now to find out about another five-letter word for Jesus – peace.

What a magnificent title – 'Prince of Peace'. That's Jesus! He is not just a peaceful person, or someone who makes us feel at ease. Jesus *is* peace – it's in His nature! Peace is not something you find by acting laid back and cool. Real peace begins and ends with Jesus. We cannot have peace with God, without Him. Gaming, sports or watching a movie can help us to escape our worries and problems for a short time, but only Jesus can give us lasting peace.

Jesus warned His disciples that they would face trouble. But before they had the chance to get all worked up and freaked out about it, He told them not to worry because He would give them His peace. Christianity is not a ticket to an easy life, but even in the toughest times, we can turn to Jesus and He can make us calm and confident.

THINK If we want peace, it's important to take time out to spend with Jesus, reading the Bible and talking with Him. He is the way to peace with God, others and ourselves.

HIS NAME IS...

SLAVE

READ: Mark 10:35–45

KEY VERSE: 'slave of all' (v44)

James and John hoped that being a follower of Jesus would give them the chance to sit back and give the orders. They'd got it totally wrong. Jesus reminded them that He hadn't come to boss them around. Neither did He expect them to run around after Him doing His chores. He had come to serve them. Not just some of them – all of them... everybody! Jesus put Himself at the bottom of the pile.

So, when there were smelly feet that needed a wash and scrub down, Jesus was on His knees with a bowl of water. When people with diseases, criminals, traitors and other not-liked people needed help, He met them, forgave them and healed them.

But the ultimate act of putting others first was Jesus' willingness to die on the cross. He gave up the number one spot and all the perks of heaven to become the lowest of the low – hated, rejected and hurt – all so we could be forgiven by God. Jesus is our servant King. He deserves to be praised!

PRAY

God, I know You want me to serve the people I know, but it isn't easy. Please help me to find ways to do this, and the confidence to go ahead with it. Amen.

DEFENDER

READ: 1 John 2:1–14

> **KEY VERSE:** 'we have an advocate with the Father – Jesus Christ' (v1)

Those facing trial need lawyers to plead their case in court. They are the ones wearing black gowns and white curly wigs. Did you realise you have a case pending? Yes, one day all of us will have to face up to God. On our own? No, we have someone to defend us.

Jesus is our defence. He is willing to talk to God on our behalf. Although we are guilty of breaking God's laws, Jesus is there to argue that we are 'not guilty'. Why? Simply because He died to take the punishment for our sin. Our sentence has been paid. The evidence for this? His blood poured out on the cross.

Jesus cares about us so much about us that He prays for us. Yes, *you* are on His prayer list! Sometimes problems or mistakes can make us feel so low that we wonder if anyone really cares or understands. Jesus knows what we are going through, prays for us and brings our situation to God the Father.

PRAY
Lord Jesus, thank You so much for being my defender. I'm amazed that You would be punished in my place. You deserve all the praise and fame. Amen.

HIS NAME IS...

PIONEER

READ: Hebrews 2:1–11

KEY VERSE: 'the pioneer of their salvation' (v10)

Can you think of any famous pioneers? Here's one you might have heard of: Christopher Columbus. He's the guy who set out to pioneer a route to India going west from Europe, and discovered North America! And there are lots of other people who have pioneered new routes, new ways of doing things, new inventions, and made new discoveries.

Who is the greatest pioneer ever? Jesus is! You might be thinking it's quite strange to think of Jesus as a pioneer. What is He the pioneer of? He's the pioneer of our salvation. He left heaven, came to earth, suffered, died and rose again to open a new route for us to join God's family. No one else could have done that. God wanted us to be saved and Jesus made it a reality by dying on the cross and rising again.

What is the greatest achievement of all time? Saving the world – and that's all down to Jesus. Because of Him, we are forgiven. He deserves all the praise!

THINK
Do you think your friends understand what Jesus was doing when He died and rose again? How can you help them to understand this more?

TEACHER

READ: John 13:3–17

KEY VERSE: 'I, your Lord and Teacher' (v14)

Teachers have lots of practice telling their pupils what to do. 'Do this... do that... be quiet... I won't tell you again... QUIET!' Teachers in Jesus' day were no different. Rabbis (the Jewish name for teachers) expected their pupils to do as they said.

Jesus was a great teacher – the greatest ever. He spoke with great power and people travelled miles to hear Him. But Jesus taught with more than words and interesting parables. He taught by example. So when He wanted to teach His disciples to serve each other, He showed them how He wanted them to do it...

He grabbed a bowl and a towel, and started washing the disciples' manky feet! Bear in mind that they would have been wearing sandals to walk around in, and the roads were not concrete – they were dusty and dirty. Ew! But Jesus showed them His attitude, and what He wanted them to be like. And if Jesus, their 'Lord' and 'teacher', treated others better than Himself, His pupils didn't have an excuse not to do the same.

PRAY Lord Jesus, I want to be like You and follow Your example. Help me to value others like You do. Amen.

FRIEND

READ: Luke 7:34–48

KEY VERSE: 'a friend of tax collectors and sinners' (v34)

We can't choose our family but we can choose our friends. When Jesus came to earth, He was free to choose His friends. Who do you think God's Son, fresh out of heaven, would want to mix with?

Jews hated tax collectors. They were traitors who worked with the Romans and cheated people out of their money. So the Jews refused to speak to them. They also kept away from people who were thought of as 'sinners', like the woman with the bad past who visited Jesus as He was eating.

Jesus saw things differently, though. He was friends with these people – not telling them that what they had been doing was OK, but telling them that God hadn't rejected them.

Stuck-up Simon the Pharisee was shocked that Jesus didn't tell this woman to clear off. Jesus then reminded Simon that we all sin. Yes, some sin much more than others. But that means that they've got more to thank God for when He forgives them. Just like the woman was when Jesus forgave her.

THINK
Have you got any bad habits that keep you away from Jesus? Talk to Him about them and ask for His forgiveness.

KING OF KINGS

READ: Revelation 19:11–16

KEY VERSE: 'KING OF KINGS' (v16)

Jews believed a mighty king, greater than King David or King Solomon, would come to defeat their enemies and make them into the greatest nation. There was good news, bad news and excellent news.

The good news: Jesus arrived as King to deliver people from the big enemy – not the Romans, sin!

The bad news: Jesus was crucified with a sign mocking Him as the 'King of the Jews' nailed to His cross.

The excellent news: Jesus rose from the dead and returned to heaven to be crowned the King of kings!

When John wrote Revelation, Caesar ruled the world. Christians obeyed Caesar, but they worshipped Jesus as the King of kings. Jesus was much more important to them than anyone else. When Caesar ordered Christians to worship him and turn their backs on Jesus, they refused. Thousands of Christians were put in prison or fed to the lions for refusing to say that anyone other than Jesus was the King of kings.

THINK
Have you ever been teased for following Jesus? While we don't get thrown to the lions, we do sometimes face insults. Try talking to a Christian friend or youth leader about this.

HIS NAME IS...

LORD OF LORDS

READ: Revelation 19:16

KEY VERSE: 'LORD OF LORDS.' (v16)

It's the same key verse today as yesterday. It's not that we don't think you read it carefully enough yesterday, but that there is another revelation about Jesus in the book of Revelation.

In Bible times, many kings were known as 'lord'. The title meant 'one who is in control'. The word 'Lord' is used thousands of times in the Old Testament to describe God. Moses reminded God's people that 'the LORD your God is God of gods and Lord of lords' (Deut. 10:17). There were hundreds of gods that people worshipped, but they were all fakes and God was more powerful than any of them!

In the New Testament, Jesus is called 'Lord' hundreds of times. But more even better – Jesus is the 'Lord of lords'. He is greater than Caesar, Herod or any power. The first Christians openly said that Jesus was the 'Lord' and completely believed that.

Jesus is above every other power but He still wants to be our friend. How great is that?!

PRAY Jesus, You are Lord of everything. You're higher up than anyone in power in the whole world. Please be Lord of my life, too. Amen.

LORD JESUS CHRIST

READ: Acts 2:22–36

KEY VERSE: 'Jesus... both Lord and Christ' (v36, NKJV)

The title 'the Lord Jesus Christ' does not appear in any of the Gospels, but when the Holy Spirit came at Pentecost, He started to be known by this great title more. The first Christians called Jesus 'the Lord Jesus' or the 'Lord Jesus Christ'. We have already discovered what these words mean on their own, but look at their power when they're thrown together:

Lord – the ultimate authority, Lord of lords.

Jesus – Saviour, saving us from sin.

Christ – anointed by God to be King – King of kings.

Looking at that, we can start to understand why the first Christians were so dedicated to telling others about Jesus.

Christians do not follow a brilliant man, or a hyped-up superhero, but the Lord Jesus Christ. He is Lord of all creation! He is our King, our master, our everything. Even those in heaven who have power fall down to worship Him, respecting and admiring Him (Rev. 5:8–13).

THINK
Unfortunately, many people in the world don't see the name of Jesus as important, and even use His name as a swear word. Let's make a choice to always do our best to respect the name of Jesus.

HIS NAME IS...

ABOVE ALL OTHER NAMES

READ: Philippians 2:5–11

> **KEY VERSE:** 'the name that is above every name, that at the name of Jesus every knee should bow... and every tongue acknowledge that Jesus Christ is Lord' (vv9–11)

Who's your favourite famous person? Maybe they're an actor or actress, a footballer, a singer... whatever! Have you ever wondered what their life is like? Here's a secret: you know something about their future that they might not know.

One day everyone, absolutely *everyone* will kneel with respect in front of the Lord Jesus. That means every celebrity, all the world's rulers, all the sporting heroes, every school bully, anyone and everyone. There's not a person alive who won't meet Jesus one day. Many will face Him as their judge. Those who have believed in Him will face Him as their Saviour. And there's a big difference in what those experiences will be like.

Never forget that there is only one name in the whole of heaven and earth with the authority to save us from our sin – the name of the Lord Jesus Christ (Acts 4:12)!

PRAY Lord Jesus Christ, Your name is above every other name. I worship You right now and want to tell You that I believe You are Lord of everything. Amen.

SORRY

READ: Psalm 51:1–19

KEY VERSE: 'Create in me a pure heart, O God' (v10)

When things go wrong, when we mess up, we can't just press a button to make everything right again – we have to sort things out and that usually involves saying sorry.

Of course, this can be one of the toughest things to do. We naturally want to pretend we've done nothing wrong saying, 'It wasn't my fault.' Or, 'That person deserved it.'

The psalm today is believed by many to be written by King David. He messed up big time. He was a cheater and a murderer. He tried to carry on as normal, pretending he'd done nothing wrong, but eventually it all hit him. He'd behaved badly, not only against other people, but against God. He felt terrible! He couldn't turn back time, but at least he could get right with God.

If we don't admit we've done anything wrong then we're trapped – we can't grow as Christians. That's a big shame and it can even tear us away from God. But when we admit our mistakes to God, the burden of guilt is lifted and we can feel so much better!

PRAY
God, You love me so much and forgive me freely. Thank You. Please clean out my heart and make me new today. Amen.

PSALM

RELAX

READ: Psalm 131:1–3

KEY VERSE: 'I have calmed and quietened myself, I am like a weaned child with its mother' (v2)

So, you've just been born and what happens? Suddenly you are thrown out of a lovely, safe, warm and comfortable home and into the cold, fresh air. Where's your lovely warm home gone? And what about your endless supply of food? Now you have to ask for it (cry a lot!).

The thing about babies is that when they finally get fed, they relax. Cuddled up with their mums, nice and snug, they are very, very happy!

Weaning is the stage of a baby's life where they are no longer on milk but start to eat other food. This psalm shows us a picture of a happy child who has learnt to trust his mother to provide this food for him. It shows us that when we come close to God and relax in His company, then we are a bit like a happy child. God loves us, protects us and feeds us. Just like a mother enjoys the bond that grows between herself and her child, so God enjoys it when we chill out and enjoy His company.

THINK
What do you think it means to spend time relaxing with God? Take some time now to enjoy just hanging out with Him — it's so good for you!

PSALM

RUN TO YOU

READ: Ephesians 6:18–20

KEY VERSE: 'And pray in the Spirit on all occasions with all kinds of prayers and requests' (v18)

Have you ever felt pulled in different directions? Sometimes life can be a bit confusing, but there's one place you can take all your questions...

Did you know that God *loves* to listen to you? It doesn't matter that He knows everything already, He just loves to sit and listen to everything you have to say, down to the tiniest detail. He also has *the* most brilliant answers, but sometimes He helps you figure it out for yourself too.

Talking through things can really help us to sort out our jumbled thoughts and feelings, and God has all the time in the world to spend with you. He's never too busy; with Him there are no silly questions. Your needs and wishes are important to Him. Sometimes we don't get the exact answers we want, but the answers God gives are always the best thing for us in the long run. And like in any relationship, the more you speak to Him, the more you know Him.

PRAY
Father God, I come to You now with everything going on in my life. Please help me with _____.
I'm so thankful that You listen to me. Amen.

TALKING WITH GOD

SHAKEDOWN!

READ: Acts 4:23–31

KEY VERSE: 'After they prayed, the place where they were meeting was shaken. And they were all filled with the Holy Spirit and spoke the word of God boldly.' (v31)

Peter and John had been ordered by the Jewish authorities to stop talking about Jesus or there would be serious, and we mean *serious*, consequences. But they weren't shaken by their experience. Instead, they met with other Christians to plug in to the ultimate power source: God. And what did they say? 'Sovereign Lord...' That was a good start. It was the same as saying, 'Lord, you are the real boss, You are in control of the situation...' They had the creator of the universe on their side, so why worry about a few trumped up men in fancy robes?

The group of believers didn't ask for an opt-out option on sharing about Jesus, or for God to zap their enemies. They asked God for the power to obey Him and fearlessly tell the world about Jesus. God heard them, answered their request and dispatched the power supply they needed – so much of it that it nearly brought the house down!

THINK Is there something you need to pray for today? Strength? Courage? Wisdom? Asking another Christian to pray with you can be really helpful.

THE INTERPRETER

READ: Romans 8:22–27

> **KEY VERSE:** 'We do not know what we ought to pray for, but the Spirit himself intercedes for us through wordless groans.' (v26)

Fumbling for words? Don't know what to say? Still learning 'prayer' language? Even if you're shy, overwhelmed or new to the ways of prayer, you don't need to worry. Help is near!

One of the names Jesus' followers called Him was Rabbi, meaning 'teacher'. He taught a completely new, wonderful way of approaching life. But in learning something new, we need constant practice. Often we have a tutor, and that's where the Holy Spirit comes in.

Prayer is an absolutely essential skill for every Christian to have. It is the key to everything else because prayer is how we communicate with God. And if we can't communicate with God, we're not going to be able to live *for* God. That's why He sent His Spirit to coach us on how to pray. He's even there in those times of frustration when we just don't know how we feel – let alone what to pray – stepping in to translate the feelings that we can't put words to.

PRAY Lord, I don't always find it easy to pray. Thank You for sending Your Holy Spirit who puts the power into my prayers. Help me to listen to Him. Amen.

TALKING WITH GOD

IN IT TOGETHER

READ: Genesis 1:26–30

KEY VERSE: 'Then God said, "Let us make mankind in our image, in our likeness, so that they may rule over... all the creatures that move"' (v26)

When you create something as a group – for school or just for fun at home with a friend – what's the very first thing you do? You talk about it, don't you? Without communication, it would be chaos and a waste of effort! Besides, half the fun is in the talking about it! Right back at the beginning of time, God made a stunning world for His children, then said, 'It's over to you... Go explore, create and rule!' We are co-workers or partners with God, joint-guardians of this earth!

But God lets us choose how we live. We can live only for ourselves, doing our own thing and ignoring Him (look where that got Adam and Eve!) – or we can accept the offer to join with Him, live a meaningful life, and be on talking terms with the creator of the universe!

THINK Do you consider yourself to be on God's team? He wants us to be – it's the best team to be a part of! How often do you talk to your God, your team leader?

MIRROR IMAGE

READ: Psalm 8:1–9; 115:16

KEY VERSE: 'The highest heavens belong to the Lord, but the earth he has given to the human race.' (115:16)

Ever been told you look like someone else? Maybe a relative, or maybe just someone from TV! Well, we really *were* made to remind people of someone else. But who?

You guessed it – people are made in the image of God, crowned with glory! When the rest of creation saw Adam, they saw a reflection of God. Just as the moon has no light of its own but reflects the light from the sun, Adam was simply reflecting God. And (at first, anyway) he kept in close contact with God so he could rule the earth under God's guidance.

So what went wrong? Basically, Adam and Eve believed a lie from the devil, stopped trusting in God and disobeyed Him, destroying their relationship with God. But when Jesus defeated Satan on the cross, He took us back into God's family. Being in God's family means we have His Spirit at work in us, and the more time we spend with God, the more we'll be like Him.

PRAY
Father, thank You for creating me in Your image. That is such a privilege. Help me to keep talking with You so that I can live under Your guidance. Amen.

PSALM

USE YOUR SWORD!

READ: Luke 4:1–13

KEY VERSE: 'Jesus answered, "It is written: 'Worship the Lord your God and serve him only.'"' (v8)

Oh, my goodness! Doesn't reading today's passage make you think what a massive liar the devil is?! He'd never do anything nice for anyone, especially Jesus!

Everything that comes from Satan's mouth is dripping with lies (he's even known as the father of lies). If Adam and Eve had realised this back in Eden, the world would not be in the mess it is today – so let's make sure we learn from their mistake!

The brilliant thing here is Jesus' responses to Satan's temptations. Every lie of an offer is met and defeated... with Scripture. Jesus used God's Word as His weapon against enemy attack, and the devil was disarmed. When we know and speak the truth of God's Word, we will win hands down, every time.

This is really important for us to remember as we pray. If any lies about God pop into our head and tempt us to stop talking with Him, we can slam them down with a good bit of Bible!

THINK
Do you think the Bible is important? Your Bible is a message from God to you, so open it up, read it out loud and speak His truth into your life!

RAIN, RAIN... HURRY UP!

READ: 1 Kings 18:1–4,41–44

KEY VERSE: 'the word of the LORD came to Elijah: "'Go and present yourself to Ahab, and I will send rain on the land."'

Things start out promisingly for Elijah, chosen by God to pull Israel back from the edge of self-destruction. To punish some evil behaviour, Elijah prays for a stop to all rain. Sure enough, three and a half years pass without a drop. His point made, he now prays for the rain to start again, and God tells Elijah to get ready.

But first there's a show-down on Mount Carmel: 450 bad guys lined up against Elijah and God (vv22–24). The bad guys rave around their altar but their false god doesn't respond. Elijah prays, God barbecues his offering and the bad guys get wiped out. But still no rain... So Elijah gives a faith-filled forecast of thunderstorms, then gets his prayer on!

Drumroll... nothing, even six prayers later. Time to quit? Never! The seventh prayer leads to a single cloud starting a huge downpour. God *always* listens to our prayers – but sometimes He doesn't answer them when or how we expect Him to.

PRAY

God, I know that You always hear me. Help me to not give up when my prayers don't seem to get answered. Keep me talking with You. Amen.

TALKING WITH GOD

MAKING A WAY

READ: Daniel 9:1–6

> **KEY VERSE:** 'So I turned to the LORD God and pleaded with him in prayer and petition, in fasting, and in sackcloth and ashes.' (v3)

If God has the future all mapped out and has the power to do anything He wants, is there any point in praying?

Daniel certainly thought so. Today's Bible reading finds Daniel, erm, reading his Bible! He's been a prisoner of war in Babylon for 70 years when suddenly, in the middle of his daily quiet time, he notices something in the book (well, scroll at that point) of Jeremiah. As Daniel reads he realises that God has limited the time of the Jews' being kicked out of their land to 70 years. He does some quick maths... 'That's it, time's up!'

So what's his next move? He enters into serious prayer talks with God, pleading for the Jews' freedom. Prayer opens doors for the power of God to move through, and Daniel knew that. When we decide to trust God and partner with Him, that's when things get really exciting!

THINK Is there a certain person or situation that you need to pray about? Write the name/issue on a piece of paper and stick it in your Bible or on your mirror, to remind you daily.

YOUR TIME IS YOUR TREASURE

READ: Psalm 86:8–13

KEY VERSE: 'Teach me your way, LORD, that I may rely on your faithfulness; give me an undivided heart, that I may fear your name.' (v11)

David asked God for an undivided heart. What do you think that means? We have a divided heart when our love of other things, even other people, saps our dedication to God.

Have you ever felt torn between spending time with God and watching TV or doing something else? Most of us have felt that way at times. And there's nothing wrong with those things in themselves. God wants us to enjoy different activities in life. But how we spend our time shows who is most important in our lives. When we love God with all of our hearts, when He is number one in our life, we don't allow anything to stop us from knowing Him better.

Are you managing to find time to chat to God each day? Do you see prayer as essential or optional? If you don't feel like you've got an undivided heart for God, here's the good news – you can ask Him to help!

PRAY Father, I want to spend time with You and I know You want to spend time with me. Please give me an undivided heart for You. Amen.

PSALM

SET YOUR SIGHTS HIGH

READ: John 17:1–12

KEY VERSE: 'Now this is eternal life: that they know you, the only true God, and Jesus Christ, whom you have sent.' (v3)

When Jesus faced a terrifying situation, He knew who to look to and what to say.

Jesus was under huge stress. He knew He was soon to be brutally crucified as a sacrifice for us. Yes, Jesus and the Father had planned it together – the only way to save the world – but that just meant that Jesus was even more aware of how much He would suffer. In that moment, when He felt more human than ever, Jesus looked to God to give Him the desire and strength to see things through. He prayed to His Father about it.

Prayer helps us to approach situations from a place of God's power and goodness, rather than from a place of human weakness – sometimes showing us His viewpoint, but sometimes just helping us to trust Him. Prayer isn't begging God to go along with our plans, but asking Him to help us go along with His.

THINK Do you find it easy or hard to live life God's way? If you need a big dose of His power and strength, He is right there waiting to help you. Chat to Him!

POSITION YOUR HEART

READ: Philippians 4:4–9

> **KEY VERSE:** 'Do not be anxious about anything, but in every situation, by prayer and petition, with thanksgiving, present your requests to God.' (v6)

So far, we've looked at the main reasons *why* we pray. Now let's get down to discovering *how* we should pray.

How does God want us to talk to Him? Is there a particular set of words to use? Do we need to include 'thou' to make it more holy? Or will God be OK with us using our everyday language? And do we need to stand up, or sit down?

The Bible shows us a whole load of different ways people prayed. Lying face down, standing with hands lifted up, loudly, silently, as a group, alone, in the Temple and in a field. It's safe to say that if we're going to look to the Bible for examples of how to pray, we've got a lot of choice!

Really, the only 'how' God cares about is how real and honest you're being with Him – the attitude of your heart. If you've got that right, the rest is up to you!

THINK

Think about how you normally pray. Are there certain things you always do? Do these things help you talk to God, or are they just what you thought you had to do?

TALKING WITH GOD

I WANT WHAT YOU WANT

READ: 1 John 5:1–5,13–15

KEY VERSE: 'And if we know that he hears us –
whatever we ask – we know that we have what we
asked of him.' (v15)

Wow! So prayer is basically a fast-track ticket to anything
we want, the way we want it and when we want it? Well,
not quite. If we want a successful prayer life, we need to
learn to pray in line with what God wants.

OK... so how do we know what God wants? Ask Him! If
you wanted to know what your best friend wanted or was
thinking about, you'd ask and listen to the reply.

We also have the Bible to guide us. We may not always
get specific answers to our questions (eg who should I sit
with at lunch?) but we learn God's guidelines for living.
For example, Galatians 5:22–23 has a handy list of good
things to look for in a friend) so, by knowing what the
Bible says, and talking to God about the situations we
face, we can work out what He wants us to do.

PRAY God, You're such a good Father.
Thank You for always looking out for me and
knowing what's best. Help me to listen to You
and know what You want. Amen.

PSST!

READ: 1 Kings 19:9–13

KEY VERSE: 'After the earthquake came a fire, but the Lord was not in the fire. And after the fire came a gentle whisper.' (v12)

Since we're on the topic of learning to listen to God, it would be really helpful to know what God's voice sounds like, wouldn't it? Lucky for us, Elijah's got that covered.

God wants us to be able to hear Him as He guides us down good paths, as He speaks loving words over us, as He inspires, strengthens and comforts us. So He shows Elijah how to hear His voice, and because God wrote the Bible, this is also His way of telling us how to hear Him. But why would God whisper? Well, think about it, when you're lonely, sad or frightened like Elijah was, do you want someone shouting at you – or do you want someone to sit down with you, listen and speak gently to you?

That's generally what prayer is like – not so much an out-loud voice (although God does occasionally speak to people like that), more an inner voice like the way you talk to yourself without anyone being able to hear.

THINK
Have you ever heard God speaking to you? What did He say? Writing down your prayers and thoughts can be helpful if you want to see how God speaks to you.

TALKING WITH GOD

I KNOW THAT VOICE

READ: Revelation 22:12–21

> **KEY VERSE:** 'I warn everyone who hears the words of the prophecy of this scroll: if anyone adds anything to them, God will add to that person the plagues described in this scroll.' (v18)

'How can I know whether God is speaking to me?' That's a common question. One thing to remember is that God will never contradict Himself. If you think God is telling you to do something that goes against what the Bible says, think again.

The Holy Spirit is gentle. When He speaks to you, He might warn you off something that you are doing, but he will never condemn you (make you feel guilty and give you negative labels) – any words like that come from the devil.

God loves you. He *is* love, and love is the language He speaks to His children. What He says to you will never be unloving.

The more time we spend getting to know God by reading His words to us in the Bible, and listening to that 'inner voice' in our hearts, the more easily we will recognise when God is speaking to us.

PRAY Loving Father, thank You for the help of Your Word and Your Spirit in leading me down the best paths. Help me to be able to recognise Your voice. Amen.

KEEPING IT REAL

READ: Psalm 91:9–16

KEY VERSE: 'He will call on me, and I will answer him; I will be with him in trouble, I will deliver him and honour him.' (v15)

Some people think the Bible is unrealistic, but God is as real as it gets. He doesn't say we'll never have tough days, in fact John 16:33 says that we will have troubles!

Don't worry though, He has promised that through all of the ups and downs, He will be with us and give us what we need, and He will turn it all around for good for us.

So what's prayer got to do with this? Well, remember how prayer is talking to God? When we go through a tough time, God is often the last person we go to. Weird, isn't it? Especially when we know that He has all the answers and is able to help us overcome everything. Even people who have been Christians for decades have to be reminded of this! We don't need to face hard stuff on our own, we can do it with God.

So here's your reminder: stay on the line with heaven and don't hang up!

THINK **Do you ever forget to go to God with your questions and concerns? Can you think of any practical ideas to help you to remember to talk to Him?**

OPEN HEART SURGERY

READ: Psalm 66:16–20

KEY VERSE: 'If I had cherished sin in my heart, the Lord would not have listened' (v18)

Did you notice the key word in that verse? *Cherish*. What we cherish in our heart makes a big impact on our prayer life.

To cherish something is to let it grow, to put great importance on it, to give it lots of our attention. The psalmist knew sin, but he didn't *cherish* sin in his heart. Others had sinned against him, and he had sinned against others. But when others hurt him, he didn't take the pain, anger, and 'why me' questions to heart and give them room to grow; he took them to God and asked Him to deal with them. When he sinned, he didn't try to hide his guilt and shame from God: he laid it all out to God, asking for forgiveness.

There's nothing God can't deal with. By His sacrifice on the cross, Jesus has already paid the price for our sin, and His Holy Spirit comforts us in our pain caused by sin. We just need to take it all to God and ask Him to fix it.

PRAY

Father God, forgive me for holding sin and anger in my heart. I give You all my sins and hurts now and ask You to deal with them. Amen.

STOP THE POISON

READ: Matthew 6:5–15

> **KEY VERSE:** 'But if you do not forgive others their sins, your Father will not forgive your sins.' (v15)

If a venomous snake bit you, what would you do? Would you start shouting and attempt to get your own back on the snake? Or would you get away and get medical help ASAP?

Unforgiveness is a poison to your life – that's right, *your* life. Refusing to forgive someone is like choosing to die attacking the snake instead of getting help. That might seem like an exaggeration, but think about it: when you're angry at someone, do you feel peaceful and like everything's going to be OK? No! You feel annoyed, unable to think about other things for long, trapped in this anger. Unforgiveness is bad for us.

It's also a huge blockage to your payer life, because when you refuse to forgive completely – which is how God forgave us when Jesus died for us – you're saying that His sacrifice wasn't good enough. Forgiving someone doesn't mean what that person did to you was OK. It means that you're trusting God to sort out both your hurt and their sin, in His way and timing.

THINK
Has a friend done something that really hurt you? Have you forgiven them for this? It's not easy to forgive, but God can help you.

TALKING WITH GOD

STICK AROUND

READ: John 15:1–11

KEY VERSE: 'If you remain in me and my words remain in you, ask whatever you wish, and it will be done for you.' (v7)

What fruit is Jesus talking about? It's the fruit of the Spirit – godly character traits that grow in us as we grow in our relationship with Him.

This fruit – love, joy, peace, patience, kindness, goodness, faithfulness, gentleness and self-control – is not something we have to work to produce ourselves. It's God who produces these things in our lives as we spend more time with Him. Wouldn't you love to be someone who has all of those things?

Well, you become like who you hang out with! The more we hang out with God, the more like Him we'll become. Prayer is just being in constant communication with God as He walks with you through each and every day. It's allowing Him to get rid of your rough edges so that the new, healthy shoots can push through and produce good fruit. The thing is, if we want Him to keep sorting out us out in order to produce these great things in us, we need to stick around!

PRAY Dear Jesus, it's so good to spend time with You! Help me to stick close to You so that You can produce Your goodness in me. Amen.

PAY IT FORWARD

READ: Philippians 1:9–11

KEY VERSE: 'And this is my prayer: that your love may abound more and more in knowledge and depth of insight' (v9)

Prayer is a wonderful opportunity to talk about other people behind their backs. Not to gossip about them but to talk to God about their needs.

See, the more you hang out with God, the more like Him you become and the more interested you become in the things He cares about. And what does God care about more than anything? People. As your relationship with God grows, so does your love for other people. When Paul visited Philippi on his second missionary journey, several people became Christians. Lydia and a prison jailer were among those who became Christians and formed the first Christian church in Europe. Paul wrote to them to tell them that he was praying for them. Just look at his love and prayers for them.

We are blessed to be a blessing to others. We pray, not just for the sake of our relationship with God, but for the sake of those around us and their relationship with Him.

THINK Do you mainly pray for yourself or do you remember to pray for others as well? Challenge yourself to choose three people who you will pray for every day for a week.

FROM THE TOP

READ: Matthew 16:13–19

KEY VERSE: 'I will give you the keys of the kingdom of heaven; whatever you bind on earth will be bound in heaven, and whatever you loose on earth will be loosed in heaven.' (v19)

Prayer is not a religious duty – it is part of an awesome relationship with God. It is powered by the same revelation that Peter had in today's reading: that Jesus is who He says He is – Son of the living God. Prayer is the key that opens the door to understanding the world from the view of its creator. With prayer, we end up walking in line with God, working with Him to bring a piece of heaven to earth.

In heaven, there will be no more sickness, poverty, corruption, sadness, death, violence, conflict, confusion and pain. In heaven, there will be joy, love, peace, patience, kindness, life, health, goodness and every other good thing imaginable. Let's pray that we see a bit more of heaven on earth.

God has given us the keys to open any situation to His power. The question is whether we leave the keys in our pocket, or start turning the lock.

PRAY

Lord Jesus, teach me how to pray so that Your power is unlocked in my life – not just for my benefit but for the benefit of others too. Amen.

NO MATTER WHAT

READ: Psalm 43:1–5

KEY VERSE: 'I will yet praise him' (v5)

If all music was lively and happy then it would not tell the whole story of what life is like (and most rockstars wouldn't have any songs out). This psalm was written at a time when things had gone pear-shaped. The people had let God down big time and were now paying the price — they were frightened refugees.

The worst thing about being not-yet-perfect people is that when we make a mess of things, we feel like we've let God down. It's bad enough getting into trouble, but it's worse letting down someone you love.

When we have times like this, the last thing we want to do is pray or believe that God is doing amazing things in the world, let alone that He has incredible plans for us. All we want to do is hide.

Even so, the psalmist grabs hold of the last bit of faith he has and asks God to bring great things out of a miserable situation. God is good to us — all the time — no matter what!

THINK
How are you today? If you're a bit down, ask God to help — don't try and solve everything on your own. And whether you're feeling great or rubbish, praise God today!

PSALM

MUCH MORE

READ: Psalm 132:1–18

KEY VERSE: 'The LORD swore an oath to David, a sure oath he will not revoke: "One of your own descendants I will place on your throne."' (v11)

Symbols are things that point to something much more than what they actually are themselves. A good example is a national flag. It's only a bit of cloth, but it symbolises so much more. In Old Testament times, the name 'David' wasn't like any other name, it symbolised something much more.

David, as we know, was God's chosen king of Israel. As the king, he would be used in a special way to bring about God's promise to rescue the world. God spoke through the prophets to say that he would use a 'Son of David' to carry out His rescue mission. So when this psalm talks about David, everyone who first heard it, knew what that meant. 'David' was a symbol for everything God had done, and all that He was going to do to rescue His people.

As Christians, we know that the 'Son of David' is in fact the Son of God: Jesus. He is now ruling the universe as the eternal king!

PRAY **Lord Jesus, I can never thank You enough for what You did for me by dying on the cross, and for how You still help me each and every day. Amen.**

PSALMS

INNER CIRCLE

READ: Mark 14:12–21

KEY VERSE: 'But woe to that man who betrays the Son of Man!' (v21)

Let's jump right in at the deep end looking at the days before Jesus' crucifixion. It's a dinnertime scene, and Jesus is having dinner with His closest friends for the last time before His arrest.

As Judas was one of the disciples, he was one of Jesus' *best friends*. Think about that for a moment. He had followed Jesus for three years, seen Him perform miracles, and heard Him preach about the incredible love of God. Jesus loved Judas, and at some point Judas must have loved Jesus.

We read today that Jesus knew that Judas would betray Him (v20), but had still loved him as one of His best friends. He warns Judas of how bad things would be if he did betray Him. But Judas still goes through with his plan to hand Jesus over.

Jesus allowed Judas into His inner circle, and loved Him, despite knowing that he would hurt Him. That's pretty incredible. In the same way, God brings us close to Him even though we sometimes mess up!

PRAY
Lord Jesus, thank You for allowing me to be Your friend even though I get things wrong. Your forgiveness and love for me are amazing. Amen.

CROSSROADS

THE NIGHT SHIFT

READ: Luke 22:47–53

KEY VERSE: 'But Jesus answered, 'No more of this!' And he touched the man's ear and healed him.' (v51)

So, picture this...

It's the middle of the night – something like 2am. You're a temple guard out for your night duty in Jerusalem. You're tired and crabby, but you've received a tip-off from Judas that Jesus – the 'trouble-maker' the authorities have been after for ages – is close by. This should be the easiest arrest of your career (and may earn you a promotion!).

When you get to the Garden of Gethsemane, Judas signals to you which one is Jesus. Your moment has come: time to jump in and arrest Him.

He doesn't resist. But the next thing you know, pain is blasting the right-hand side of your head. A very angry man – one of Jesus' friends – has chopped off your ear with a sword!

This was pretty much the experience of the temple guard in today's reading. But in the midst of chaos and horrible pain, Jesus – the man he has just arrested – places His hand on the spot where the guard's ear had been, and heals him. No questions asked.

That's how the Son of God responded to being arrested.

THINK How do you react when someone starts an argument with you? Do you lash out? Or do you show them kindness?

TRIAL AND ERROR

READ: Matthew 26:57–67

KEY VERSE: 'But I say to all of you: from now on you will see the Son of Man sitting at the right hand of the Mighty One and coming on the clouds of heaven.' (v64)

Let's fast-forward a couple of hours from the ear-chopping incident...

Jesus has been taken to a make-shift court. Everybody there wants Him killed. There's just one problem – Jesus is perfect. They don't have any dirt on Him to have Him crucified. They resort to calling false witnesses. The trial was clearly illegal and was part of the plot to get rid of Jesus.

Caiaphas, the high priest, was completely disgusted by Jesus' claims that He was the Son of God – so much so that he tore his own clothes in anger (as you do!). He then decided to go with the charge of blasphemy, which meant acting or speaking in a way that disrespects God. Caiaphas couldn't have been more wrong.

Jesus faced all of this for us. He willingly went through this unfair trial so that we could go free. Jesus, now our high priest, sets out to free us and not condemn us.

PRAY

Lord Jesus, thank You so much for going through such an awful situation so I could be free. I praise You for what You have done. Amen.

CROSSROADS

PASS THE SOAP

READ: Matthew 27:11–26

KEY VERSE: 'So when the crowd had gathered, Pilate asked them, "Which one do you want me to release to you: Jesus Barabbas, or Jesus who is called the Messiah?"' (v17)

The next man to step in was Pilate. He had the authority to pull the plug on the plot against Jesus, but he didn't have the backbone.

By this point it was early morning. The crowd wanted to see Jesus crucified by lunchtime, and they wouldn't stop yelling until they got their way. In stepped Governor Pilate. He tried to get Jesus to defend Himself, but Jesus made 'no reply, not even to a single charge' (v14).

It was a holiday weekend in Jerusalem, and tradition allowed the release of a prisoner, decided by public vote. So Pilate offered the mob the choice: a perfectly innocent man from Nazareth, or a convicted scumbag called Barabbas. But the crowd screamed all the louder and chose to release Barabbas. Pilate then washed his hands of the situation and gave the order for Jesus to be crucified.

THINK   The mob wanted Jesus' blood out of hatred for Him, but Jesus was willing to go to the cross out of love for them. Is love what drives you to make the decisions that you make?

FRENEMIES

READ: Luke 23:4–12

KEY VERSE: 'That day Herod and Pilate became friends – before this they had been enemies.' (v12)

Today's reading shows just how Pilate liked others to take the blame for him. He didn't like the decision he was being forced to make. So he packed Jesus off to Herod, and ended up making a friend out of an old enemy.

To cut a long story short, Pilate and Herod had not exactly been best buddies. They had probably hated each other. But when Pilate signed the death warrant of Jesus – top of Herod's hit list – he was back in his old enemy's good books. However, their jolly reunion was based upon a shared dislike for the Son of God. Not exactly a friendship built to last.

This can be a hard passage to read when you really think about what is happening here. Jesus is 'ridiculed and mocked' (v11). He was dressed up and humiliated, and no doubt shouted at and spat upon. They wanted Him to fight back. But look at Jesus' reaction – He 'gave Him no answer'. His love for us kept Him standing firm, taking all our punishment on His shoulders.

PRAY Lord Jesus, thank You for going through so much to have a friendship with me. Help me to always remember this. Amen.

CROSSROADS

THE LONG ROAD

READ: Mark 15:21–32

> **KEY VERSE:** 'A certain man from Cyrene, Simon, the father of Alexander and Rufus, was passing by on his way in from the country, and they forced him to carry the cross.' (v21)

The trek to Golgotha wouldn't have been an easy one, and Jesus had been beaten up so badly that He barely had the energy to carry His cross.

We don't know all that much about Simon, except that he was from North Africa. We can guess that he was on his way to the city for the feasts happening that weekend. He would have passed Jesus' execution parade on his travels.

The Bible tells us that Simon was 'forced' to carry the cross (v21). We don't know why, but whatever the reason, he walked alongside Jesus to the place where He was killed. He felt how heavy that cross was, and it may have given him splinters and blisters. He was there, right there, when the Son of God was nailed to the cross he had carried, suffering a punishment on behalf of the human race.

THINK It's a horrible scene to think about, but it's important for us to remember everything our Saviour did for us. If you were walking with Jesus up to the cross, what would you say to Him?

THE GAME OF THE KING

READ: Matthew 27:27–31

KEY VERSE: 'After they had mocked him, they took off the robe and put his own clothes on him. Then they led him away to crucify him.' (v31)

Let's be clear about one thing: the Roman soldiers we are talking about here were not nice people. They were dangerous, cruel and enjoyed killing people. In today's passage, the whole company of soldiers gather together in a large building and are tormenting Jesus before He is crucified.

A few of the men dress Jesus in a robe. A crown of thorns is put on His head. The rest of the soldiers shout insults at Him and a staff is placed in Jesus' hand as a mock iron sceptre. The soldiers mock Jesus more by shouting, 'Hail, king of the Jews.' Then, they begin to spit on Him and hit Him.

Again, this passage is pretty hard-going. But the thing to remember is that Jesus died for every single soldier tormenting Him. He suffered at their hands so that He could save them. People still mock Jesus today – maybe you know some people who do this. But Jesus' mission was to save everyone, no matter how bad.

PRAY

Lord, it's amazing to know that no one is too bad for You to save them. Thank You for wanting to save everyone. Amen.

CROSSROADS

THEY DO NOT KNOW

READ: Luke 23:23–43

KEY VERSE: 'Jesus said, "Father, forgive them, for they do not know what they are doing."' (v34)

It can be pretty shocking to think about what human beings are capable of. Watching the news on TV can make us very aware of this. In today's passage, we read more about the soldiers who seemed to enjoy executing people so much that they even started gambling while doing so.

We've already mentioned about their cruel behaviour. But look at the plea that Jesus shouts out to His father on their behalf: 'they do not know what they are doing.' That's love right there. The soldiers have no idea that they still have the chance to be saved and forgiven – all because of the man they are killing.

Then we see 'the criminal' – that's all we know about this guy. He's unknown, but he's clearly not one of the good guys. Despite that, he sees who Jesus is, and that's enough for Jesus – He tells the criminal that he will be welcomed into paradise.

PRAY Lord Jesus, I believe You are who You say You are. Thank You for dying such a horrible death for me. I believe You are alive today, and I want to live the rest of my life following You. Amen.

GOD'S UNDERTAKER

READ: Luke 23:50–56

KEY VERSE: 'There was a man by the name of Joseph, a member of the Jewish High Council, a man of good heart and good character.' (v50, *The Message*)

So – where have all the good men gone? Today we meet one of them: Joseph of Arimathea.

The other Gospel accounts tell us that Joseph was 'a rich man' (Matt 27:57), and a member of the council (Mark 15:43). We also know that he was a 'disciple of Jesus' (John 19:38).

Joseph was there when Jesus was on trial, but did not agree with the decision that was made. We don't know if he spoke up for Jesus or not, but going to Pilate and asking for Jesus' body would have taken some guts.

Joseph was pretty rich, too. Rich enough, in fact, to own a family tomb in Jerusalem. He believed that Jesus' body deserved a proper burial, not to be dumped in an unmarked grave. So that's what he did. He took Jesus' body down from the cross, wrapped it in cloth, and buried it.

Joseph might have felt like he'd let Jesus down, but he knew that there was still something he could do to worship Jesus – bury His body properly.

THINK Do you ever feel like you've let Jesus down? Don't let your past mistakes make you feel like you can't serve Jesus right now.

CROSSROADS

THE SPICE OF LIFE

READ: John 19:38–42

KEY VERSE: 'He was accompanied by Nicodemus, the man who earlier had visited Jesus at night.' (v39)

Joseph didn't have to bury Jesus by himself. We are told that he had the help of another guy, Nicodemus, who was an important Jewish leader. Nicodemus had tried to get Jesus a fair trial when he heard about the plot against Him. And here, we see him again, giving Jesus a funeral fit for a king.

Do you know what John 3:16 says? Lots of Christians love this verse! It says: 'For God so loved the world that he gave his one and only Son, that whoever believes in him shall not perish but have eternal life.' And do you know who Jesus was speaking to when He said that? Nicodemus! Now that's a conversation he wouldn't easily forget. Perhaps those amazing words were going through Nicodemus' head as he poured expensive myrrh and spices onto Jesus' body, prompting him to take care as he buried God's Son.

The words that are now on church walls all over the world were first spoken to good old Nic – what a brilliant claim to fame!

PRAY Lord God, thank You that I also get the chance to hear the message You shared with Nicodemus. Help me to always remember the truth of this and live by it. Amen.

WAY AHEAD OF YOU

READ: Matthew 28:1–15

KEY VERSE: 'He is not here; he has risen, just as he said. Come and see the place where he lay.' (v6)

It's been quite a weekend in Jerusalem... but the worst is over. Today we look back at the very first Easter Sunday, when it would have been a great day to be called Mary!

Picture the scene: two Marys go to visit the tomb of Jesus. They both would have really loved Jesus, and their emotions would have no doubt been all over the place. It had been one heck of an upsetting and scary few days. But just when they thought they'd seen it all, they find an angel sat on the tomb stone, having rolled it away.

Imagine that! The tomb is wide open and empty and an angel is there, just chilling out, waiting to speak to you! Team Mary were told, 'He has risen from the dead and is going ahead of you into Galilee. There you will see him' (v7).

Sorry – what?! Is this the right tomb? Is the angel talking about the same Jesus? Is this a joke? No! Jesus took death on, and He smashed it.

THINK
Mary and Mary were the first to see Jesus alive again, and they fell at His feet. What would your reaction have been if you were in their shoes?

CROSSROADS

A GIRL CALLED JO

READ: Luke 24:1–12

KEY VERSE: 'It was Mary Magdalene, Joanna, Mary the mother of James, and the others with them who told this to the apostles.' (v10)

Today we meet another woman who played a big part in the news about Jesus' resurrection going viral: Joanna.

Joanna was one of the women who gave money to support Jesus in what He was doing. The disciples had quit their jobs to follow Jesus, so the money needed to come from somewhere. Joanna had definitely helped here. She'd seen Jesus' miracles and have given Him her time, money and gifts.

What makes Joanna super interesting is that her husband, Chuza, was the manager of Herod's household! That's right, the money Joanna was giving to Jesus came from none other than the man who had pushed for Him to be killed.

Joanna got to be one of the first people to hear that Jesus was alive – most definitely not the sort of thing her husband's boss would like to hear! But did she care? Probably not, because she ended up being one of the first members of the Church – ever.

PRAY
Dear God, I want to be part of the team that makes Your good news go viral. Please use me to spread the word to other people. Amen.

A MYSTERY GUEST

READ: Luke 24:13–35

> **KEY VERSE:** 'It is true! The Lord has risen and has appeared to Simon.' (v34)

Cleopas was making his way to Emmaus, a few miles out of Jerusalem. We don't have many clues as to who his friend was (one theory suggests Mrs Cleopas) – but the two of them walked and talked together, getting on with their journey.

Reading this story, we know that it is Jesus who joins them on the road, but as far as Cleopas and his friend are concerned, they've picked up a mystery guest. Look at how Jesus just 'came up and walked along with them' (v15). He doesn't demand to be bowed down to; He just joins His friends where they are, and asks them questions. And Jesus definitely has a sense of humour here – He gets them to tell Him everything that's happened over the past few days!

Did you also notice that Jesus doesn't barge into Cleopas' home and expect to be fed? Instead, He waits for an invitation, just like He waits to be invited into our lives. It isn't until dinner is served that He is recognised for who He is. And what a shock it was!

THINK Jesus is walking alongside us, waiting for us to chat to Him even though it means telling Him things He already knows. Will you have a conversation with Him?

CROSSROADS

SOMETHING IN THE WATER

READ: John 21:1–14

> **KEY VERSE:** 'None of the disciples dared ask him, "Who are you?" They knew it was the Lord.' (v12)

The resurrected Jesus still isn't done revealing Himself to His followers.

Before the disciples met Jesus, they had been professional fishermen. Then Jesus told them to throw their nets over the other side of the boat, and they caught so many fish their nets broke. After the best catch of their lives, they quit their day jobs to follow Him.

In today's reading, it looks as though the disciples had tried to re-enter the fishing business. Their master wasn't with them anymore, they thought it was all over, and they needed to keep a low profile and put some food on the table. They'd spent the whole night fishing, still to be left fish-less, when Jesus showed up. Performing the same miracle in front of the disciples was the perfect in-joke. They realised who He was, and couldn't refuse His offer to 'Come and have breakfast' (v12).

Jesus is full of surprises and is always doing new, exciting things in people's lives. Why not ask Him to show you what He is doing in yours?

PRAY Father, I know You have so many good things in store for me. Help me to notice when You are doing something new in my life. Amen.

THE NEW GUY

READ: Acts 1:15–26

KEY VERSE: 'the lot fell to Matthias; so he was added to the eleven apostles' (v26)

Warning! This one isn't pretty. Judas didn't get a happy ending at all. But his departure left a spot open in the 12 disciples – and prophecies from years and years ago said that this spot would need to be filled. So, who got the job?

Picture this: you've been around in Jerusalem for a while, and are well aware of the awesome stuff that Jesus has been doing. You know about the healings and miracles, His death and resurrection, and you want that spot on the dream team. There's only one other guy who's in with a chance. Of course, you'd prefer it if they didn't decide by throwing dice, but you trust that it's God who gets the final say.

That's what it was like for Matthias! But God knew how loyal Matthias had been behind the scenes and pulled him into the group at the right moment. The disciples had started their decision-making off with an important prayer: 'Lord, you know everyone's heart. Show us' (v24). Wow – what a prayer!

THINK
The next time you face a decision, why not try praying a similar prayer? 'Lord, You know my heart. Show me what You think.' Give Him the ultimate control.

RELEVANT

READ: Acts 5:27–42

KEY VERSE: 'For if their purpose or activity is of human origin, it will fail. But if it is from God, you will not be able to stop these men' (vv38–39)

Here we meet a chap called Gamaliel. He was a Pharisee but in today's reading the man speaks sense.

Reading on through the book of Acts, the good news about Jesus is spreading fast. Jesus has returned to heaven, the Holy Spirit has come on the day of Pentecost, people are getting healed from sickness, many are accepting Jesus as their Saviour, and the anti-Jesus club is getting nervous. Once again, the Temple guards are blood-thirsty.

Gamaliel was 'a teacher of the law who was honoured by all people' (v34). And whether he meant to or not, he saved the disciples. What he said went something like this: 'Leave them be, chaps. If this is all a big lie, it will blow over. Don't go mad about it. That way, just in case it's actually true, you won't have picked a fight with God.'

We know that it wasn't a lie. Jesus is alive! Over 2,000 years later we're still talking about Him. He's relevant, He's adventurous and He's amazing.

THINK
Write down some of the ways that Jesus has had an impact on the world we live in today. You might be surprised how many there are!

WE ARE FAMILY

READ: Psalm 133:1–3

KEY VERSE: 'How good and pleasant it is when God's people live together in unity!' (v1)

Imagine two brothers. They fight constantly about the tiniest things. One day, a boy comes along and starts a fight with one of them. The other brother sees the threat and immediately jumps to his brothers' defence! Even though they were more than happy to fight each other, when someone else threatened one of them, their true loyalty shone through. They suddenly realised who they were – brothers who loved each other.

Today's reading is all about how important it is for us, God's children (who are a family!), to love each other. Because together we are a light showing God to the world. When we fight we look just like any other family. But if we love each other, we will shine – and others will see God through us.

Obviously it's not always easy to love people, even other Christians! Sometimes, like the brothers in the story, we need to remember who we really are – God's children – before we can do it.

Do you find it easy to get on with other Christians? Are there some you don't like so much? Talk to God about it.

PRAY Father God, please help me to be patient with other Christians especially. Please remind me that we're all family. Amen.

PSALM

ON TOP OF THE WORLD

READ: Psalm 134:1–3

KEY VERSE: 'May the LORD bless you from Zion' (v3)

The singers of this psalm had climbed up the hill to Jerusalem, and now they're worshipping God in the Temple. Not only are they on top of the mountain, they're on top of the world!

Some people think that Christianity is all about suffering and hard work. Well, admittedly there is some of that, but this is knocked out the park by joy! The joy of being in God's presence is like nothing else. He is so amazing and yet He's so keen to be close to us.

Worship isn't just an extra bit added onto our Christian life, it's the whole point of being a Christian. That doesn't mean it's all about just singing songs... it means knowing God is close to you, loving being with Him and listening to Him (reading the Bible and listening to good Christian teaching can help you worship God too).

You could perhaps say that our main reason for being alive is to praise and give glory to God by enjoying knowing Him forever. When we enjoy knowing God, we are worshipping Him!

THINK Do you enjoy knowing God? We can know and worship God more when we include Him in every day of our lives, talking with Him and living in His joy-filled way.

PSALM

AMNESIA

READ: Judges 3:7–11

KEY VERSE: 'But when they cried out to the LORD, he raised up for them a deliverer' (v9)

You might have notice throughout the Bible there's a recurring story: God's people think they can live without Him. It all descends into chaos. God's people go running back to God. Things are good for a while, until the amnesia kicks in and the people go off and do their own thing again. And so on...

The book of Judges is all about some of the temporary leaders of Israel. It's gory, it's not for the faint-hearted, and it's got a lot to say to us.

Forty years had gone by since the Israelites were released from Egypt. Moses and Joshua were dead – leaving a generation of people whose memories were starting to get a bit foggy when it came to remembering the awesome things God had done for them.

Today's verse shows the centre of it all: when God's people cry out to Him, He answers them and delivers them. It's classic human behaviour to let things get messy before asking for God's help, forgetting about Him until He's the only 'help' option left. Do you ever do this?

PRAY
Lord Jesus, thank You for always doing great things in my life. Please help me to never forget about them and, more importantly, never forget about You. Amen.

ROLLERCOASTER RIDE

POTENTIAL

READ: Judges 1:8–15; 3:7–11

KEY VERSE: 'The Spirit of the LORD came on him' (3:10)

Here we meet Saleb, who had an interesting strategy for getting his daughter married off: whoever wins the battle wins themselves a wife!

Othniel loved a challenge, so he led the battle against the Canaanites and won the woman, Aksah. But Othniel didn't have much else going for him – he wasn't exactly raking in the money. In fact, Aksah had to ask her dad for a patch of land so she and her new hubby could enjoy a decent life.

When the Israelites 'did evil in the eyes of the LORD' (3:7) and got themselves in real trouble, it was time for Othniel to step in as the hero: 'The Spirit of the LORD came on him, so that he became Israel's judge and went to war' (3:10). Not only did God help Othniel win the battle, Othniel also ruled peacefully until his death 40 years later.

So what was Othniel's secret to success? It wasn't his impressive talents or his plot of land. It was the Holy Spirit helping him that made Him successful.

THINK Is there anything that you have to do right now that looks really hard? Perhaps some homework or a test? Ask God to send His Spirit to be with you as you do these.

NO GUTS, NO GLORY

READ: Judges 3:12–23

KEY VERSE: 'Ehud... drew the sword... and plunged it into the king's belly' (v21)

This is your warning: this story doesn't paint a pretty picture. The Israelites had been off the rails again – worshipping false gods, being captured by the Moabites, and then begging God to rescue them. This time it was Ehud who put on the judge's hat.

After 18 years of the Israelites suffering under the horrendous rule of Eglon, God sent Ehud to get rid of him. And Ehud made it look easy! Using the trick of a secret message, he managed to get him one-on-one. Ehud, armed with a double-edged sword, stabbed Eglon in such a way that 'the king's bowels emptied' (v22, NLT). Yep, that does mean what you think it means! Ehud then locked the king in the room and calmly escaped from the enemy headquarters. He had completed the first part of his mission.

Did you know that God says His Word is like a double-edged sword? What that means is that it gets deep into our thoughts and feelings and helps us to discover right from wrong. Have you ever experienced the Bible doing this for you?

PRAY
Father God, thank You for the power of the Bible. Help me to remember to keep on reading it. Amen.

ROLLERCOASTER RIDE

ARE YOU OK IN THERE?

READ: Judges 3:24–30

KEY VERSE: '"Follow me," he ordered, "for the LORD has given Moab, your enemy, into your hands."' (v28)

While Ehud made his escape, the unsuspecting servants thought their king was still on the loo (no, we're not making this up). By the time the penny had dropped, it was too late: Ehud had rallied the Israelites and was leading them into battle.

Spurred on by the belief that God had already given them victory, Ehud and his troops kicked the mighty Moabites out of the land. The Israelites put God first and enjoyed 80 years of peace.

Each time the Israelites asked God for forgiveness, He gave them back their freedom. And while they obeyed Him, they lived in peace. It really isn't rocket science and you'd have thought they'd get it eventually — walk away from God and you walk away from His freedom, get back to God and you get back to His freedom. But human beings have always had terrible memories, along with the ability to massively mess things up. We've all done things our way instead of God's way at times.

THINK Ask yourself if there is anything you think you need to stop doing. Talk with God about the things that are hardest to resist doing and ask for His help and forgiveness.

HERE WE GO AGAIN

READ: Judges 4:1–4

KEY VERSE: 'Again the Israelites did evil in the eyes of the LORD' (v1)

Oh, come on! As soon as Ehud popped his clogs, the Israelites fell back into some seriously dodgy behaviour patterns. And when they pushed God out of the picture again, things went pear-shaped.

The people hadn't learnt from their mistakes. Without Ehud to lead them, they left an era of God-given peace and spiralled into 20 years of misery. The Canaanites, with their 900 chariots, turned up to bully the Israelites and showed no mercy.

Who did the Israelites go running back to? You guessed it – God. And this time He wasn't going to raise up a mighty man to save their skins. Nope, he sent in a wonder woman.

It might be a bit boring reading the same story over and over again, but just imagine how God was feeling watching His people do the same thing over and over again. Look how kind, patient and forgiving He was – they were always messing up, He was always welcoming them back. No matter how many times we ask Him, He always forgives us when we are truly sorry.

PRAY Father, I'm sorry for _____.
Thank You for Your never-ending love and forgiveness. Help me live the way that You want me to. Amen.

ROLLERCOASTER RIDE

WARRIOR WOMAN

READ: Judges 4:4–16

KEY VERSE: 'the LORD will deliver Sisera into the hands of a woman' (v9)

The Israelites had been pushed around for 20 years by the heavily-armed Canaanites. But Deborah wasn't scared of the Canaanites. She was filled with the Holy Spirit and was a prophet. God had told her that He was going to defeat the enemy, and she believed Him.

Brave Deborah rallied the troops and set them charging towards 900 heavily-armed chariots. The enemy chariots couldn't withstand the attack from the Israelites, spurred on by Deborah. And the Israelites won the victory.

Deborah was the only person prepared to do what God said, and God backed her all the way! God calls all sorts of people to be leaders, no matter your age, gender, qualifications or experience. In this case, He chose Deborah – a woman from Israel, who went on to pull off an incredible victory. And God can use you too! No one is perfect, but if we can trust God, be humble and be kind— there's no limit to what God will do through us!

THINK God asks all sorts of people to be leaders of His people, and it makes their jobs a lot nicer when those who lead respect them. Do you respect your leaders?

TRICKS AND TRUST

READ: Judges 4:17–24

KEY VERSE: 'But Jael, Heber's wife, picked up a tent peg and a hammer... She drove the peg through his temple into the ground, and he died.' (v21)

Only one man escaped from Deborah and her army – Sisera, the cruel enemy commander. Deborah told the troops that the Lord would deal with Sisera – did He keep His promise?

Deborah trusted God, while Sisera trusted his mates. The enemy commander hid from the Israelites in the tent of his friends Heber and Jael. He thought he was safe with Jael. But it turned out she was on the other team! Not wanting to be caught with the most-wanted man in her house, she murdered him (rather imaginatively) in his sleep. As for the Israelites, God had given them their freedom again and they lived by His rules – but for how long?

Deborah put her trust in the living God, but Sisera put his in 'friends'. Who do you trust more? The big test comes when your friends put you under pressure to act in ways that God doesn't like. Remember that God won't let you down, but people might.

PRAY Father, help me to know I can trust You. Thank You for always being there for me, no matter what. Please help me to be trusted by others. Amen.

ROLLERCOASTER RIDE

WHO WILL SAVE YOU?

READ: Judges 10:6–16

KEY VERSE: 'Again the Israelites did evil in the eyes of the Lord. They served the Baals and the Ashtoreths' (v6)

Deborah's impressive leadership brought peace, but would the next generation listen to their parents and continue living for God, or would they fall back into the same old habits? Take a guess...

It's incredible how quickly we can forget God's goodness, and the Israelites were no exception. Not only did they cut God out of their lives, but they replaced Him with every other false god you could come up with. Anything and everything was considered cool, except for God. He didn't like their way of life and it wasn't until the Israelites showed that they were truly sorry, by destroying their false idols, that God showed mercy.

It can be tempting to cut down on our time with God when we think we don't 'need' Him because we're doing OK. Often it's not until we have a mini crisis that we really want to make contact with Him again. We sometimes treat God like a doctor who we only visit when we really have to. But actually, He wants to be our friend.

THINK **Do you see God more as your doctor who you call on when something's wrong, or your friend who you stick with through life?**

AN UNLIKELY HERO

READ: Judges 11:1–11

> **KEY VERSE:** 'So Jephthah went with the elders of Gilead, and the people made him head and commander over them.' (v11)

Have you noticed that often God chooses the most unlikely people to do His work? Well, the Israelites needed a judge to scare of their enemies – and the man for the job was one who they'd previously kicked out.

If there was anyone who had a bad start in life it was Jephthah. Jephthah suffered a lot of hurt and rejection as a child. He was born because his father had an affair with a prostitute, and he was treated as an outsider by his half-brothers. He had become an aggressive hard man, ready to fight anyone who gave him a tough time. Yet God chose Jephthah as the next judge.

Do you ever feel like the bottom of the pile, or that nobody will ever take you seriously? Then you're in the best position to serve God! On the other hand, have you ever ignored someone because they don't seem that impressive on paper? Remember that God will use anyone for His purposes – and He seems to really like the people no one else thinks of!

PRAY
Father, please use me today. Help me to be confident in who You made me to be, however I feel. Thank You for loving me. Amen.

ROLLERCOASTER RIDE

THINK IT THROUGH

READ: Judges 11:29–40

> **KEY VERSE:** 'I have made a vow to the LORD that I cannot break.' (v35)

Today's reading might be one of the most heart-breaking passages of the Bible – and it all comes down to Jephthah not thinking things through before making crazy promises, and not realising what God is actually like.

Jephthah had been on good terms with God. But instead of trusting what God would do for him, he felt he needed to make a deal with God. Well, God won the battle for him, as He was going to anyway, but Jephthah thought he needed to make a sacrifice – which turned out to be his daughter. How twisted he'd got it all! It was horrible, desperately sad and such a waste.

Do you think God actually *wanted* Jephthah to murder his own child? Of course not! Never! And if Jephthah had done his homework and really thought about the situation, he would have known this.

While it's important to follow God with all your heart, He doesn't want us to make Him careless promises that we can't keep. We don't need to try and make deals with Him – He's already on our side. If only Jephthah realised that.

THINK
Have you ever jumped into something without thinking it through first? It's important to always think about the decisions we make, and what God actually wants.

DEDICATION

READ: Judges 13:1–5

> **KEY VERSE:** 'You will become pregnant and have a son whose head is never to be touched by a razor' (v5)

The Israelites returned to their selfish ways (again) and it cost them their freedom for 40 years. Their rulers, the Philistines, were big, muscle-bound iron men. As always, God had a rescue plan.

Samson's parents hadn't been able to have kids, but God had other ideas. Samson's birth was announced by an angel with instructions that he was to live his life in total dedication to God by taking the Nazirite vow. The long and short of it: no booze and no haircuts allowed. As a Nazirite, Samson would show his dedication to God by never shaving. He was born and bred as one of God's judges, destined to 'take the lead in delivering Israel from the hands of the Philistines' (v5).

These days, people don't tend to take the Nazirite vow, but there are other ways in which we can show our commitment to God. What behaviour do you think He might want you to steer clear of? How does your life show the world you are a follower of Jesus?

PRAY Lord God, You are amazing and know the best way to live life. Help me to stand out to people as someone who follows You. Amen.

ROLLERCOASTER RIDE

A MATCH NOT MADE IN HEAVEN

READ: Judges 14:1–7

KEY VERSE: 'Samson went down to Timnah and saw there a young Philistine woman.' (v1)

So baby Samson grew into big, strong, hairy Samson, with super-human strength! Now he was at the age where he was looking to marry. God had forbidden His people from marrying anyone who didn't love Him too. After all, isn't it a good idea for to be on the same page as the person you're married to? But when a Philistine woman caught Samson's eye, God's rules seemed to go out the window.

God was going to use Samson's bad attitude as a chance to disrupt the Philistines. He had a plan. And on his way to his first date, Samson had a run-in with a lion – but God gave him the strength to tear the lion apart with his bare hands (v6). Now that *is* strength!

Sometimes the thing we want most is not what's best for us in God's eyes, and that can be hard to take. But remember, a football match has rules so the game can be fun and go well. That's the same with God's rules for life and relationships.

THINK Do you think you would find it easy to listen to what God says about relationships? It's important to always know that He wants to protect you.

RIDDLE ME THIS

READ: Judges 14:8–20

> **KEY VERSE:** 'Out of the eater, something to eat; out of the strong, something sweet.' (v14)

Samson's way of life meant he was forbidden to touch any dead creature. But when he passed the lion he had ripped apart three days before, and noticed it was filled with bees and honey, he scooped himself a snack. Uh-oh! Another rule broken.

Having married a woman he shouldn't have, Samson was about to discover a side to his wife that he hadn't seen before. When he refused to give away the answer to his riddle, Mrs Samson threw a week-long tantrum! When Samson finally gave in, she went and told all the Philistines – and later ran off with the guy who'd been best man at the wedding. Samson's reaction was to go absolutely crazy, unleashing his rage on 30 men. He wasn't having a good day.

Samson ignored God's rules about relationships, and he ended up getting really hurt. Think about your friendships. Have you ever felt you've been let down or that you've messed up? Pray about these and ask God to help you take a practical step in making amends with the person or people.

PRAY Father God, please help me to be close to the right people and to be a good friend to them. Amen.

ROLLERCOASTER RIDE

WEAPON OF CHOICE

READ: Judges 15:9–17

> **KEY VERSE:** 'With a donkey's jawbone I have made donkeys of them.' (v16)

First, let's rewind. Samson felt like a right fool when he discovered he had been rejected. The Philistines had humiliated him. He kept up his tough-guy image, but inside he was deeply hurt and very insulted by all that had happened. To add to this betrayal, his fellow Israelites were prepared to hand him over to the Philistines to save their skins.

God was not going to let the idol-worshipping Philistines humiliate Samson anymore. Although Samson had let God down, God was not going to let Samson down. He broke the ropes that tied Samson's arms together and gave him the superhuman strength to defeat his enemies with an interesting weapon – a donkey's jawbone!

We can become so tied up with feelings of anger or bitterness that God can get squeezed out of our lives. But remember that God will never let you down, even when you've let Him down. He has the power to free you from any shame, fear or anger in your life – and He wants to.

THINK Are you feeling angry or upset about something that's happened to you? Remember that even when you've really messed up, you can always talk to God.

WHY, WHY, WHY, DELILAH?

READ: Judges 16:4–22

KEY VERSE: 'he did not know that the LORD had left him' (v20)

After being betrayed by his nagging first wife, you'd think Samson would learn his lesson and be a bit pickier on the dating scene. But he was about to be fooled by a beautiful woman for the second time. Clearly Samson had a weakness for Philistine women. Being emotionally involved with the enemy was just a way of life for him! He had vowed to put God first all his life and his long hair was a symbol of that commitment. But when it came to a choice, Samson chose his girlfriend over God.

Having always had God on his side, and having made it out of many tricky situations, somehow Samson thought pushing God down to second place wouldn't change anything. But when he woke up with a skinhead, his God-given superhuman strength was gone. The consequences were painful.

There's a good reason God asks us to put Him first, above everything and everyone: He never, ever lets us down. He is totally trustworthy. He is incapable of lying or tricking us, and He will never betray us.

PRAY Lord, thank You for being so trustworthy and loving. When I'm tempted to go a different way, help me to remember that You want what's best for me. Amen.

ROLLERCOASTER RIDE

BRING THE HOUSE DOWN

READ: Judges 16:23–30

KEY VERSE: 'Sovereign LORD, remember me.' (v28)

Samson's hair was a symbol of his commitment to God. When he forgot about that commitment, he lost his hair, eyesight, freedom and strength. Now a prisoner of the Philistines, Samson finally twigged that God was in charge and God knew best.

Samson re-dedicated his life to God. While being mocked and humiliated in the Philistines' temple to their false god, he called out to God as his 'Lord over all' for a final charging-up of supernatural strength. It was to be an epic finale. Samson became strong enough to pull down the pillars of the temple and it collapsed on itself, flattening everyone inside it one big crush.

God never forgets us, even when we really walk away from Him. When we truly regret what we've done and meet God on His terms, our relationship is made good again. God forgives us and has a plan for us, no matter what we've done. His arms are always wide open.

Samson's strength came from God – and He can give you a big dollop of strength too!

THINK Is there a tough situation you're facing today that you need some of God's strength for? Take some time to talk to Him about this.

GOD LOVES AN UNDERDOG

READ: Judges 6:11–32

KEY VERSE: 'Tear down your father's altar to Baal and cut down the Asherah pole beside it.' (v25)

What a rollercoaster ride our journey with the Judges has been so far! Now we're heading in reverse for a while to our next stop: Gideon. He was one of the greats – and what makes it even better is that his is a classic underdog story. In order to recruit Gideon in the first place, the angel of the Lord had to get pretty creative – this guy was going to take some convincing. For starters, Gideon was quite literally hiding in a cave, all too aware of his own weaknesses. To look at, he wasn't an obvious leader – let alone a hero or judge!

Gideon was convinced that surely God wouldn't want to use a nobody like him to rescue Israel, but God had other ideas. He would give Gideon the strength he needed to complete the task, all he wanted Gideon to do was be willing. That's the thing about God – His ideas are always better than ours, and He'll use whoever He wants to bring them about. That includes you – yes, even YOU!

PRAY **Father, please help me to be brave and go for it when You ask me to do something – I know You can give me what I will need. Amen.**

ROLLERCOASTER RIDE

WITHOUT A SHADOW OF A DOUBT

READ: Judges 6:33–40

KEY VERSE: 'he squeezed the fleece and wrung out the dew – a bowlful of water' (v38)

Have you ever had a moment where you've doubted your faith? Even after he'd been persuaded that God might actually have a plan for him, Gideon was still doubting his beliefs and believing his doubts. But God patiently reassured Gideon not once, but twice.

Totally relying on God is no small thing and can be quite scary. So it's OK to go to Him with our doubts and questions, and ask Him to confirm something. That's what Gideon did with the fleece – He was asking God for a clear sign to make sure that he was on the right track.

Notice how God didn't give Gideon a major telling-off when he came to Him with his doubts. God knows that our trust in Him can be shaky at times, but is happy to reassure us that He is in control. No matter how afraid we might be, our powerful and mighty God is also incredibly kind and understanding. He's our Father who wants to reassure us of His goodness.

THINK Do you have doubts about anything to do with God right now? Talk it through with God and another Christian.

A FEW GOOD MEN

READ: Judges 7:1–8

KEY VERSE: 'With the three hundred men... I will save you... Let all the others go home.' (v7)

Over the next few days, we'll be looking at one of the most epic and unlikely battle defeats in military history! You couldn't have worse odds than Gideon and his soldiers did here...

Gideon knew he would have a fight on his hands. The might Midianites – over 120,000 of them – were camped ready to raid Israel. He bravely rallied up 32,000 men to head them off, but that meant he was still outnumbered 4–1. God would help them out, right?

God rarely works out a problem in the way we expect Him to. Instead of sending more men to level the playing field, He brought down the numbers in Gideon's army to just 300! They were now outnumbered 400–1. And with these ridiculous odds, God told Gideon He would give them victory.

It's when there's absolutely no way we can solve a problem on our own that our faith in God is tested. Gideon had only got God's word that He would win the battle, but that was all he needed.

PRAY
Heavenly Father, I worship You because there is no one else like You. Help me to trust You even when the odds seem against me. Amen.

ROLLERCOASTER RIDE

AGAINST ALL ODDS

READ: Judges 7:9–14

KEY VERSE: 'If you are afraid to attack, go down to the camp... and listen to what they are saying.' (vv10–11)

So the odds for Gideon winning this battle were stacked against him, 400–1. Though he trusted God, it was hard not to be terrified! But God found a way to get word to Gideon that everything was going to be alright.

By doing a little night-time eavesdropping at the enemy camp, Gideon discovered that God was already getting under the skin of the Midianites. Rumour was spreading in their camp that the God of the Israelites was going to crush them. This was great news for Gideon! He had trusted that God would give them the victory in theory, but now he was prepared to put his faith into practice. His fears were gone and he took time out to worship God.

Faith makes such a huge difference to how we see life. One minute Gideon was a nervous wreck, the next he was praising God for giving them victory – before the battle had even taken place. That's how confident he was that God would work things out.

PRAY Father God, I know that You are always working for my good. Thank You for all the ways You've helped me in the past, and all the ways You will do in the future. Amen.

MAKE SOME NOISE

READ: Judges 7:15–24

KEY VERSE: 'A sword for the LORD and for Gideon!' (v20)

It was the day of the big battle, and God had a completely brilliant strategy up His sleeve. The plan was to make a racket so huge that the Midianite would believe they were about to be wiped out by a ginormous mega-army. 'Blow your trumpets, smash those pots and scream your little hearts out, boys!' The enemy troops were so panicked and confused that they turned on each other! Those who ran away found that their escape routes were blocked by the Israelites.

It had looked impossible at the beginning, but God kept His promise and won another famous victory for the Israelites. And it was all made possible by a few good men who trusted in God and made some noise.

At the beginning of his story, Gideon was a glass-half-empty kinda guy, always seeing the worst. But by choosing to believe what God had to say about him, stepping out in faith, praying about his decisions and trusted in God's wild and whacky plans, Gideon went down in history. It wasn't easy, but God always gave him the back-up he needed.

THINK God is not the slightest bit boring. Do you think that being a Christian makes life way more adventurous, or way more boring?

ROLLERCOASTER RIDE

AMNESIA... AGAIN

READ: Judges 8:32–35

KEY VERSE: 'They... did not remember the LORD their God, who had rescued them' (vv33–34)

Have you ever made a mistake, promised yourself you would never do that again, and then and done it again anyway? Despite having lived in victory and peace under Gideon, the Israelites soon went back to their old ways (surprise, surprise!). Though God had helped Gideon to chase the Midianites out of Israel and bring them 40 years of peace, a new generation was growing up. When Gideon died, the Israelites showed no loyalty to him, his family or his God – and went shopping for something new to worship.

Baal was a big hit with all the nations around them. Half human, half bull, Baal wasn't a good-looking carved image, but he appeared to bring good harvests. God had forbidden His people to worship false gods, but the new generation of Israelites didn't care. It can feel a lot easier to keep on going and growing with our Christian faith after a 'spiritual high' – an answer to prayer, a miracle, or an amazing time away at a Christian event. But as time passes, it's important to still remember the good things God has done.

PRAY Lord, You are so good to me! Please help me never to forget the brilliant things You've done, even as time passes. Amen.

COUNTER CULTURAL

READ: Judges 21:25

KEY VERSE: 'everyone did as they saw fit' (v25)

The book of Judges definitely has its up and downs, and today we're looking at the very last verse. It's a shame that the book doesn't end on a high, but it's still got a lot to show us.

There are some pretty bonkers things happening in Judges, but what's the most disturbing is how similar the Israelites were to some people today. People's idea of right and wrong is always changing, and most people do what they want. So how can *we* live for Jesus in a world full of people living for themselves?

If history tells us one thing, it's that people will always mess up — just look at the book of Judges! Knowing that we have a loving God to forgive and rescue us is what makes all the difference, but we need to be prepared to live for Him. It's a challenge, for sure — but when we put God at the centre of our lives, not ourselves, people will start to pay attention. It's then that with God's help we'll change the world around us for the better.

THINK
How might God be calling you to live differently for Him today? Write down your ideas and chat to another Christian about them!

ROLLERCOASTER RIDE

DUST YOURSELF OFF

READ: Psalm 130:1–8

KEY VERSE: 'If you, LORD, kept a record of sins, Lord, who could stand? But with you there is forgiveness' (vv3–4)

Have you ever tried really hard at something only to find it's not worked? Well, most people know what it feels like to fail every now and then! It's actually a good thing! How? With God, realising you've failed is a very good place to get to know Him better. That is what this psalm is all about.

The people of Israel knew what failure was. God had rescued them and given them His law. Because of this they knew the world was in a total mess, broken, sick and damaged beyond repair. They knew they could never fix things and that, deep down, human beings had failed! Their only hope was that God would do something to help. In verse 8 you can see how strong that hope was.

God has chosen to forgive those who admit their failure to Him. This is not because we have a right to forgiveness, but because He is extremely loving and kind. We can have a completely fresh start, thanks to God.

PRAY Lord, thank You that You love us so much, however many times we make a mess of things. Thank You that I don't have to be scared of failing. Amen.

HONESTLY

READ: Psalm 123:1–4

KEY VERSE: 'I lift up my eyes to you' (v1)

Today's psalm starts off cheery, talking about friendship with God, but then it goes downhill a bit as the psalmist talks about how tough things have been. Was the psalmist right to do that? When we worship God, should we really talk about our struggles too?

Do you ever find that you can't be yourself with people? Maybe it's like that in your class at school, with some of your friends or even at home with your family. We can all be guilty of telling people what we think they want to hear. Why do we do it? Well, it's usually because we're worried of what they'll think of us if we're honest.

The sad thing is that we can get so used to doing this with other people that sometimes we hide our feelings from God. We can worry that He won't accept us if we're really open with Him.

But that's the amazing thing about psalms. They're honest to God. Yes, about how great He is, but also about how incredibly tough life can be at times.

So to answer that question, yes we can talk to God about our struggles. We can talk to Him about anything!

THINK There's no better time than now to start being honest with God. Try writing down whatever you want to say to Him.

PSALM

LET'S GO

READ: Psalm 122:1–9

KEY VERSE: 'I rejoiced with those who said to me, "Let us go to the house of the LORD."' (v1)

This psalm was sung by Old Testament believers as they climbed a hill to Jerusalem, where they worshipped God. In the Old Testament, Jerusalem wasn't just a capital city, it reminded the people of these promises of God:

- That God would bring healing to the whole world through Abraham's children.
- That God is with His people.
- That God was going to do something miraculous to sort out Israel's problems and, at the same time, the problems of the whole world.

Today we are reminded of the same things when we talk about Jesus. He is bringing healing to the world, He has given us the Holy Spirit to be close to us, and He is the great King who mends our lives.

We don't have to climb a hill to meet with God, He is with us all the time. But what we can do is go to His promises. When we *feel* God is distant, even though we *know* He's not, let's go to His promises and trust Him. He's never broken a single one – and he never will.

THINK
Do you ever experience times when God doesn't feel near? What might you do when this next happens?

PSALM

ASSURANCE

READ: 2 Timothy 3:14–17

KEY VERSE: 'continue in what you have learned and have become convinced of' (v14)

Long Bible words can make your brain feel like a can of mushy peas, unless you know what they mean. We're going to take a look at some of these words and make sense of this the jargon. First up is the word 'assurance'.

Christians might sometimes have doubts that they really belong in God's family. Does He kick us out when we mess things up? How can we really *know* that we are saved?

The Bible says that if we love Jesus and follow Him, He forgives us and gives us eternal life. And when you become a Christian, the Holy Spirit makes His home inside you! The Holy Spirit helps us to know that God is with us.

Timothy wasn't convinced he was a Christian just because Paul said so. He knew he was saved by Jesus because the Holy Spirit was at work in him, making him more like Jesus. He knew God's Word and believed it too.

Satan hates it when we start to understand just how loved we are by God and he'll do anything to persuade us otherwise! But you can be confident that God loves you.

THINK **Have you ever doubted that God has actually forgiven you? His forgiveness is real when we turn to Jesus. Believe it!**

JARGON BUSTER

ABUNDANT LIFE

READ: John 10:1–10

KEY VERSE: 'I have come that they may have life, and have it to the full.' (v10)

Jesus came to earth to deliver abundant life – a way of living that is longer and deeper than anyone thought possible.

Although most us will live happily into our old age, the sad truth is that life can end at any moment. But abundant life doesn't go out of date. When our human bodies switch off, God gives us a new body and a new home with Him forever.

Lots of people feel like something is missing from their life. When Jesus talks about abundant life, He means living a life that is full of the Holy Spirit! Now that's living!

The Bible is full of God's promises to give us a future and a hope (Jer. 29:11); to never leave us (Heb. 13:5); and to make things work for good (Rom. 8:28). Until we let God into our lives, they are incomplete. But when we invite God's Spirit to live in us (wow!) our emptiness becomes full to the brim with good stuff – God's stuff. Abundant life.

PRAY Holy Spirit, come and fill me with life – abundant life. Please show me the best way to live, full of You. Amen.

ADVOCATE

READ: John 14:15–27

KEY VERSE: 'I will ask the Father, and he will give you another advocate to help you and be with you for ever – the Spirit of truth' (vv16–17)

The word 'advocate' might not crop up as often as some other biblical words. Other Bible translations might say 'Counsellor' or 'Helper' in this verse instead. But what does it mean?

Put simply: the Holy Spirit stands alongside us. God fights our corner. When we're up against it in life, we can ask the Holy Spirit for help. He makes us winners, because Jesus has won. We get to share in His championship and raise the trophy with Him! If we trust Jesus it means that when God looks at us, He sees Him!

The Holy Spirit advocates for us in prayer to. In Romans 8:26 it says the Spirit even helps us when we know we want to pray, but we can't seem to do so. He steps in and prays on our behalf – how amazing is that?! When we just don't have the words, our advocate fills in the blanks. He is on our side.

THINK
How often do you speak up for other people? Is there someone who needs you to stand alongside them at the moment?

JARGON BUSTER

CONSCIENCE

READ: 1 Timothy 1:18–20

KEY VERSE: 'holding on to faith and a good conscience, which some have rejected and so have suffered shipwreck with regard to the faith' (v19)

Our conscience is a partnership with God that helps us know right from wrong. Have you ever done something you shouldn't have and felt regret afterwards? That's your conscience speaking!

In today's reading, Paul talks about two men who had ignored God's warning and made a right mess of their lives because of this. Instead of admitting they had messed up and asking God to forgive them, they'd shut Him out. If we don't want to make a mess out of our faith, we need to keep listening to God.

Paul told Timothy to hold on to a good conscience. When you know God's telling you what to do, don't avoid the issue – sort it out with Him. He's given us a Bible packed with info on right and wrong – so get to know it! If we get closer to God, we'll become more like Him. Hold on to God and you'll hold on to a good conscience.

PRAY
Dear God, help me to get Your ways into my head, so that my conscience lines up with what's right. I want to listen. Amen.

CONFESSION

READ: 1 John 1:1-10

KEY VERSE: 'If we confess our sins, he is faithful and just and will forgive us our sins and purify us from all unrighteousness.' (v9)

When we think of confession, we might think it just means confessing our sins, but really, there's more to it. We do need to confess where we've gone wrong to God. But it's also about lining ourselves up with God's truth and living (and speaking) according to the truth.

We're not perfect. We never will be. We can't do this on our own. Put bluntly: without Jesus, we're not good enough for God. But remember what we said about our advocate? God doesn't look at us and want nothing to do with us. He sent His Son to save us so we can be forgiven.

Confession is also accepting the truth about God. He's awesome. Perfect. Holy. Spotless. He is God.

The first Christians made sure they were openly 'confessing' that Jesus is Lord. It wasn't a secret they kept. So many people have the wrong idea about God. They don't understand who He is. Let's spread that word about how great God really is. If we really believe that this is the truth, then let's confess it!

THINK
Is there anything you know you need to confess *to* God? Is there anything you know you need to confess *about* God?

JARGON BUSTER

DISCIPLE

READ: John 8:31-36

KEY VERSE: 'Jesus said, "If you hold to my teaching, you are really my disciples."' (v31)

Did you know that the word 'disciple' is used nearly three hundred times in the Bible? Depending on your Bible translation, the word 'Christian' is only used about three times. So, what is a disciple? It's a follower or learner.

The first 12 disciples of Jesus dropped everything to follow Him. They literally *followed* Him everywhere He went. They watched how He lived. They asked Him questions. They learned all they could about life; how to love people; how to change the world.

Jesus is a great teacher. He knows learners make mistakes. His first 12 were always messing up. James and John had anger problems, Peter was always saying the wrong thing, none of them were perfect. And after three years together, they all ran away! They should have been crossed off the list of suitable disciples, but Jesus loved them, helped them with their issues, and turned them into champions. And it's the same for us too. We are all disciples of Jesus when we decide to follow Him.

PRAY Lord Jesus, thank You for being the best teacher ever. You know the areas that I need to grow more in, so help me to learn from You. Amen.

FAITH

READ: Romans 10:9–17

KEY VERSE: 'faith comes from hearing the message, and the message is heard through the word about Christ' (v17)

God doesn't leave fingerprints. You can't take photos of Him, record His voice, or touch Him. People will tell you there's no 'proof' for God. How do you deal with that?

God's creation is living, moving, growing, talking evidence of His power (Rom. 1:20). But people today aren't impressed, and instead they see our existence as a gigantic cosmic accident. Why doesn't God show His face every now and again? The truth is that God did make an appearance through Jesus coming to earth. Witnesses wrote down what happened, and that's how we've got a lot of the New Testament. And God wants us to trust what the Bible says about Him.

We become Christians by believing that Jesus can save us from our sin (v9) – we trust Him. That's what we call *faith*. There's so much about life that we don't understand – and may not ever understand until we make it to heaven. But no one who trusts God will ever be let down (v11).

THINK Have you had anyone tell you that there's no proof for Christianity? What would be a good way to respond to this? Tip: start by looking at the life of Jesus.

JARGON BUSTER

GRACE

READ: 1 Corinthians 15:1–11

KEY VERSE: 'But by the grace of God I am what I am, and his grace to me was not without effect.' (v10)

Grace isn't that prayer you quickly mumble so you can tuck into your dinner. In the Bible, 'grace' is what is meant by God's love for us. A love we don't deserve.

Paul is a star example of God's grace in action. He'd hated followers of Jesus, even ordering for them to be killed. Paul was basically a terrorist, targeting Christians. If there was ever a guy who deserved to be shown no mercy from God, it was Paul.

So what did God do – let him rot away in jail? Send a lightning bolt strike him down? No! God introduced him to Jesus and forgave him! Amazing or what?

Paul knew that he didn't deserve God's kindness. So he didn't want to waste it or take it for granted. The more Paul understood God's grace, the more he became like Jesus and told others about Him. Let's do the same with God's grace to us – become more like Jesus, and tell more people about Him.

Remember this: if God could love Paul, He can love anyone.

PRAY Lord Jesus, I just can't thank You enough for grace! Thank you for saving me even though I don't deserve it. Amen.

GOSPEL

READ: Romans 1:8–17

KEY VERSE: 'I refuse to be ashamed of sharing the wonderful message of God's liberating power unleashed in us through Christ! For I am thrilled to preach that everyone who believes is saved' (v16, TPT)

The news is often so full of bad news that we can wonder where the good news has gone. Well, here's some...

The word 'gospel' means 'the good news about Jesus'. What a great news story to tell! God sending Jesus to die for us so we could live. Jesus told His disciples to release this story everywhere. The bad news is that we were cut off from God. The good news is that Jesus has made a way for us to get together with Him!

In Greek, the word for 'gospel', *euggalion*, became the Latin word *evangel* – where we get the word 'evangelist' from. An evangelist is someone who tells the good news. That someone includes you and me. We've got a job to get on with! The most important job in the world – telling everyone about Jesus. Paul says he wasn't ashamed of the gospel. Why would we ever be ashamed of our incredible, powerful God who saves us?!

THINK
Who could be the first/next person you tell this good news to? Pray for them to listen and then share with them what Jesus has done for them!

JARGON BUSTER

JUSTIFIED

READ: Romans 5:1–9

KEY VERSE: 'Since we have now been justified by his blood, how much more shall we be saved from God's wrath through him!' (v9)

Every morning millions of people get up and head for the mirror. Why? Because we care what we look like, don't we?

Before we became Christians we looked pretty bad in God's sight. Sin had made us a right mess – and there was nothing we could do about it. But God stepped in and sent Jesus, who died and rose again – providing a way for our mess to be cleaned up. Because of Jesus, when God looks at us now it's like we've never messed up. He died so we could be forgiven! His sacrifice has made everything all right again. Jesus wipes the slate clean.

In verse 6, Paul explains it really simply: 'just at the right time, when we were still powerless, Christ died for the ungodly.' We can't make ourselves right again, only Jesus can do that. And He did – even though we didn't deserve it. Are you thankful for that?

PRAY Thank You, Jesus, for justifying me by dying on the cross and rising again. I praise You for making a way for me to be forgiven! Amen.

LOVE

READ: John 21:15–19

KEY VERSE: 'The third time he said to him, "Simon son of John, do you love me?"' (v17)

The Bible uses two Greek terms when talking about of love: *phileo* and *agape*. *Phileo* love means to like someone or be friends with them. *Agape* love is loving others without expecting anything in return. *Agape* love is used to describe God's sacrificial love for us.

Why are we spending today talking about love? Isn't the whole topic just a bit too soppy? Well, no! The kind of love that the Bible shows is a strong, powerful love that sent Jesus to the cross for us. So it's worth looking into.

Before this meeting in John 21, Peter had disowned Jesus on three occasions to save his own skin. The New Testament was originally written in Greek, in which several different words (each with a different meaning) are used for the English word 'love'. Jesus asks Peter, 'Do you love me?' He's talking about the *agape* form of love. Peter responds the first two times using the *phileo* word. Jesus doesn't want us to just *like* Him, but *love* Him – with an all-out love that overtakes everything else in our lives.

THINK How would you describe your love for Jesus – is it *agape* or *phileo*?

JARGON BUSTER

MEDIATOR

READ: 1 Timothy 2:1–7

KEY VERSE: 'For there is one God and one mediator between God and mankind, the man Christ Jesus' (v5)

Have you ever been in the middle of two people who aren't on good terms?

The word 'mediator' is made up from two words, 'middle' and 'go'. And that's why Jesus is described as our mediator – He's the middle man going between us and the Father.

In order to come close to our holy God, we need to get our problem of sin sorted. Jesus Himself took the punishment for our rejection of God. What an amazing friend He is! He built a bridge in the gap between us and God, and takes us over it. We could never do that without Him. Because of Him, there's no issue between us and God.

Today's passage also tells us that Jesus gave Himself 'as a ransom for all people'. He came for *all people*. So once again, we're reminded this isn't a gift to be greedy with, but to share with other people. The greatest favour we can show anyone is to introduce them to Jesus. Jesus said 'I am the way' (John 14:6). He meant it. He is the only middle-man, and everyone needs to know this.

THINK How could you be a mediator today? What would it look like to be the mediator between your friends and Jesus?

PRAISE

READ: Ephesians 5:18–20

KEY VERSE: 'always giving thanks to God the Father for everything, in the name of our Lord Jesus Christ' (v20)

Praise is saying thanks and giving God credit. The Bible is always reminding us to 'praise the Lord'. That's because we need reminding!

God doesn't need us to pat Him on the back or raise His self-esteem. What we say doesn't make God feel any better about Himself. But praise helps us to focus on God instead of ourselves. And that's good for us! Praise says out loud that God knows best. He's the King! He cares about us. He deserves to be at the top!

By praising God in tough times, we avoid the trap of feeling sorry for ourselves. By giving thanks in every situation, we announce that God is in control. He won't let anything happen to us that He can't turn around and work out for our good.

Praising God can be hard at times when your friends are being weird, you're grounded, or you've just lost a game. But the Holy Spirit can help us to praise God throughout everything.

PRAY
Lord Jesus, You are worthy of my praise! It's impossible to say everything You have done for me, but I am so grateful. Amen.

JARGON BUSTER

REDEEMED

READ: 1 Peter 1:13–19

KEY VERSE: 'it was not with perishable things such as silver or gold that you were redeemed from the empty way of life' (v18)

REDEEMED

When the New Testament was written there were over six million slaves in the Roman Empire. Some slaves had the option of buying their freedom for a sum of money. But sometimes the owner would arrange that slaves would only have enough money to buy their freedom when they were too old to work.

The price of a slave's freedom was agreed, and when it was paid they were redeemed. As slaves were poor, this often meant someone else paying for them. We still use the word 'redeemed' to mean 'settling the cost'.

The Bible says that Jesus is our redeemer – He paid the ransom to set us free. And the cost of our freedom was not paid with a cash, coupons or clubcard points – it was paid with the blood of Jesus on the cross. What does He want in return? Us to love Him.

THINK Do you ever feel like you're not very valuable? Lots of us can feel like that, but here's the truth: you are so valuable that Jesus died just so you would be His friend!

REPENTANCE

READ: Acts 3:17–20

KEY VERSE: 'Repent, then, and turn to God, so that your sins may be wiped out' (v19)

Some people confuse the word 'repent' with 'remorse'. Remorse is simply feeling sorry for what we've done. Repenting is more than that – it's a big U-turn in God's direction. Have you ever seen someone walk down a street, realise they're going the wrong way, and awkwardly turn right back round? In the Bible, to repent is to change your heart and mind – to choose to walk away from your sin and accept that God's way of doing things is right and perfect.

In today's passage from Acts, Peter is explaining the gospel to people – that they need to turn away from their old ways of living.

But that's not all – Peter says that when they do repent, God doesn't keep a big folder in a filing cabinet in heaven with a record of what they've done wrong. God wipes their sins away. That's right – He gets a big shredder out and destroys those records! So when we repent, we tell God we're sorry and run away from our sin, and He forgets all about it. That's how amazing God's forgiveness is!

PRAY Father God, help me to see the things in my life that are wrong. I want to leave them behind. Amen.

JARGON BUSTER

REVIVAL

READ: Psalm 85:1–6

KEY VERSE: 'Will you not revive us again, that your people may rejoice in you?' (v6)

Most first aid courses teach you how to give the 'kiss of life'. Those who have only just stopped breathing can sometimes be revived if you can get air back into their lungs.

Not only can bodies be revived, but relationships can be too. When the Bible uses the word 'revival' it's usually to do with our friendship with God. When we drift off into disobeying God, we need Him to wake us, shake us and breathe His new life into us.

We all need to be revived – woken up by God. Throughout history there have been huge revivals where thousands of people have asked Jesus into their lives! Psalm 85 is a prayer for revival. God's people had gone off to do their own thing. Their relationship with God had fizzled out and the joy had gone missing from their lives. So they humbly asked God to forgive and revive them. They needed reviving, not just help surviving!

THINK
Do you feel a bit 'sleepy' in your faith? Maybe it's become the same old, same old? Think and ask God about ways that you can wake up a bit more in your faith.

RIGHTEOUSNESS

READ: John 16:5–15

KEY VERSE: 'When he comes, he will prove the world to be in the wrong about sin and righteousness and judgment' (v8)

Mutter the words 'right' and 'just' very quickly and you get the word 'righteous'. To be righteous means to be completely right because we are right with God.

God knows what is good – He *decides* what is right, and He thinks right and acts right.

So, are we righteous? We all like to think we're right. We even say we are. But that's our opinion. Righteousness is being right by God's standards. Jesus told His disciples that the Holy Spirit would show them right from wrong. Without His help we can't appreciate how good God is and how much we fall short in comparison. It's the Holy Spirit who shows us that we are not as smart as we think, and guides us to Jesus to sort it out.

Jesus is our righteousness – our way of being made right with God. We can't become righteous on our own. Only Jesus has the power to deal with the 'not right' and make us all right. So where are you? Just not right? Or right with God – and just thankful to Jesus?

PRAY Jesus, thank You so much for making me 'right'. Help me to live the right way – for You! Amen.

JARGON BUSTER

SANCTIFICATION

READ: John 17:13–19

KEY VERSE: 'Sanctify them by the truth; your word is truth.' (v17)

Have you ever used a pen that leaks? The ink gets on your fingers or stains the lining of your pockets. It's a real pain. We're like a leaking biro when our lives are not fully put in God's hands. Instead of being focused on doing what God wants, we leak off to do our own thing, often leaving a mess behind us.

To be sanctified is to be made holy, completely washed clean by God – and that means to be set apart, different from everyone else, for God. In a pocket full of leaking biros, the sanctified pens are the good-as-new ones.

The moment we become Christians, we are 'justified' – forgiven and made right. God has made us holy, but we still need to chase after holiness. In today's reading, before His death, Jesus is praying to His Father (God!) to sanctify us 'by the truth' (v17). That's His prayer for us – that we be pure and set apart. We'll mess up, but we can keep on trying.

THINK Do you ever feel pressure to follow the crowd and do things that you know aren't good? Make a plan for how you will try to be different, because of God, next time this happens.

SALVATION

READ: Acts 4:8–12

KEY VERSE: 'Salvation is found in no one else' (v12)

It's at the centre of our faith, but what does salvation actually mean?

We can't get into heaven on our own – there's no way we'll ever be good enough. The Bible says that the 'wages [penalty] of sin is death' (Rom. 6:23) – we need a Saviour! We need salvation: to be saved from an eternity spent separated from the love of God, and to have our relationship with God mended now.

Peter and John risked their lives to tell the Jews that Jesus – the man they'd crucified – was alive, with the power to give them eternal life instead of death! The Jews hoped their good work would save them, but there is only one way to be saved, and that is through Jesus. After speaking about the penalty of sin, Romans 6:23 goes on to say, 'but the gift of God is eternal life in Christ Jesus our Lord'. Wow!

But salvation is optional. We have to grab hold of this gift. Jesus died in our place and came out on top – He can save us and sort our relationship with God out, if we ask.

PRAY

Lord Jesus, thank You for saving me! I want You in my life today and every day. I receive Your forgiveness and choose to follow You. Amen.

JARGON BUSTER

WISDOM

READ: 2 Chronicles 1:7–12

KEY VERSE: "'Give me wisdom and knowledge, that I may lead this people, for who is able to govern this great people of yours?'" (v10)

If you could ask for anything in the world, what would it be? King Solomon didn't come up with a wish list to make him rich, popular or a style icon. He asked God for something very rare – wisdom.

Wisdom is using knowledge the right way – God's way. It's seeing life from God's point of view. Usually when we are faced with a decision, we look at the options from our own point of view. What's best for me? Wisdom looks at things differently. It knows that God knows best and turns to Him for answers. Wise people put God first.

Wisdom views others as God sees them. It sees what people really need. And being wise isn't about being popular, but about doing right. Whose view on life are you going with? Yours or God's? Solomon put God in the top spot and found that all the other things he needed came his way too.

THINK
What's more important to you – being popular, or doing right? Which one do you think would be the best way of living life, and why?

LOSE CONTROL

READ: Psalm 127:1–5

KEY VERSE: 'Unless the LORD builds a house, the work of the builders is wasted.' (v1, NLT)

Do you like rollercoasters? Some people love them, some absolutely hate them! Part of the reason for their hatred of them is the feeling of having no control.

The singers of today's psalm were on their way to worship God. They were getting themselves ready by remembering that they are totally in God's hands. He controls everything, we don't. This can be a scary thought!

No one likes to admit that they can't control things. But the simple fact is we don't have complete control over anything – what's going to happen today, tomorrow or even what happens inside our own bodies. But the great thing is we don't' *need* to. Because someone far more qualified does!

God is in charge of our lives. That doesn't mean we shouldn't care about anything. But it does mean that when we make plans we should make sure God is behind them, if He's not they won't get anywhere. God has good things in store for us, things we couldn't even imagine!

PRAY
Father God, You know me inside and out. You know what's best for me and You know what makes me happy. I trust You. Amen.

PSALM

LOOK OUT

READ: Psalm 96:1–13

KEY VERSE: 'Sing to the LORD a new song' (v1)

Do you like hearing new music, or do you prefer the songs you already know?

This psalm tells us to sing a new song to God. Why? Well, for the same reason that people are always releasing new songs into the charts — partly because old songs get boring after a while, but also because there's always something new that can be said about life. We always need new songs about God because He is so amazing that no song on its own can say it all!

So what does this psalm focus on about God? The main thing it says is that God is the king of the universe and that He is coming to make everything right: 'he comes to judge the earth' (v13).

Christianity isn't about trying to make ourselves as nice as we can compared to everyone else. Following Jesus is about looking out for God who is on His way to sort the world out. Jesus is coming back! This songs show how the world around us is waiting for God to come. So let's look around us and see what God is doing.

THINK **What did you think most about yesterday? Were you concerned with others or were your thoughts mostly about yourself? Today, try to turn your focus to the world around you.**

PSALM

SERVANT OR FRIEND?

READ: John 15:9–17

> **KEY VERSE:** 'You are my friends if you do what I command.' (v14)

Heroes. World-changers. Champions. Jesus assembled a bunch of misfits to be His disciples, who would change the world forever.

The terms 'friend' and 'servant' might seem like opposites, but today's reading shows us the strange-but-true relationship between being a friend and being a servant. One minute Jesus is giving the disciples commands, but the next minute He's telling them they are His friends, not His servants!

So which is it? Well... both. If you saw someone who was in trouble, wouldn't you help them if you could? That's serving them! Serving is what we do to give someone something they need.

Watch any superhero film and you'll notice that their aim is to 'help' (serve) people. And next to these heroes there are quite often friends who work with them to bring good into the world.

Our world is full of hurt people who need help. Jesus invites us to serve with Him to change the world.

We are invited to join Jesus the superhero's mission!

PRAY Dear Jesus, You are God of all, but You came to serve us. That's awesome! I want to be a member of Your world-changing team. Amen.

HERO ACADEMY

WHO, ME?

READ: Mark 3:13–19

> **KEY VERSE:** 'He appointed twelve [disciples] that they might be with him' (v14)

Who would definitely *not* be on Jesus' team to save the world? Bad-tempered bigmouths? Cowards? Doubters? Cheaters? Thieves? In another surprising turn of events, that's exactly who Jesus chose.

God loves to take the 'nobodies' and turn them into 'somebodies'. Jesus could have had the talented, loyal, brainy ones. But instead, He chose the misfits to stay with Him and learn from Him – and they ended up changing the world! Today, 2,000 years later, their work still affects us – you might even go to a church named after one of them.

Jesus turned them into legends. How? He assembled a team that He could train. He was ready to get stuck in and spend time working with then. He was keen to encourage, help and defend them. Even more, He was about to show them how to do amazing things in the power of His name. Did they mess up along the way? Of course they did! But Jesus used their mistakes as learning opportunities. That's the kind of friend Jesus is. He chose you, sticks with you and helps you. Always.

PRAY Lord Jesus, thank You for being such a good friend. You're always with me, helping me, even when I make mistakes. Help me to stick with You. Amen.

YOU GOTTA SEE THIS!

READ: John 1:35–42

KEY VERSE: 'The first thing Andrew did was to find his brother' (v41)

When you find out some amazing news, what's one of the first things you do? You tell people! Do you know who's a shining example of this in our passage today? Andrew. He's more interested in getting the word out than getting credit for being the first to know the word on the street.

Did you know that it was actually Andrew who first realised the Jesus was the Christ and believed in Him? He was so amazed he even went to go and grab his brother, Peter, to tell him all about Jesus.

Andrew was getting along great with this person who was the Saviour they'd all been waiting for – for centuries!

Jesus had invited Andrew and his mate back to where He was staying, and they spent the whole day chatting. When Andrew realised Jesus was looking for people to join His academy, he signed up straight away. And instead of hiding his friendship with Jesus, what's the first thing he did? He ran off to share the news!

THINK **If you're really honest, do you want your friends to know Jesus? The more we know Jesus and realise how amazing He is, the more desperate we become for everyone we love to know Him.**

HERO ACADEMY

FOOT RUB, ANYONE?

READ: John 13:1–17

KEY VERSE: 'Then, Lord... not just my feet but my hands and my head as well!' (v9)

Remember the foot-washing occasion? Well, we're back here again because this was a very important part of the Jesus' academy (disciples) training. To us, it seems quite random for Jesus to fill up a bowl and start washing people's feet. But back then, having someone wash your feet when you went into a house was just normal. Kind of like taking your shoes off at the door. But it would be a servant who got their hands dirty.

Jesus and the disciples had all been in the house for a while, but someone had forgotten to bring the servant with the foot spa. No one had offered to do this grim job, so Jesus grabbed a bowl and started washing everyone's smelly feet. Peter was mortified. He didn't mind anyone else doing it, but not Jesus! When Jesus pointed out that this was an act of friendship, Peter suddenly wanted a full hose down. Jesus taught Peter an important lesson about friendship – caring for others instead of being obsessed with our own image.

PRAY

Lord Jesus, thank You for showing us how to serve each other. Help me to serve You by serving others. Amen.

STRONG LOVE

READ: John 13:33–38

KEY VERSE: 'By this everyone will know that you are my disciples, if you love one another.' (v35)

Sporting teams wear team colours. Schools have uniforms. Nations have flags. What shows that we are part of Jesus' crew? Love. Of all the things that could have shown the world that the disciples were on God's team, the one thing that Jesus said would identify them as 'His' was how they loved and looked after one another. Why on earth would Jesus choose love as His mascot? Doesn't that make the team look a bit... weak?

Not at all. Love is strong, because God is love. He is all about love and friendship. Love is who God is: Father, Son and Holy Spirit all living together in perfect love and unity. To love, *really* love – 'putting the needs of others before yourself' kind of love – is to be like God. Humans fail, but love doesn't. Jesus knew that. In fact, as He told the disciples He didn't have much longer left with them, what He wanted to remind them about was love.

THINK
Jesus said that people would know we are part of His team if we love each other, if we treat each other with God-like love. Do you find it a challenge to love people?

HERO ACADEMY

BACK ON THE TEAM

READ: John 21:4–14

KEY VERSE: 'As soon as Simon Peter heard... he... jumped into the water.' (v7)

Have you ever felt dropped or betrayed by a friend? Pete's just spent three years with Jesus, learning about love, truth and forgiveness. Then, at the first whiff of trouble what does he do? He knifes a guard, chopping off his ear. Not his finest moment!

He boasts that he'll never leave Jesus, but when Jesus is being arrested, he scarpers. When people recognise him, he tells them *three times* that he's never even met Jesus. He abandons Jesus completely, leaving Him to die. All in all, a really bad few days.

After all that, you'd think that friendship would have gone out the window, right? But Jesus knew Peter was going to mess up, and He was ready to forgive Him already!

Peter felt like the world's biggest failure and traitor, but Jesus wanted Peter to take his place back in the team. He didn't hold a grudge, instead He went out of His way to rebuild the friendship. When people let us down, Jesus wants us to forgive them and do all we can to be friends with them again.

PRAY
Jesus, help me to forgive those who have treated me badly, just like You did for Peter and still do for me all the time. Amen.

IT'S JUST THE BEGINNING

READ: John 21:15–19

KEY VERSE: 'Then he said to him, '"Follow me!"' (v19)

Think about the ending of any action film that is followed by a sequel. The heroes have won one battle, but appearing more enemies are starting rise up and more people will need to be saved. The heroic team gather together, knowing that their job is not finished. Then the leader asks, 'Are you with me?' The team answer: 'We're with you – to the end.' They know what they are fighting for, and they know that defeating the enemy will be worthwhile.

Today's passage is like that scene. Peter had already tried running away from Jesus – and it left him grieving, alone and utterly lost. So when Jesus offers Peter a second chance to follow Him by asking 'How much do you love me, Peter? How much of your life are you willing to give to my mission?' – Peter's response is, 'Everything, Lord. I'll go anywhere and do anything for You. I dedicate everything to Your mission.' (And he's for real this time.)

THINK God has tasks for you in His mission, even right where you are. It could be anything from helping others to telling them about Jesus. Are you with Him?

WHAT'S IT GONNA TAKE?

READ: John 14:5–14

KEY VERSE: 'Don't you know me, Philip, even after I have been among you such a long time?' (v9)

Meet Philip. He was there when Jesus used His supernatural powers to feed over 5,000 people with a kid's packed lunch – impressive stuff? Phil wasn't convinced. Even after seeing Jesus perform many, many miracles, Phil still couldn't wrap his head about Jesus being God's Son. It didn't make sense to him. He just couldn't figure out how being Jesus' friend made you God's friend. Unless Jesus was God... 'Prove it,' said Philip. 'Let me see God, then I'll believe.'

Jesus flips this around and says 'Phil, if you get on board with me and choose to believe despite your doubts, you'll do even more amazing stuff than I'm doing. You'll get to know God and get rid of your doubts as you go!'

Philip shows us that it's possibly to be around someone for a long time without really getting to know them. But when we do, everything changes. This can also happen to people who have been around church for a long time – even all their lives – but don't actually know God personally.

PRAY **God, please help me get to know You more. I want to be part of Your adventure, not a side-line spectator. Amen.**

THE ROUGH PART OF TOWN

READ: John 1:43–51

KEY VERSE: 'Nazareth! Can anything good come from there?' (v46)

Before Philip started having his doubts, he was someone who got people signed up to Jesus' disciple academy. This brings us to Nathanael, the first person Phil got to fill out the forms. But Nathanael says, 'Hold up, Phil. Not so fast. This guy's from *Nazareth*? I think you've lost it. Nothing good comes from that dump.' You see, Nazareth was not known as the home of heroes. It was the sort of town you only went to when you were on your way somewhere else.

Jesus knew what Nathanael was thinking, but was nice to him anyway – even giving him a compliment! By building up the person who had tried to knock Him down, Jesus turned the situation around in seconds. Nathanael then knew that Jesus was someone special – none other than God's Son, the King of the Jews – and what an honour it was to be invited to join His academy!

When we appreciate people for who they are rather than where they come from, we might be unlocking the door to some great friendships and adventures!

THINK Do you know someone who you've thought 'I will *never* be friends with them'? Why not start praying for this person?

HERO ACADEMY

THUNDER AND LIGHTNING

READ: Luke 9:51–56

> **KEY VERSE:** 'Lord, do you want us to call fire down from heaven to destroy them?' (v54)

Have you ever argued with someone because they'd said something to you; you then came back with something to them, and so it continued? This is basically what the Samaritans and the Jews were like. They'd been in a fight for so long that they now wanted nothing to do with each other. They all thought that they were right and the others were wrong.

When James and John wanted to punish the Samaritans for rejecting Jesus by burning them to a crisp with fire from heaven, Jesus put them in 'time out'! He hadn't come to start a fight, but to put an end to one. Both the Jews and the Samaritans were His beloved children. He planned to offer His forgiveness both groups of people, so He wanted them to get along.

Jesus warned James and John that they would have to get over what had gone on in the past, because eventually it would be their job to reach out to the Samaritans and share the good news with them.

PRAY Father God, when I'm in an argument with someone, please remind me that we are all your children. Help me to find ways to resolve any fights well. Amen.

SUCCESS IS SERVICE

READ: Mark 10:32–45

KEY VERSE: 'whoever wants to become great among you must be your servant' (v43)

It seems that James and John had selective hearing. Jesus had just told them, 'The time is coming when I will be captured, tortured and killed before rising three days later' – but all they heard was, 'The time is coming... when the Song of Man will rise'. They fast-forwarded over the uncomfortable, painful parts and skipped straight to the bit where Jesus became famous, and they wanted some of that fame!

Jesus tried to explain to them that a lot of the time, ruling over others isn't all it's cracked up to be. And when He explained to them what it was really like, they were up for it!

The rest of the disciples heard fairly quickly what had been happening, and they weren't happy with James and John. So Jesus got them all together to clear the air. He told them, 'Being my disciple isn't about getting fame and fortune, it's about supporting and looking after each other. I don't want to conquer the world, I want to save it – by giving my life.'

THINK

Have you ever wanted to be famous? Sometimes people want fame because they want to feel loved and important. But here's the thing: God offers you all that anyway!

NO MATTER WHAT

READ: John 11:7–16

KEY VERSE: 'Let us also go, that we may die with him.' (v16)

Jesus and His disciples were headed for a place called Bethany, but some had serious doubts about going there. It was really close to Jerusalem (where people were plotting against Jesus), and last time they were in town they'd only just escaped a stone-throwing mob!

Jesus knew this mission wasn't going to be easy. His time leading the academy on earth was coming to an end — He was about to defeat death for His team to have the strength and power to deal with whatever was ahead of them.

Jesus' team just could not get their heads around His final mission — shouldn't they come up with another plan? But Jesus wanted to go to Bethany to see His friends Mary and Martha and bring their brother Lazarus back from the dead.

We will face hard times, but we can face them with God's strength. Thomas was amazed by Jesus' attitude. He told the rest of the team to stay together and support Jesus. Their leader had never let them down before and it was time for them to step up.

PRAY

Father, help me to always be there for my friends, celebrating with them when everything's great but also being there when things are really tough. Amen.

BRINGING OUTSIDERS IN

READ: Luke 5:27–32

KEY VERSE: 'Why do you eat and drink with tax collectors and sinners?' (v30)

We often think of being a disciple as something we choose to do. But back in Jesus' day, rabbis chose their disciples. It was like being picked for a team, only the best would do. So Jesus' choice of disciples – fishermen who never went to school, notorious bad guys... and now tax collectors(?!) – well, that just didn't make sense to the Pharisees.

Tax collectors were hated, *really* hated, because they worked for the Romans – the invaders of Israel. Most of them were thieves, stealing from their own people and pocketing the money for themselves. So when Jesus chose Matthew to join His academy, the Pharisees were fuming! But Jesus explained His choice to them: 'I haven't come to choose those who think they are OK with God. I've come to lead those who want to change their ways and be made right with God. *They* are my disciples.'

Wow! You know what that means, don't you? Mistakes that we have made in the past won't stop Jesus from loving us and wanting us on His team.

THINK If Jesus came to your school or town, who do you think the people He would choose for His team would be? Would you choose the same people?

HERO ACADEMY

HE SEES YOU

READ: Mark 15:40–41

KEY VERSE: 'James the younger' (v40)

There were two guys called James in Jesus' academy. One was called Son of Thunder and nobody dared to mess with him. The other was named James the Younger, sometimes even James 'the Less' – charming! It's not always easy being the youngest or the shortest of a group of people (perhaps family, friends or team), and James would have known this well. We don't know much about him but we do know that he was one of the twelve disciples. Just like the others, when he had received the Holy Spirit, he went and changed the world!

So often we compare ourselves to others, thinking they are better than us and that there's no way we could possibly do anything good. Have you ever felt like that? Maybe you've got a hobby but you know other people who also have that hobby, and when you look at what they can do, you feel like you're 'less' than them.

Remember, no one is too small or too 'less' to God, and no one escapes His notice. God had a purpose for James and He has a purpose for you.

PRAY God, thank You that I can play an important part in Your plans. Help me to serve You with every chance I get. Amen.

WAITING FOR THE 'GO' ORDER

READ: Acts 1:12–14

KEY VERSE: 'They all joined together constantly in prayer' (v14)

Meeting Jesus after He'd risen from the dead definitely lifted the disciples' spirits. Even Thomas now believed that with Jesus back in the driver's seat, nothing could stop them! Jesus had promised the team that when He got to heaven He would send back-up – the Holy Spirit – to encourage them, train them, help them and get them going!

So what were they all to do while they waited to meet the Holy Spirit? They met together all of the time and talked to God. If there was an award for praying, this lot would have got it. And it wasn't just men, women were part of the team too. These were the ones who hadn't abandoned Jesus when He was arrested, but had stuck by His side through it all.

God's academy is made up of all sorts of people who can use their different skills to change the world. For that, there's a very important thing we need to do: pray together. Whether that's at youth group, church, home or school – let's make praying together a priority.

THINK Do you pray with other Christians much? If you don't, think about if you know any Christians your age that you could team up with to talk to God.

HERO ACADEMY

AN EARLY EXIT

READ: John 12:1–8

KEY VERSE: 'Why wasn't this perfume sold and the money given to the poor?' (v5)

One member of Jesus' academy never made it to see the victory moment when Jesus defeated death. Instead, he was swayed over to the dark side: greed. Jesus not only told the poor about God but also gave to them, and Judas' job was to look after the team's money. But having access to this money was too tempting for Judas, and he couldn't stop himself from stealing some of the money.

When Judas saw Mary pour very expensive perfume on Jesus' feet, he was horrified that all that money had been wasted.

So Judas found another way to get his money: he sold out Jesus for cash. After that, Judas didn't buy his dream house. In fact, he tragically ended his own life. Jesus knew that Judas would go down this path, and it made Him sad to see it.

When we do things wrong, Jesus doesn't kick us out, but we sometimes kick ourselves out by running away. If we own up to how we get tempted to do things which aren't right, Jesus is always there waiting to forgive us and lead us forward in life.

PRAY

Lord God, You know I get tempted to _____. Please forgive me and help me through this. Amen.

POWER UP, PEOPLE!

READ: Acts 2:1–4

KEY VERSE: 'All of them were filled with the Holy Spirit' (v4)

Jesus had promised the disciples that He would send a new person to be with them in the mission to tell the world about Jesus. On the feast of Pentecost the whole team assembled. God chose this moment to introduce the person He had promised – and what a dramatic first impression He made on them! The gangly group were immediately transformed into heroes. Fear was turned into fearlessness, doubt was turned into daringness. All simply because of this 'new' guy's presence. So who was He?

It was God Himself. He came down in Spirit form to live inside each of them, fuelling them meet every challenge head-on and win! And if they slipped up, the Holy Spirit was there to show them where they had got it wrong and get them back on track. God living in them made a huge difference to the disciples and gave them the power they needed to get the good news of Jesus out into the world.

THINK We have the same Spirit of God living in us today. He loves to fill our lives and get us going forward for God, for His people and for those who don't know Him yet. Do you notice Him?

HERO ACADEMY

THERE'S NOTHING HOLDING ME BACK

READ: Acts 2:42–47

KEY VERSE: 'All the believers were together and had everything in common.' (v44)

The introduction of the Holy Spirit began a new era for the disciples. They were now called apostles, and their job was to bring in new disciples from every nation. The Holy Spirit was guiding them and showing them how to follow Jesus in all their lives. No more arguments over who was the best – they now served each other as friends. And this offer to follow Jesus was for everyone.

Each member of the community was seen as valuable for his or her unique and important role. They supported each other, cared for each other, enjoyed spending time together, worshipped together and studied God's Word together. And together, they followed God with every part of their lives – just as Jesus had showed them. Nothing held back.

This display of team power impressed others, and every day more people believed that Jesus was alive and joined up to live His way, to fight evil and stand up for those who had been hurt, to live lives that made their creator and Saviour happy.

PRAY Jesus, thank You for saving me, and for helping me to join the greatest mission ever – telling people about You! Amen.

RAISE IT UP

READ: Psalm 113:1–9

KEY VERSE: 'He raises the poor from the dust and lifts the needy from the ash heap' (v7)

This psalm was sang during the Passover party time, which celebrated God setting the Israelites free from Egypt. It's likely that Jesus sung this with His disciples the day before He was crucified (Mark 14:26). What do you think these words would have meant to Jesus as He got ready to die?

All through time, God has shown Himself to be the one who brings hope into impossible situations.

He breathed life into some dust and created human beings! (Genesis 2)

He promised an elderly couple, who weren't able to have kids, that they would have more descendants than would be possible to count! (Abraham and Sarah – Genesis 12)

He loved a bunch of refugee slaves and made them into a great nation!

In His teaching He is always looking out for those who are poor, hurting, sick and those without parents.

Because of these things it shouldn't surprise us that God has power over death. He raised Jesus from the dead. And if God can overcome death, He can overcome anything!

THINK God can do the impossible. What situations that seem impossible could you raise up to Him in prayer today?

PSALM

TO THE RESCUE

READ: Psalm 126:1–6

KEY VERSE: 'Restore our fortunes, Lord' (v4)

Do you sometimes see things around you that make it seem like your beliefs about God aren't true? The people of Israel believed that God was going to fix things for the whole world and that Israel, particularly Jerusalem, would be the place He would it. But, even though they believed this, what they actually saw was Israel invaded by a massive army, torn to bits and Jerusalem smashed to ruin! Either they could give up and forget about God or they could carry on believing. What would you do?

These people didn't base their lives on what they saw but by what they *believed*. They had faith. They were thrilled because God had brought them back to Zion (another name for Jerusalem) years after terrible invasion. But they had returned to a pile of rubble! That is why they asked God to 'restore' their 'fortunes'. Even though everything was a mess, they knew that God would do something great, that He was still at work to restore Israel and the world!

God is at work right here, right now, in the world and in His people.

PRAY Lord, I've seen how You restore people and places. Please help me to believe that You are doing the same in my life and the world around me. Amen.

PSALM

I NEED A MIRACLE

READ: 1 Samuel 1:1–11

> **KEY VERSE:** 'In her deep anguish Hannah prayed to the LORD, weeping bitterly.' (v10)

Say hello to Samuel. This guy was someone who heard God speak all the time, and maybe the coolest thing about him is that he got started *young*. Sam being born was a bit of miracle – his mum, Hannah, couldn't have children and was heartbroken about it.

In those days, not being able to get pregnant was something really embarrassing that people looked down on. But the worst thing about it? Hannah's husband's other wife, Peninnah, had no problem having children – and loved rubbing it in Hannah's face with rude comments. Why? We know that Hannah's husband loved her – and for his favourite wife to be the childless one was pretty special. Peninnah was jealous.

So what did Hannah do? Hannah unloaded how she was feeling onto God. She broke down in front of Him and told Him what it was that she really, *really* wanted. God listened to her. He knew Hannah wasn't a failure, even if that's what she felt like. And He was about to show her just how important she really was.

THINK **What do you do when someone makes you feel a bit rubbish? Take a leaf out of Hannah's book (or technically Samuel's book!) and talk to God – you won't regret it!**

SAMUEL

OH, BOY

READ: 1 Samuel 1:12–20

KEY VERSE: 'Hannah became pregnant and gave birth to a son. She named him Samuel' (v20)

What do you look like when you talk to God? When Eli, the high priest, saw Hannah crying by the tabernacle entrance, he assumed she'd had too much to drink and got emotional. But Hannah had been having a chat with God about how miserable she felt and what was upsetting her. Eli couldn't hear her words but he could see the state she was in.

He didn't interrogate her to get the latest gossip to pass on. Instead he said, 'Go in peace', and then prayed that God would help her with whatever she was upset about. What a difference prayer makes! Hannah's puffy-eyed look was replaced with a smile. Her appetite came back and she worshipped God.

Hannah told God that if He gave her and her husband (Elkanah) a son, she would dedicate her son to Him. A while later, she found out she was pregnant! She had a boy and called him, 'God has heard me' – or 'Sam' for short. It was her way of giving God credit for answering her prayer, and the start of Samuel's life of being dedicated to God.

PRAY Dear Lord, I'm so glad that I can talk to You about everything and anything. Thank You for taking me seriously and never ignoring me. Amen.

DEDICATION

READ: 1 Samuel 1:21–28

KEY VERSE: 'So now I give him to the LORD. For his whole life he shall be given over to the LORD.' (v28)

Have you ever been to a dedication? It's basically a service where the parents make a promise to God to raise their children His way – but Samuel's dedication was a bit different!

God had given Hannah her bouncing baby boy, but would she now forget God? Hannah had promised Him that she would give the boy back to Him. That meant sending young Sam to train as a priest at the tabernacle. It must have been tough to give Sam to Eli the priest to look after, but Hannah kept her promise. Sam, probably only just five, settled into his new home.

Just as Hannah had promised, Sam *never* had a haircut. Did this make him turn into a long-haired rebel? No. It was a sign that he was different to everyone else and that he served God. And he lived up to the hairstyle! From day one, Eli taught Sam how to worship the Lord.

THINK Can you think of anything God gives us that He wants us to give back to Him? How about our time and talents – do we use them for ourselves, or does God get a say?

SAMUEL

NEVER GIVE UP

READ: 1 Samuel 2:1–11

> **KEY VERSE:** 'There is no one holy like the LORD; there is no one besides you; there is no Rock like our God.' (v2)

Why did Hannah put God first and hand her only son over to train as a priest? You don't return gifts you've been asking for, do you? Hannah's prayer explains it.

Before Hannah became a mum, she had been absolutely miserable. She'd been made to believe she was a failure and had probably wondered if God actually cared about her. But even at her lowest point, she had still trusted God with her future.

Hannah's prayer in today's reading is a great big 'Thank You' to God. Hannah knew what God was like, and she felt secure with Him. She understood that God was her rock, He was in charge and He knew everything. God guarded her and looked after her, and she knew He would look after Sam too. It was the thought of this that made it easier to let Sam go.

Talking through difficult situations with God makes a big difference. A few years after blubbering out a prayer, Hannah was praising God. He never gives up on us, so don't ever give up on Him.

PRAY Father God, thank You for never giving up on me. Help me to keep talking to You however I'm feeling. Amen.

ALTAR BOYS

READ: 1 Samuel 2:12–26

KEY VERSE: 'And the boy Samuel continued to grow in stature and in favour with the LORD and with people.' (v26)

Preacher's Kid Syndrome is the term used for when a preacher's kid goes off the rails. And today's reading shows us two serious cases of this! Sam was training to be a priest, but sadly some right crooks were doing the same thing. And the worst of the lot were Eli's sons!

Hophini and Phinehas took full advantage of being the high priest's sons. Their greediness meant they stole the meat from the sacrifices given to God, threatening people who tried to stop them. Not only that, they were also messing around with the local girls. When Eli gave them a proper telling-off, it went in one ear and out the other. Because of this, God kept his distance and rarely spoke to His people.

Young Sam didn't get involved in any of Eli's sons' stupidity. He listened to Eli and worshipped God. He knew the tabernacle was a worship centre – where people met with God – not a place to get girls' numbers and steal meat for a barbecue. Samuel lived to please God and do his best for others.

THINK When people are causing trouble do you tend to follow the crowd and join in, or do you stand out and not get involved?

SAMUEL

DIALLING SAM

READ: 1 Samuel 3:1–10

KEY VERSE: 'Then Samuel said, "Speak, for your servant is listening."' (v10)

God had a message for His people, but He wanted a new spokesperson – our very own Sam! As Eli lost his eyesight, young Sam had become his guide. God, however, had greater plans for the young lad – to become a guide to the nation.

Samuel knew about God, knew His laws by heart, worshipped Him, but had never heard His voice. So when he heard someone calling him, he thought it was Eli. He woke up Eli three times in the night before Eli clocked on to the fact that God was the one calling Sam.

God is quite often trying to get our attention but a lot of the time we don't realise it's Him, or we even ignore Him. Perhaps we don't want to go along with God's plans so it's easier to pretend He's not saying anything.

Samuel was ready to listen to God, no matter what He was about to hear. Let's try and do that too. Reading the Bible is one way of telling God we're ready to listen, just like Sam was.

PRAY Lord God, I want to hear Your voice. Help me to listen out for You, pay attention to what You say and be ready to respond. Amen.

MESSAGE: SAM

READ: 1 Samuel 3:11–21

KEY VERSE: 'The LORD was with Samuel as he grew up, and he let none of Samuel's words fall to the ground.' (v19)

Being the bearer of bad news is never easy, and often it's the messenger who gets the bad reaction. God's message was a hard one to hear. There was bad news for Eli. You can't ignore God and get away with it. Samuel learnt that Eli's wicked sons were going to be history – and Eli, who had failed to sort them out, would lose his job as high priest.

Sam's first reaction was to keep the message quiet. We all tend to keep quiet about how God disagrees with things people are doing. It's never an easy topic to talk about. Eli told Samuel that it is a serious matter not to share a message from God. So Sam gave him God's message.

Eli didn't argue or get angry. He accepted that God knew best.

When God continued to speak to Sam, the nation was buzzing and they named him as a prophet. Overnight Samuel became God's voice to the nation. Sam spoke God's words with God's help. God made people sit up and listen to young Sam.

THINK God still speaks to young people and He wants young people to speak for Him. Are you letting God speak to others through you?

SAMUEL

STOP THE ROT

READ: 1 Samuel 7:2–9

KEY VERSE: 'He cried out to the LORD on Israel's behalf, and the LORD answered him.' (v9)

Watching your friends do something that is bad for them, having warned them against it, is really hard. Samuel grew another 10 years' worth of hair before the Israelites realised how far from God they had got and started turning back to Him.

They had been defeated by the overgrown hulks from Philistia and the ark of God was captured. It was then that the Israelites realised how foolish they had been to stop trusting God.

What was Sam doing during this low point in the nation's history? Praying that God's people would learn their lesson and turn back to Him. When they finally started to listen, here's what he told them to do:

1. Be willing to follow God in all your life (v3).

2. Be determined to let God stop the rot of sin.

The Israelites obeyed, trashed their false idols and quit their wild drunken raves.

Sam brought them together to own up to their guilt and make a sacrifice of a lamb in order to be forgiven. Now, it is Jesus who has been our sacrifice for forgiveness!

PRAY

Lord Jesus, thank You that You always want to forgive me, even if I've wandered away from You for a while. Amen.

GATE-CRASHED

READ: 1 Samuel 7:10–17

KEY VERSE: 'Thus far the Lord has helped us.' (v12)

Have you ever noticed that when you get closer to God, difficulties often start popping up? That's because Satan does his best to put us off putting God first in our lives.

The long-haired prophet was now recognised as the nation's leader. But as he prayed, the Philistine hulks arrived to gate-crash the party. How did Sam cope with the Philistine bully boys arriving on the scene just as he was offering a burnt sacrifice to God? Did he stick the offering in the microwave and run? No. Sam talked with God about the problem.

Samuel knew that God had the power to save them and make them victorious. Sure enough, God thundered in and the Philistines were off like lightning. With God's help, the Israelites had no trouble fighting them off.

Afterwards, Sam set up a statue to remember God's incredible and gracious deliverance of them. He didn't make out life would be easy from then on – there would be other struggles and difficulties, but God had helped them in the past and would help them again.

THINK How much has God helped you in your life? Why not talk to a friend about some times when God has helped you? Samuel thought it was a great idea to remember these, so give it a go!

SAMUEL

KING ME

READ: 1 Samuel 8:1–9

> **KEY VERSE:** 'And the LORD told him: "... it is not you they have rejected, but they have rejected me as their king."' (v7)

Time had been ticking away and Sam's long hair had started to turn grey in colour. In his old age, Sam was still an honest guy, but his sons were crooked judges. Everyone knew that Sam's lads were being given money to find the innocent guilty and the guilty innocent. There was no way they wanted those crooks leading the nation.

The problem got even worse. All the other nations had tough-talking kings leading them. The Israelites had a king – God – but He was invisible, and Sam apparently didn't look hard enough.

The Israelites wanted a king they could see. The fact that God had fought for them, protected them and helped them, suddenly counted for nothing.

Sam was not impressed when they told him. But rather than lose his cool, he talked it through with God. He told Sam not to take their comments personally; they were rejecting Him, not Sam. God wasn't going to force them to make Him king – that's not His style. He would let them learn the hard way that it's best to have God in charge.

PRAY Lord God, You are my King – even though I cannot see you, I choose to believe and trust in You. Amen.

THE ROYAL FAIL

READ: 1 Samuel 8:10–22

> **KEY VERSE:** 'But the people refused to listen to Samuel. "No!" they said. "We want a king over us."' (v19)

You'd think it was a no-brainer: God in charge, or a man. Surely there was no contest. But, shocker: human beings messed up again. To be fair to Sam, he really did warn them. They had two options:

With God as king, they would know they would be seen as part of His family. He would encourage them use their talents out of a genuine love and care for them. He would want the best for them. And He wants freedom for them.

With a human as king, they could risk having someone who didn't care about them. He might force people to do all sorts of jobs they hated and maybe couldn't even do. He could decide to take all their money if He wanted to. He might even take away their freedom.

Sam was disappointed (and probably gobsmacked) when the Israelites voted for a human king, but he took his feelings to God. The Israelites needed to learn their lesson: God in second place is always second best. Why? Because He genuinely loves and cares for us.

PRAY
Lord, I don't always find it easy to follow You in every area of my life. Help me to be more open to You. Amen.

SAMUEL

TALL SAUL

READ: 1 Samuel 9:1–14

KEY VERSE: 'Look, in this town there is a man of God… Perhaps he will tell us what way to take.' (v6)

Just a couple of weeks into this One Year, we read about King David and the dodgy king in charge before him (Saul). Well, here's how Saul got the job! The Israelites had voted to be ruled by a king, and it was down to Sam to find him. How would he do that? By asking God, of course!

Saul was head and shoulders above everyone else – literally. He was a skyscraper. But as he came from a downtown tribe, the young donkey keeper wasn't an obvious choice for the throne.

All Saul was trying to do was find some runaway donkeys, but he was out of ideas. His servant helpfully suggested that Sam, the respected man of God, was in the area and perhaps he could ask God where the donkeys were. Brilliant. Saul turned his attention to tracking Sam down, and he was successful – he bumped into the man himself on the way to lead a worship service.

What should we do when we don't know what to do? No matter how big or small the decision, it's wise to ask for God's help. We can trust Him.

THINK Do you only talk to God about the big stuff? Try including Him in some of the smaller things in your life, too. If it matters to us, it matters to Him.

THIS IS THE MAN

READ: 1 Samuel 9:15–27

> **KEY VERSE:** 'When Samuel caught sight of Saul, the LORD said to him, "This is the man I spoke to you about; he will govern my people."' (v17)

Sam was on his way to lead a service when a tall stranger appeared and started quizzing him about donkeys on the run. But Sam wasn't weirded out – he'd been expecting Saul.

The day before, God had told Sam that He would sending along a stranger from the tribe off Benjamin – for Sam to anoint as king! Sam was so full of faith that he'd even done his food shopping that day to prepare – so when Saul arrived on the scene, all God had to do was give him the green light.

Before Saul knew it, his donkey disaster had been sorted, and he was the guest of honour at a banquet at Sam's house. Sam didn't look at Saul's qualifications, his reputation or his image. God had chosen Saul to be the first king of Israel and that was good enough for Sam.

Sometimes we have to make decisions about people – who we're friends with and how much time we spend with them. It's good to draw from God's advice for these decisions.

THINK Do you trust God to show you the right people to have in your life? He knows everything and He knows best!

SAMUEL

A KING-SIZED HEART

READ: 1 Samuel 10:1–16

KEY VERSE: 'The Spirit of the LORD will come powerfully upon you… and you will be changed into a different person.' (v6)

Saul was king-size in height, but what about his character? Sam knew that God would give Saul a king-sized heart! Sam had anointed Saul as the future king of Israel, but Saul wasn't as confident as he looked. He needed some encouragement, and God gave him some.

First he was met by some men who told him that the donkeys had definitely been found. Just in case the thought of it was keeping Saul up at night, God got rid of any doubts. Then Saul was met by two men who offered him bread. God had *all* his needs covered. Finally Saul met up with a group of prophets praising God. He didn't keep his distance but did as Sam had asked and joined in. To everyone's surprise, he started speaking words from God. The Holy Spirit had powerfully met with him! Saul was a changed man, and this was big news. He was not alone. God was with him.

God is with us and is happy to encourage us so that we can be confident too!

PRAY Lord God, please work in my life to encourage me and get me ready for the awesome plans I know You have for me. Amen.

KING HIDE'N'SEEK

READ: 1 Samuel 10:17–26

KEY VERSE: 'And the LORD said, "Yes, he has hidden himself among the supplies."' (v22)

The big day was fast-approaching. Saul was about to be made king. But Sam had one small problem: Saul hadn't shown up. Awkward. Although God's Spirit was upon him, Saul let his fears run away with him, and *he* ran away with them.

By now Sam had lots of experience in how to deal with a crisis: pray. God wasn't going to be stood up, and so He told Sam where Saul was hiding. But notice that Sam didn't think any less of Saul. He introduced Saul as 'the man God had chosen' (v24) – not 'the man that ran away' Sam knew that God doesn't give up on us – even when we let Him down. And God changed the hearts of the bravest men in the country so that they respected their new king.

Have you ever avoided something you had to do because you were afraid? Fear can get in the way of what God wants to do in our lives. But He knows why we are afraid and wants to replace this fear with strength.

THINK **When you've got something important to do, do you feel afraid? God doesn't want us to run away – He can help. Talk to Him about your fears.**

SAMUEL

A FAREWELL SPEECH

READ: 1 Samuel 12:1–5

> **KEY VERSE:** '"You have not cheated or oppressed us," they replied. "You have not taken anything from anyone's hand."' (v4)

Sam willingly stepped down as leader to let King Saul take charge. It was time for Sam to give one last speech – a recap of his career.

Kings, rulers and leaders everywhere had one thing in common: a million opportunities to do whatever they wanted. Holding the top spot meant they could have all the freebies they wanted, take all the money they wanted, and give the good jobs to whoever they wanted. But Samuel was different. He was honest! All he cared about was pleasing God. There were no dodgy deals or shady secrets. Sam was the real deal.

God *is* truth. He cannot lie or cheat. He's never out to trick us. And God helps us to follow His example.

It's tempting to want to get away with anything we can – conning teachers with some rather creative excuses, lying to parents about where you're going, making up lies to cover your tracks. It takes real guts to be open and honest. God can give us those guts.

PRAY
Lord Jesus, give me the guts to only speak the truth. Help me to follow Samuel's example of an honest life – I know that's the best way to live. Amen.

REIGNING AND RAINING

READ: 1 Samuel 12:6–7,16–25

> **KEY VERSE:** 'far be it from me that I should sin against the LORD by failing to pray for you' (v23)

Sam had given his goodbye speech, but it wasn't long before he was needed again. The Israelites had insisted on having a king, and God had given them what they demanded. But Sam knew this was a huge mistake. Their hopes were in shaky Saul who nearly hadn't even made it to his ceremony to become king!

No one could have been prepared for what happened next: God showed that He still reigned in power by sending rain – lots of it! It flattened their harvest and their egos with it. They realised what a mistake they had made by kicking God off the top spot in their lives.

Sam didn't say, 'I told you so', but encouraged the Israelites to put God first – even though they had a king to serve as well. God wouldn't give up on them just because they'd given up on Him. And neither would Sam. Even though they had disappointed him, Sam promised to keep praying for the people.

THINK Sam knew it was important to pray for people who have hurt us. How do you feel about people who have put you down? Often the last thing we want to do is pray for them, but just try it.

SAMUEL

UNDER PRESSURE

READ: 1 Samuel 13:5–15

KEY VERSE: '"You have done a foolish thing," Samuel said.' (v13)

The Israelites wanted a king to lead them into battle and now they had one – but it wasn't plain sailing. The Philistines had 30,000 chariots and all the latest weapons. What did the Israelites have? One sword and spear between 600 of them. Fantastic. So what did they do? Pray for God to deliver them? Nope. They hid in caves and bushes, going out of their tiny minds with fear.

Sam was on his way to make an offering and ask God for help, but was delayed. Saul got impatient. He was panicking, his troops had run away, so he did things his way. He played priest and made their offerings himself – something totally against God rules.

Sam arrived the scene and asked the question nobody likes to hear: 'What have you done?' (v11). No matter how hard the situation, you don't find the right way by doing wrong. When you mess around with God, you don't win. God had lined up the next king already: a king who would do things His way.

PRAY Lord Jesus, help me not to panic under pressure and mess up. Help me to be calm and remember that You know best, and always go with your way of doing things. Amen.

LOOKING SHEEPISH

READ: 1 Samuel 15:1–19

KEY VERSE: 'I regret that I have made Saul king, because he has turned away from me and has not carried out my instructions.' (v11)

It's a horrible feeling working hard at something, only for someone else to get the credit! Thanks to God, Saul had a surprise win against the Amalekites. So what did he do? He set up a shrine so that people would give credit to him. He stole the glory from God and he absolutely loved it.

Saul hadn't even obeyed all of God's battle commands. God had said not to take the enemy's sheep and cattle. But the king had come up with what he thought was a better idea – take the sheep and cattle but only use them as sacrifices to God.

God spoke to Samuel about how disappointed in Saul he was. And Sam wept. The king was out of order for disobeying God. And it was Sam's job to tell him. Saul came up with his reasons for ignoring God and doing his own thing. He tried to make out he was putting God first. But he was lying, and Sam wasn't impressed. Sam simply asked, 'Why?'

THINK Do you ever think you know better than God? When God tells us to do something, He doesn't need us to come up with our own version of the plan!

SAMUEL

EXCUSES, EXCUSES

READ: 1 Samuel 15:20–35

KEY VERSE: 'I was afraid of the men and so I gave in to them.' (v24)

Saul kept coming out with excuses for taking the sheep and cattle, but Sam wasn't buying it for one minute. Saul tried to make it sound like he'd actually done something good for God, but he shouldn't have tried to reword God's instructions. It's never a good idea to hold on to things God has told you to ditch.

Suddenly Saul changed his story and came up with a new excuse: it wasn't his fault. He had been put under pressure by the troops and was too scared to say 'no' when they wanted to take the sheep and cattle for themselves. He didn't want to seem like a killjoy.

Sam didn't humiliate Saul in public, but he privately warned him that he was no longer fit to be king.

Saul caved into pressure from people because he wanted to be popular so badly. So he turned his back on God just to look good. Is that something you've ever done? It can feel awkward to have to stand up for good and for God, but in the long-run it's always worth it!

PRAY Heavenly Father, help me to value what You think above what any of my friends think. I know that pleasing You is more important than being popular. Amen.

EAT, SHEEP, HARP, REPEAT

READ: 1 Samuel 16:1–13

KEY VERSE: 'People look at the outward appearance, but the LORD looks at the heart.' (v7)

It was time for Sam to find the future king of Israel, and he learnt the important lesson of not to judge a book by its cover.

The favourite candidate: Eliab. He had everything going for him – good looks, macho muscles – you name it, Eliab had it. And as Jesse's oldest son, he was first in line to inherit his father's property. On paper, this was the guy. Thankfully, Sam wisely brought God on the judging panel and learnt that all was not as it seemed. Eliab's looks masked the fact that his heart was not right with God.

The last choice: David. Yes, he was healthy and handsome, but literally no one rated his chances. People didn't care that he could look after a flock of sheep – all they saw was a sheep-spotter who liked to chill out with his harp.

Who did God choose? David. Why? Because he loved Him and had a strong faith. That's what made him stand out. After listening to God, Sam anointed David as king.

THINK What do you spend more time on – looking after your appearance or looking after your heart? David was the strongest king of all and he looked after his heart by hanging out with God in prayer.

SAMUEL

WEAPON OF CHOICE

READ: 1 Samuel 19:18–23

KEY VERSE: 'so he sent men to capture him. But when they saw a group of prophets prophesying... the Spirit of God came on Saul's men' (v20)

When Saul heard about David being God's choice, he was fuming – and when the young giant-slayer became a national hero, he sent out an assassination squad to get him. So David ran off to find Sam. How would Sam protect David from Saul's hitmen? Did he get his prophets setting traps and rolling our barbed wire? No, he brought out the big guns – prayer and praise!

As Saul's men moved in, Sam and his prophets prayed to almighty God. The hitmen didn't know what had hit them. They came out with their arms in the air and surrendered to God. The next minute they were joining in with the prophets.

Saul then sent in two more divisions, and the same thing happened. For the final attempt, he went in himself. But one more blast of prayer from the prophets had Saul speaking to God, too! In the meantime, David snuck away to find a new hiding place.

Prayer really does work and it's a weapon you've got access to!

PRAY Dear God, help me to remember that prayer is the most powerful weapon on earth. Thank You that I can talk to You any time. Amen.

A LIFELONG HABIT

READ: 1 Samuel 25:1; Hebrews 11:32–34

KEY VERSE: 'Now Samuel died, and all Israel assembled and mourned for him' (1 Sam. 25:1)

Eventually the time came when Samuel prayed his last prayer on earth. The whole nation gathered to mourn the man they had grown to love and respect. Sam is listed in Hebrews as one of the great men of faith. What a great reputation! Through faith, Samuel achieved so much. What was his secret?

Sam started talking with God as a child, and prayer became his lifelong habit. Difficult questions? Pray. Problems? Pray. Battles? Pray. Rejection? Pray. Sam prayed and prayed and prayed. It was his answer to every situation life threw at him. He didn't think he knew best, he wanted God's opinion. And Sam's prayer list had everything and everyone (good and not so good!) on it.

Sam stuck by God's side, respecting His decisions and giving Him all the praise and glory. Throughout his whole life, Samuel's motto was: 'Speak, Lord, I'm listening.'

Want to be a world-changer? Start with prayer. Like Sam did, you can bring every situation to God. Don't hold back, make use of the awesome privilege of talking to God!

THINK Do you have a prayer list? If not, write down some people and things to start praying for. Keep this somewhere you'll see it and get praying!

SAMUEL

WHAT A BOOK!

READ: Psalm 119:145–152

KEY VERSE: 'Yet you are near, LORD, and all your commands are true.' (v151)

Sam was a guy that was definitely close to God, and one of the main ways that we can get closer to God is by reading the Bible. Do you ever feel guilty about not reading it? Well, this psalm has 176 verses about how psalmist loves reading the Bible! 'How can I ever be like that?' you may ask...

Well, this psalm was actually written by someone who had messed up – phew, we're not alone! He's 'strayed' from God and wants to find his way back.

When he talks about how much he loves God's Word, what he's saying is that he loves God's character. When he says that he wants to read God's Word, it really means he wants to be near Him.

The Jews believed that when they read their Scriptures, that God was there with them. Reading the Bible brings us close to God and invites Him to speak to us. The Bible helps us to get to know Jesus. Because of that, the Bible is really, really important!

PRAY
Lord, thank You for Your Word! Please help me to understand it better so I can feel closer to You. Amen.

I CAN SEE!

READ: Psalm 73:1–3,22–28

KEY VERSE: 'Yet I am always with you' (v23)

If there's one word to describe how today's psalm writer felt, it would be, 'GRRRRRRR!' He was angry and bitter. He was so mad that he nearly walked out on God!

He had almost made a mistake out of anger, but as he sang he realised that God was helping him all along. God was the one who kept him from making the big mistake! Although he had been fed up with God, God had been right there with him.

God has an amazing plan for our lives but the devil wants to spoil that. As Christians we can get attacked by invisible forces that will try to make us see things the wrong way.

The singer of this psalm got close to God and then saw everything clearly. God is with us no matter how bad we feel, and even if we forget it, He is still with us. Even when we ignore God, He still looks after us. And when we ditch our pride and pray to Him, He opens our eyes to see things how He does – and that can make all the difference!

THINK In what ways do you think God has looked after you behind the scenes? Give Him some credit for it!

PSALM

THREE FOR THE PRICE OF ONE

READ: Genesis 1:1–5

KEY VERSE: 'and the Spirit of God was hovering over the waters' (v2)

There is one God but He is three persons – each one unique. God the Father, God the Son (Jesus) and God the Holy Spirit. We learn a lot about God as our heavenly Father, and we appreciate Jesus as God in human form. But what about God the Holy Spirit? What do we know about Him?

Well, the Holy Spirit didn't just arrive on the scene at Pentecost. He is God, and has always existed. At the beginning of time, God the Holy Spirit was involved in planning out our universe. The Spirit was hovering over the waters, ready for action! Before He started work, there was nothing except darkness. After He started work, there was light, power and purpose.

At just the right time, God got the wheels moving on a plan for creation and humanity that is still going on. We may not totally understand the 'how' of creation but we know 'who' made it possible – 'God created' (v1). The Holy Spirit is never dull or boring. He is amazingly creative, and out-of-this-world powerful!

PRAY Father in heaven, I want to let Your Holy Spirit work powerfully to carry on Your incredible, creative work in my life. Amen.

POWER UP!

DIVINE INSPIRATION

READ: Exodus 31:1–11

KEY VERSE: 'I have filled him with the Spirit of God, giving him great wisdom, ability, and expertise in all kinds of crafts.' (v3, NLT)

When we look at the incredible diversity in creation we realise that God was not a dull, unimaginative creator. For example, it is estimated that there are over a million different species of worm alone. God could have made one worm and thought, 'That'll do' but oh no, God wanted to make a million different types!

The Holy Spirit doesn't only inspire and help preachers and teachers, He inspires the imagination of creative people such a Bezalel and Oholiab who were more the artistic sort. The work on the tabernacle was to be of the highest standard – God never accepts second best. So, He sent His Holy Spirit to be with the craftsmen to give them the creative ideas and skills needed to achieve excellence. Just look at the range of artistic skills that the Holy Spirit got involved in: design, metalwork, wood carving, jewellery, sewing... the list goes on! It was the craft show to end all craft shows.

THINK God has unlimited ideas and He wants you to be creative too. Whether you are good at art, sport, music, writing or something else, think how you could use your skills to serve God.

GODLY INFLUENCER

READ: Numbers 11:16–25

KEY VERSE: 'I will take some of the power of the Spirit that is on you and put it on them' (v17)

God had sent His Holy Spirit to help Moses be a great leader. The Holy Spirit made Moses bold, wise and fair. People respected his leadership and took all their problems to him.

Realising that he was a few steps away from turning into an over-worked agony aunt, Moses asked God for help. God responded by choosing 70 men to share the work. And to make sure that they would do a good enough job, God gave them His Holy Spirit. The Holy Spirit rested on Moses and the 70 leaders, giving them the management skills and power that they needed.

When God tells a Christian to do something, He never leaves them to do it on their own. The Holy Spirit lives in Christians to help them succeed in carrying out God's plans. God has a plan for each one of us. But He doesn't dump the plan on us and run. He gives us what we need, and is there every step of the way.

PRAY Lord, I thank You for giving me Your Holy Spirit. Help me to rely on You to show me the best way to deal with the people and situations in my life. Amen.

WHO LET THE DONKEYS OUT?

READ: 1 Samuel 10:1–8

KEY VERSE: 'The Spirit of the LORD will come powerfully upon you' (v6)

We heard about Saul not long ago. Here we see him before we went off and did his own thing without God. To recap, this is how the story started...

Israel wanted a king. Meanwhile, Saul, a country chap from one of the least important families in the land, was asking Samuel for his help locating some runaway donkeys. Saul had no idea that God had told Samuel to anoint him as king. So he was amazed when Samuel got the oil out to put on his head and told him that God wanted him to rule over His people. Saul was only looking for his donkeys, not looking to become king!

Samuel told him not to worry about the donkeys – they were fine. God even gave Saul some reassurance that He was with him, ending with Saul being filled with the Holy Spirit. All of this happened so that Saul could be absolutely sure that this was God's work.

If He was to become king, Saul needed to know God powerfully in His life. The Holy Spirit was God living inside of Saul, and that was a game-changer.

THINK Do you need God to reassure you that He is with you today? Speak to Him and tell Him how you're feeling.

POWER UP!

HEART TRANSPLANT

READ: 1 Samuel 10:9–11

KEY VERSE: 'God changed Saul's heart' (v9)

Saul's life was turned upside down and inside out by God's Holy Spirit. One minute he was a loser, running around after lost donkeys; the next, he was a winner, the first king of Israel, speaking God's words like a prophet.

Saul was tall, dark and handsome (1 Sam. 9:2). He would look great in all the royal pictures. But this was not the main thing the nation wanted – they wanted a leader to unite them and defeat their enemies. God needed to change Saul from the inside out to make him into the person He wanted him to be. Where did God start? He gave Saul a new heart, then He sent the Holy Spirit to power up his life. The change was sensational. Saul felt and acted like a new person.

God still changes lives in the same way today. First He has to deal with our hearts. That's why we need to ask God to forgive us and make us holy. Jesus died on the cross so that God could do just that for us. Not only does God clean out our lives, but He sends His Spirit to give us the power to live for Him.

PRAY

Father God, maker of everything, please help me to welcome the Holy Spirit to come and power up my life. Amen.

WARNING SIGNS

READ: Nehemiah 9:6,21–31

KEY VERSE: 'By your Spirit you warned them through your prophets.' (v30)

How often do you get told off for doing something wrong? Those who do the telling off are often actually helping us by making us realise our mistake, and that's what the Holy Spirit is like.

Today's reading is part of Ezra's prayer in which he gives a ten-minute history of the Jews. It's a sad cycle of events. First, God rescues the Jews from Egypt and cares for them. But the Jews turn away from God. So, God warns them He will punish them if they do not turn back to Him. He gives them time to do this. However, when the Jews continue to disobey, He takes away their freedom. The Jews then cry out to God to forgive and save them. God, being a loving God, rescues the Jews and cares for them... and so on.

The Holy Spirit sometimes shows His love for us by warning us when we are heading into dangerous territory. He might do that through something we read in the Bible, our conscience, or through other people. God patiently gives us time to change our ways because He only ever wants what's best for us.

THINK Has God been trying to get your attention about something you've been doing recently? Take time to sort it out with Him.

GOD'S SPIRIT BRINGS LIFE

READ: Psalm 104:1–4,27–30

KEY VERSE: 'When you send your Spirit, they are created' (v30)

Have you seen any of the episodes from the *Blue Plane* or *Planet Earth* series? These really popular documentaries captured amazing footage of nature and animals, often never seen before, from around the world. Using the best cameras, they show the spectacular variety of living creatures on our planet. The sea, air and land are filled with life – and it's amazing to see this.

Of course these programmes show how important it is that we all take care of our planet, but who's making sure that creation is all being held together still? David, the writer of this psalm, knew the answer. It is God the Holy Spirit who continues the cycle of life, generation after generation. God's Spirit brings colour, variety, laughter, enjoyment and purpose to creation.

David knew that every creature looks to God to give them the food that they need (v27). Similarly, we can look to our Father to provide for us.

THINK Are you a creative person? Take a look at the world around you – what do you think is the best part of God's creation?

HERE, THERE AND EVERYWHERE

READ: Psalm 139:1–12

KEY VERSE: 'Where can I go from your Spirit?' (v7)

The Holy Spirit knows all about us. He even knows what we are going to say before we say it. Can we do a runner and get away from Him if we want? This Hebrew worship song explains that we can't get away from God's Spirit. There's nowhere we can go to avoid Him. But the writer didn't see that as a problem, instead he'd found a reason to party!

Why should we want to avoid someone who only wants the best for us – someone who cares, guides, protects and helps us? This song is raving about the fact that God the Holy Spirit is here, there and everywhere. Whatever the situation, God is around to support us through it. Isn't that awesome?

The writer was bowled over at the thought of God's Spirit going ahead of him to guide and also following behind to protect. Christians have the excitement of knowing the Holy Spirit lives within them, giving all the support and strength they need. Who wouldn't want that extra help in their lives? Let's not shy away from the Holy Spirit but welcome His guiding presence.

PRAY Father, You know everything about me and You still accept me! Help me to remember that and to be completely open with You. Amen.

POWER UP!

SPIRIT-LED PATHWAYS

READ: Psalm 143:1–10

KEY VERSE: 'may your good Spirit lead me on level ground' (v10)

David was trapped. His enemies were hunting him down. He was surrounded. He felt weak and scared as he hid in a dark cave. A meeting of the escape team was called.

David knew he could only move under the cover of darkness and along dangerous mountain trails full of bumps, ditches and drops. So he invited the Holy Spirit onto the escape team. He wanted the Holy Spirit to show him the next move he should make; to guide him along safe routes. And with the Holy Spirit's help, David was able to plan ahead knowing that God would be with him every step of the way. The great escape was a success. His enemies never caught up with him.

Sometimes we too don't know what to do next. Thankfully, we have God's Holy Spirit to lead us. We can talk with God about all our plans and ask for His advice, and then wait for the go-ahead from Him. Then, we can be sure that the Holy Spirit is moving in front of us, removing any obstacles from the path ahead.

THINK
What are your future plans? It's always best to keep God in our planning, so why not talk to Him about these plans?

PSALM

CARING HOLY SPIRIT

READ: Isaiah 61:1–3

KEY VERSE: 'The Spirit of the Sovereign LORD is on me' (v1)

One of the jobs of the Holy Spirit is to teach us what God wants us to know, and show us what God wants us to do. The Holy Spirit gave Isaiah some exciting challenges. The prophet knew exactly what God wanted from him. Isaiah had been given a pretty long job description, but he was eager and felt honoured to have been selected by God for the task. God knew that there was a lot of sadness and he wanted Isaiah, His man on the ground, to 'comfort all who mourn' (v2).

Years later in His hometown of Nazareth, Jesus stood up in the synagogue and read the same words the Holy Spirit had given Isaiah (Luke 4:18–19). Jesus knew that God had sent Him to do all these things too. Look through the list in the reading again. Can you think of examples when Jesus preached good news to the poor, comforted those with broken hearts etc?

The Holy Spirit can show you what God wants *you* to do – that's really exciting!

PRAY Holy Spirit, I want to be like Isaiah and Jesus who knew that they should care for others. Help me to know exactly how You want me to do this. Amen.

HAS THE HOLY SPIRIT GOT YOUR ATTENTION?

READ: Ezekiel 1:1,26–2:2

KEY VERSE: 'the Spirit came into me and raised me to my feet, and I heard him speaking to me' (2:2)

We have discovered that the Holy Spirit is incredibly creative. He has many ways to grab our attention and communicate with us. Just look what happened to Ezekiel...

Each person's experience of being filled with God's Spirit is different. Ezekiel was shown a vision of God that sent him flat on his face, and then was whooshed to his feet to hear the Holy Spirit. It was an absolutely bonkers (in a good way!) story. God also works in far less dramatic ways; it could be a gentle nudge or feeling like we should say something to someone. While we may not have visions like Ezekiel, his experience helps us understand the Holy Spirit more.

The Holy Spirit reveals God to us. He helps us understand what the Father is like. And He transforms us. Like a tornado swirling around us to lift us up, He can change the way we think, feel and act to make us more like Jesus.

THINK The Holy Spirit speaks to us, showing us how to live. Are you open to hearing from Him? What might He be giving you a nudge about?

OUT WITH THE OLD, IN WITH THE NEW

READ: Ezekiel 36:24–28

KEY VERSE: 'I will give you a new heart and put a new spirit in you' (v26)

Some people spend a long time thinking about what they look like, what trainers they've got, how their hair is styled, and what people think of their whole look. There's nothing wrong with making an effort to look good, but it is good to be aware that what really matters is what our heart looks like.

God is more concerned with our hearts than appearance. And it's actually sometimes our hearts that need a revamp. This is where the Holy Spirit comes in!

He can replace our cold hearts with hearts that have love and joy in them. Doesn't that sound good? And we don't get any old second-hand heart either. Did you notice the number of new things the Holy Spirit wants to bring to His people? New hearts, new desires, new Spirit, new love... So often our hearts are cold and ignore God. But doing that is like ignoring a notification to update your phone – if you ignore it, you're missing out! Allow the Holy Spirit to update your life and bring new things into the mix.

PRAY Father, please help me to be willing to change. Fill me with Your Holy Spirit and give me a heart update! Amen.

POWER UP!

DRY BONES

READ: Ezekiel 37:1–10

KEY VERSE: 'I will make breath enter you, and you will come to life' (v5)

It's a spooky reading, this one. Skeletons rattling around in a valley. You've been warned!

No, it's not a movie – it's a dramatic picture of God working in people's lives. Here we have a fantastic picture of how God would gather the currently land-less people of Israel together in their own land, and give them the power to live for Him! At that time, the Israelites must have felt like dry bones – lifeless and useless. But God wanted them to know that He could bring them back to life.

This is also a dramatic picture of what God does for us today. Without God we're skeletons – lifeless. When we come to God for forgiveness, He not only puts our lives back together but He also send His Holy Spirit to give us life and power. God loves to bring life to His people. When they fall apart, He wants to bring them back to life through His Spirit, and turn them into world-changers.

THINK Do you feel like you need more of God's power and life? If so, ask God for that extra zing in your life – ask for more of the Holy Spirit.

OFFER OPEN TO ALL

READ: Joel 2:15,28–32

KEY VERSE: 'I will pour out my Spirit on all people' (v28)

We have breezed over some Old Testament examples of God's Holy Spirit empowering people to do fantastic things. But it was only a few people who experienced the Holy Spirit so powerfully. They were Holy Spirit 'limited editions'. Then God gave Joel a Holy Spirit forecast: the heavens would open and the Holy Spirit would pour down all over the world. He would flood the lives of young and old, rich and poor, male and female. Yep, everyone would be getting a holy drenching! No longer would God's Spirit be limited to one nation. Anyone, anywhere, anytime, would be able to experience God working in them.

Then, when Jesus came to earth, He forecast that the Holy Spirit would be like a stream of living water flowing through those who believed in Him. After Jesus had returned to heaven, the Holy Spirit came as promised. He flooded into the lives of the early Christians. And today the Holy Spirit is still ready to flow through anyone who trusts in Jesus as their Saviour – anywhere, anytime.

PRAY
Holy Spirit, It's amazing that You are alive in all Christians. I want to know more of You, so please flood my life today. Amen.

POWER UP!

ACCESS ALL AREAS

READ: John 14:15–24

KEY VERSE: 'the Father... will give you another advocate... the Spirit of truth' (vv16–17)

Jesus knew He was about to be captured and killed, and that afterwards He would rise from the dead and return to heaven. But what would happen to His disciples? How would they cope without Him to help them? Jesus had some comforting news.

God wasn't going to abandon the disciples. He loved them too much to do that. They would not be left alone with no one to care for them. Once Jesus had returned to heaven, God was going to send the Holy Spirit. The disciples had already experienced the Holy Spirit living *with* them – now they were going to experience the Holy Spirit living *in* them!

Jesus described the Holy Spirit as a comforter or counsellor. Not someone to say, 'There, there, never mind,' but a close friend to help, advise, lead and just be there, just as Jesus had done. The best news? When we become Christians, the Holy Spirit sets up a home in us too. He's with us all the time and is eager to be our guide through life!

THINK If the Holy Spirit is living inside you, are there any rooms of your life that you don't want Him to have access to? Why?

PERSONAL TUTOR

READ: John 14:25–27

KEY VERSE: 'the Holy Spirit... will teach you all things and will remind you of everything I have said to you' (v26)

Have you ever wondered what it was like when Matthew, Mark, Luke and John started writing the books about Jesus? Were they panicking, knowing how many people would eventually read these books, desperately trying to remember all the details? No, God sent the Holy Spirit to teach and help those who wrote the Bible. He reminded them of the things that Jesus had said and done.

The Holy Spirit is not the kind of teacher who comes in ready to tell someone off. Instead He is a one-to-one personal tutor. He works at our pace and is very patient. If we don't understand something, He won't bite our heads off but will take time to explain. He knows what is in the Bible and what it means. And if something is too hard for us to understand at the moment, He'll come back to it with us another time.

The Holy Spirit treats life as one big lesson in getting to know God. The more we ask Him to teach us, the more we learn.

PRAY Holy Spirit, please explain to me the things that I don't understand about the Bible. Thank You for being so patient. Amen.

POWER UP!

HOLY SPIRIT BACK-UP

READ: John 15:18–27

KEY VERSE: 'the Spirit of truth who goes out from the Father — he will testify about me.' (v26)

Jesus had warned His disciples that they were in for a hard time. Some people would absolutely hate them. Christians would be picked on for no reason. And they could expect to be beaten up, put in prison, teased, robbed, and possibly murdered – just because they loved Jesus. But why? Jesus explained that He is the reason people would hate them. God's enemies really, *really* hate Jesus and will do everything they can to make life hard for people on His team.

What does this look like for us today? Well, it's different. But let's be realistic, we still might be picked on and have horrible things said to us just because we are Christians.

So should we quit now before it gets too personal? No way! Jesus promised He would send the Holy Spirit to comfort those who are having a hard time for loving God. The Holy Spirit would encourage Christians, remind them of Jesus and give them strength to carry on living for Him.

THINK Do you get scared that if people know you're a Christian they'll give you a hard time? Lots of people feel like this, but the Holy Spirit can help you and be with you – speak to Him!

KEEPING US ON TRACK

READ: John 16:5–11

KEY VERSE: 'When he comes, he will prove the world to be in the wrong about sin and righteousness and judgment' (v8)

The Holy Spirit acts as God's police force on earth. He knows when we break God's laws. There is no need for an investigation, He moves straight in to arrest us. He makes us feel uneasy about what we've done.

Scared? You shouldn't be! The Holy Spirit wants to set us free from our bad habits so that we can live well. Sadly, we can ignore the Holy Spirit's attempts to help us out, keeping on doing the wrong thing. But if we go down that path, the evidence against us piles up. The good news is that as followers of Jesus, we can ask for forgiveness. Then when God the judge looks at us, He says, 'not guilty'!

The passage today talks about sin and righteousness. We are given an awesome, exciting relationship with God, and the Holy Spirit wants to keep us on the right path so that we can experience all the good stuff He's got in store for us!

PRAY

Holy Spirit, thank You for looking out for me and pointing me in the right direction. When I mess up, help me to sort things out with You. Amen.

POWER UP!

JESUS' NUMBER ONE FAN

READ: John 16:12–15

KEY VERSE: 'He will glorify me' (v14)

Many people seem to have a low opinion of Jesus. Some use His name to swear. Others laugh at what He's done for us. Most people seem to want nothing to do with Him.

But not the Holy Spirit! He has a message for the world: Jesus is God! Treat Jesus' name with respect! Jesus is the greatest! Give Jesus credit for all He has done. Look at Jesus! Come to Jesus! Praise Jesus! Give glory to Jesus!

The Holy Spirit runs Jesus' fan club. He helps us to show our love for Jesus.

He supplies us with information about Jesus and updates us on what He is doing. He likes us to go to events where Jesus is praised and talked about, and where everyone there loves Him! He arranges VIP access to Jesus for us, and starts off some great conversations.

The Holy Spirit works non-stop behind the scenes to bring our attention to Jesus. He absolutely loves it when we respect and praise Jesus – so do that now!

PRAY Jesus, You are so amazing. I never want to forget how You died on a cross for me so that my sins could be forgiven and I could follow You. Thank You. Amen.

A HOLIDAY TO REMEMBER

READ: Acts 2:1–4

KEY VERSE: 'They saw what seemed to be tongues of fire' (v3)

Before Jesus returned to heaven, He made a promise: 'In a few days you will be baptised with the Holy Spirit.'

Jerusalem was full of Jews from all over the world who had come to celebrate a festival. Jesus' followers were all together waiting for Jesus' promise to happen. First, there was a sound like a tornado. Jesus had described the Holy Spirit as being like wind (John 3:8) – invisible, but the effects of it can be seen. Like the wind, the Holy Spirit is invisible, but we can see what He does in people's lives.

Next came fire! It appeared over their heads. John the Baptist had predicted that Jesus would baptise His followers with Holy Spirit fire. Fire symbolised spotlessness and power.

The Holy Spirit powered up the first Christians to tell the holiday crowds about Jesus. They started speaking to them, but the words coming out of their mouths were not Greek, they were the languages of the people they spoke to – it was a miracle! There's nothing that can stop Jesus being talked about when the Holy Spirit is at work.

THINK
The Holy Spirit can help you talk to the people you know about Jesus too. In what way do you need His help for this?

POWER UP!

COMMON LANGUAGE

READ: Acts 2:4–13

KEY VERSE: 'Amazed and perplexed, they asked one another, "What does this mean?"' (v12)

Have you ever tried to learn a new language? At Pentecost, the Holy Spirit helped the first Christians express their love for God in languages they hadn't even had lessons in!

After Jesus went back to heaven, the disciples got together and kept a low profile. They didn't want to be recognised now it seemed to be all over. The Holy Spirit changed all that. This disciples were able to speak, with no fear, in languages they'd never learnt a word of! Their cover was blown. Holiday-makers rushed to find out what on earth was going on.

'Hello! Bonjour! Güten tag! Welcome to our talk about the miracles of God, available in all languages!' It was like God had invaded the school language department. Holiday-makers were listening in their own languages, and Google translate didn't get a single hit!

The Holy Spirit wants to bring Jesus out into the open in our lives too. He wants to take away our fear and give us bravery to tell people about Him.

PRAY Holy Spirit, You are the giver of the best gifts. Please give me exactly what I need right now so that I can show the world Jesus. Amen.

REASONS TO BE THANKFUL... 1,2,3

READ: Acts 2:14–21,37–39

KEY VERSE: 'The promise is for you and your children and for all who are far off' (v39)

Remember Joel? He was the prophet who preached that the Holy Spirit was coming to live in anyone who had been forgiven by God. At Pentecost, Peter remembered Joel's words, stood on a chair and started preaching...

The Holy Spirit fired up Peter to preach a long (but hardly boring) sermon. It was deep stuff! Not even one joke was cracked. Peter launched straight into his first point. He said that in God's eyes, everyone was out of order. And it was time to turn back to God.

The time came for the radical second point – only Jesus can deal with our sin and can forgive us. And to complete the original three-point sermon – those who turned from doing whatever they wanted to believe in Jesus would receive the Holy Spirit! As 3,000 people responded and said 'Yes' to this, they all received the Holy Spirit. Joel's prophecy was beginning to be fulfilled.

There is only one way to get right with God – by turning away from selfish living, believing in Jesus and receiving the Holy Spirit.

THINK
What tends to turn your attention away from God the most?

POWER UP!

RIGHT SKILLS FOR THE JOB

READ: Acts 6:1–15

KEY VERSE: 'choose seven men from among you who are known to be full of the Spirit and wisdom' (v3)

As the Early Church grew, problems occasionally cropped up. Christians from Greek backgrounds felt they were not being treated as well as those from Jewish backgrounds. New leaders would need to be chosen to sort out these problems so the apostles could concentrate on teaching and praying.

These leaders would need to make sure things were managed fairly, properly and effectively.

A leader had to be a certain sort of person, living their life in a good way. But most of all, they needed to be full of the Spirit and known for being like this.

Being a church leader is a very important job. It's also a very hard job – think about everything they have to do! Sundays are just the tip of the iceberg. So it's essential that leaders are filled with the Holy Spirit so that they can be successful not just in the main service, but in everything else they are called to do.

THINK Do you know any of the leaders in your church? Whether it's the main leader or the youth leader, why not pray for them now? They need a lot of support and encouragement.

CHANGE OF HEART

READ: Acts 8:1–8

KEY VERSE: 'Philip went down to a city in Samaria and proclaimed the Messiah there.' (v5)

One of those chosen to be a leader was Philip. He was a man powered-up by the Holy Spirit. Just look how that changed his attitude towards people!

Jewish people like Philip avoided going to Samaria. Years of rivalry and arguments had meant that Samaritans and Jews hated each other. But the Holy Spirit changed how Philip saw the Samaritans. They were people that Jesus had come to save, just like Philip. Samaritans needed to hear about Jesus and receive the Holy Spirit. So Philip boldly went where no Jew dared to go – Samaria. The Samaritans could not get enough of Philip. A Jew who loved them… this was amazing! A Jew who performed miracles in Jesus' name… this was jaw dropping! A Jew who wanted them to be filled with the Holy Spirit… this was just incredible!

Philip was a man with an attitude. An attitude of love to those he had once hated. It led to a great revival (remember that word? Look at day 219 if you've forgotten)! Samaria – a place with a bad reputation – became the place to be!

PRAY Father, I know that You love absolutely everyone. Please help me to shine Your light to anyone and everyone. Amen.

POWER UP!

A MOMENTOUS MOMENT IN THE MIDDAY SUN

READ: Acts 8:26–40

KEY VERSE: 'So he invited Philip to come up and sit with him.' (v31)

Philip is leading the most successful Jesus mission outside Jerusalem. Hundreds have turned to Christ. Where next? A bigger mission in a larger city? No, a dusty road in the desert. Why had God called Philip away from the crowds to wander among the cactus plants? Philip knew God had a purpose in sending him to a giant sandpit, and he soon found out what it was.

God had made an appointment for Philip to meet an African man who as searching for Him. Philip chatted to him and used the Bible to explain that Jesus had died as a sacrifice for sin. The man was so keen to learn more that Philip sat with him and shared the good news of Jesus.

This man was convinced Jesus was God's Son. He even found a water hole to be baptised in then and there. Afterwards, he set off to share the good news with the rest of Africa. Philip's one-to-one chat hand launched the gospel to a new continent – a day well spent!

THINK When there's an opportunity to talk about Jesus, do you take it? The Holy Spirit will give us 100% support when we want to bring glory to God's Son.

A BREAK-UP?

READ: Psalm 22:1–2, 16–31

KEY VERSE: 'he has not hidden his face from him but has listened to his cry for help' (v24)

There are loads of songs about love on the radio today, but not all of them are happy. Relationships can break down sometimes – friends can fall out, a parent can walk out on their family – and it can really, really hurt. This psalm has that feeling – only, it's about God. The writer feels that God has abandoned him. He is in a bad way. The worst thing is that when he cries out to God, God doesn't' answer (v2)!

This might be how you feel sometimes. It is how Jesus felt when He was on the cross – He even cried out some of this psalm just before He died (Mark 15:34).

But there is more to this psalm than just pain, there is hope! Although the singer feels deserted by God, he knows what God is really like. God is faithful, He will never leave His people and, no matter what, He's still got the power! Look at verses 27–31. No matter how we might feel, God is right there, listening to us, guiding us and helping us.

PRAY Lord, please help me to have hope in You and realise You always listen to me, even when I feel You are distant. I trust You completely. Amen.

PSALM

BE CLOSE

READ: Psalm 84:1–12

KEY VERSE: 'How lovely is your dwelling-place, LORD Almighty!' (v1)

Is there anyone you know who really gets on your nerves when you've been around them for a long time? Something amazing about God is that He actually chooses to be close to us. Why does He love us? Maybe we will never know, but we do know that He does love us enough to want to spend *forever* with us!

This psalm is by an Israelite looking at the Temple in Jerusalem. He knows that the Temple is the place where God is, in a very special way, and that is the reason he loves the sight of it so much. He and the rest of God's people (and even the birds!) love being close to God – there's nothing like it!

Here's the incredible news for us: everything the Temple was to the Israelites – God's home and the place where people had their sins forgiven – is found in Jesus Christ. Because of Him, our sins are forgiven, and with Him, God is with us.

If we belong to Jesus, then God the Holy Spirit is living in us. We all need God to be close – it's what we're made for.

THINK Is spending time with God something that you enjoy, or something that feels like more of a chore? Talk to another Christian about this!

PSALM

WRECKING BALL

READ: Nehemiah 1:1–4

> **KEY VERSE:** 'I mourned and fasted and prayed before the God of heaven' (v4)

Meet Nehemiah – an ordinary guy who God chose to rebuild the smashed walls of Jerusalem. The book begins with Nehemiah finding out some pretty bad news. He lives in Persia, but his home city – Jerusalem – is a pile of rubble.

Over 100 years earlier, the Babylonians had put a wrecking ball to Jerusalem, knocking down its walls and setting it on fire. The Jews were captured and made slaves. Then the Persians took control of the Babylonian empire, deciding to allow some of the Jews to take back Jerusalem. They rebuilt the Temple but didn't get round to rebuilding the walls. Then, an attempt was made to rebuild the walls, but the enemies of the Jews stopped this by knocking down any remaining parts of the old walls. News of this then reached Nehemiah and he was devastated.

Nehemiah's name means 'God comforts' – and he knew it. Yes, he was really upset to learn that Jerusalem's walls were still in ruins – but what did he do? He lived up to his name, and turned to God for comfort.

THINK **When you receive bad news, what's the first thing you do? How long does it take for you to talk to God about it? Doing so really is the best idea!**

CONCRETE FAITH

A LITTLE RESPECT

READ: Nehemiah 1:4–7

KEY VERSE: 'the great and awesome God, who keeps his covenant of love with those who love him and keep his commandments' (v5)

When things don't turn out how we want, or we get some bad news, it's easy to start feeling sorry for ourselves.

The news about Jerusalem was a drop-kick to the chest for Nehemiah. But he didn't have a go at God for the ways things were. Instead, he put his feelings to one side and spoke to God with respect.

Nehemiah had been a servant to King Artaxexes (try saying that out-loud!). He certainly wouldn't burst into the king's throne room and start shouting at him. He would always bow down and show the king respect. So he showed even more respect for the King of kings by calling Him 'God of heaven, the great and awesome God' (v5).

Bad news can cause us to wonder if God really cares about us, but Nehemiah didn't let his feelings take over the facts. He knew God loved him. He didn't pin the blame on God or anyone else. The first thing he did was sort out His relationship with God by owning up to his own sin.

PRAY
Heavenly Father, I'm sorry for when I get too focused on myself and forget to speak to You in the way You deserve. Please help me with this. Amen.

PART OF THE PLAN

READ: Nehemiah 1:8–11

KEY VERSE: 'Give your servant success today by granting him favour in the presence of this man.' (v11)

Nehemiah knew he needed planning permission from King Artaxerxes to get the walls up. Amazing news – he's been working in a job where he's got access to the king! Bit of a coincidence, eh? So Nehemiah asked God to work behind the scenes so that when he spoke, the king would be happy with what he said.

The Jews had been warned over and over again about how if they kept turning away from God, they would be kicked out of their country. Did they take any notice? No. So no huge surprise when they were invaded and taken over.

But God didn't write them off. When they turned back to Him, He made it possible for them to return. Nehemiah knew this and He understood that right now God was keeping His promise of bringing the Jews back to Israel. Even better – he realised that God was way ahead of him and had promised to make Jerusalem strong again. And he wanted to be a part of that.

THINK
What plans do you have for your future? Sometimes we can get so busy with our own planning that we forget God's got a ready-made plan.

CONCRETE FAITH

TIMING IS EVERYTHING

READ: Nehemiah 1:11–2:20

KEY VERSE: 'the king asked me, "Why does your face look so sad when you are not ill?"' (2:2)

Nehemiah prayed for an opportunity to speak with the king about the ruined walls of Jerusalem. But it didn't happen straight away —in fact it took *four months* for him to get an opportunity.

Could you have waited that long? We have quite an impatient culture these days – we expect things to happen instantly. And sometimes we can treat God like a drive-through restaurant – we say what we want and we expect it a minute later.

Nehemiah had examined the three options open to him. Option one: he could go and speak to the king without being given an opportunity – something that probably wouldn't have gone down well. Option two: forget about it all and assumed that God didn't care. Option three: wait patiently, trusting God.

He chose the third option. But often we can choose the first or second option: either jumping ahead and not trusting God's timing, or just walking away from the whole thing. Imagine if Nehemiah had done that? We'd have a very different story on our hands if he had!

PRAY Father God, help me to trust Your perfect timing. I know that Your ways are better than mine! Thank You. Amen.

AGAINST THE ODDS

READ: Ezra 4:11–23; Nehemiah 2:2

KEY VERSE: 'I was very much afraid' (Neh. 2:2)

God had given Nehemiah a golden opportunity to speak to the king and ask for planning permission. So why would he be afraid?

Nehemiah knew that this conversation had come up for the king before, and it hadn't gone down well. King Artaxerxes thought that if Jerusalem got some new bricks, the people would stop paying him taxes. In fact, he was so determined that Jerusalem should not be rebuilt, that he made himself the only person with the power to give the OK on any building work.

No wonder Nehemiah was shaking –his chances of getting the green light were looking pretty slim! But the thing to remember was that God had made the building plans, and He was backing Nehemiah all the way. So Nehemiah, ever so slightly nervous, went to ask the king.

When we have an opportunity to speak with others about Jesus or stand up for God, it can be tempting to run away from the situation. But God promises to be with us and gives us the right words to say.

THINK Is God asking you to speak to someone about Him? What might be holding you back from doing so?

CONCRETE FAITH

GET SPECIFIC

READ: Nehemiah 2:3–8

KEY VERSE: 'And because the gracious hand of my God was on me, the king granted my requests.' (v8)

Imagine how wobbly Nehemiah must have felt when the king of all Persia looked him in the eye and asked him, 'What is it you want?'

When you pray, do you know what you need – and do you dare you ask for it?

Nehemiah sent a quick 'help me' prayer to heaven before replying to the king. He'd had several months of waiting to figure out his plans – so even though he was nervous, he was ready for the questions that might follow. He knew what he needed.

The king – head of the biggest business empire of all time – was so impressed with Nehemiah's plan that he approved it there and then. Did Nehemiah let the success go to his head? No, he gave the credit to 'the gracious hand of my God' (v8).

God wants more than for us to just say that we'll serve Him. He's given us the brains we need to think about the details – not just about what we need, but about what others need too. Then we can ask Him for those things.

PRAY Lord, thank You for giving me a mind that can think! Please help me to use it to see what my friends and I really need. Amen.

THINKING IT THROUGH

READ: Nehemiah 2:9–15

KEY VERSE: 'I had not told anyone what my God had put in my heart to do for Jerusalem.' (v12)

With God's help, Nehemiah finally had his planning permission. The next step was to view the burnt-up site. Even though he had the king's approval in writing, Nehemiah knew that there would still be people who didn't like God's plans for Jerusalem's comeback. So he brought in a security guard for some extra peace of mind. Nehemiah then did his inspection under the cover of darkness – if he did it in the daylight the news would have spread like wildfire.

Where did he start this undercover work? Dung Gate. The people who had named Jerusalem's gates hadn't shown much imagination. You could buy fish at Fish Gate, find sheep at Sheep Gate and go to the fountain at Fountain Gate. So you can imagine what Dung Gate meant (clue: it wasn't the nicest-smelling gate).

Nehemiah gives us the details of his inspection – and he'd clearly put a lot of thought into God's work. He used his head and worked out the best way to get things done.

THINK It's worth talking things through with God whenever we start something new. Are you in a new situation? Ask God to help you figure out what needs to happen.

CONCRETE FAITH

READY, STEADY, BUILD

READ: Nehemiah 2:16–18

KEY VERSE: 'Let us start rebuilding.' (v18)

Nehemiah had kept his mission a secret, but now it was time to roll up his sleeves and unroll the plans. He didn't know how the Jews around Jerusalem would react to the DIY project, but he knew that there were two reasons why they hadn't gone through with it before:

TOO BUSY – In the past, workers had preferred to put more effort into building their business rather than Jerusalem's old ruins.

TOO SCARED – The troublemakers from other lands didn't want the Jews to have a capital city that they could defend. So they wrecked every attempt to rebuild the walls. Not wanting to risk being killed, the Jews quit whenever the troublemakers came knocking.

So what got them eager to get going this time? God used Nehemiah to ignite some team spirit. Nehemiah got all God's people together and told them why getting the job done was important. He explained how God had answered his prayers and given all they needed – and that even the king was on board. Immediately, the ruins became a building site (v18). You don't hang around once God's given the green light.

PRAY Dear God, I know that You have big plans – and I want to work for You. Help me to be ready when it's time to get to work! Amen.

KNOW WHO YOU WORK FOR

READ: Nehemiah 2:19–20

KEY VERSE: 'The God of heaven will give us success.' (v20)

Are there any people in your area who are known as troublemakers? Sure enough, as soon as Nehemiah's builders started, the troublemakers showed up. Let's see who they were...

SANBALLAT THE HORONITE – This guy, named after 'Sin' (the Babylonian moon god) was governor of Samaria. He lived up to his Sin-ful name by going against everything God wanted to do. He wanted to add the area to his territory.

TOBIAH THE AMMONITE – This geezer was the Persian governor of the area before Nehemiah showed up. He saw Nehemiah as a threat. He was half Jewish and had lots of Jewish friends, but always put what he wanted before God's plans.

GESHEM THE ARAB – This mobster was the chief of the desert tribes of northern Arabia. Since the time of Abraham, the Arabs have been at odds with the Jews.

In the past, the likes of these guys would have been enough to make the workers go home. But Nehemiah stood up to the bullies as they shouted insults. Nehemiah said, 'The God of heaven will give us success' (v20). He wasn't being cocky – just completely trusting God.

THINK Do you ever get laughed at or insulted for following God?

CONCRETE FAITH

GRAFTERS AND SHAFTERS

READ: Nehemiah 3:1–5

KEY VERSE: 'but their nobles would not put their shoulders to the work under their supervisors' (v5)

Nehemiah had a pretty mixed group on the building site, and they seemed to split into two teams...

The first team — Eliashib (high priest) and his fellow priests — were very hard workers. They turned up and quickly got to work preparing the Sheep Gate. This was the gate through with sheep were led to be sacrifices in the Temple for sin. Years later, Jesus, 'the Lamb of God', was led out of Jerusalem through this gate to become the ultimate sacrifice.

The men of Jericho travelled miles and miles each day to lend a hand, too. Following the example of the priests, thousands got stuck in to work on the walls.

The second team — men of Tekoa — were asked to repair a section of wall near the Fish Gate. Most of them gave a hand, but a few of the officials opted out. They obviously thought they were far too important to get their hands dirty or take orders from Nehemiah's leaders. So they sunbathed while others sweated.

Nehemiah noted down those who worked and those who didn't.

PRAY Lord Jesus, You are God and yet You went through so much for us! Please help me to get stuck in to Your work. Amen.

YOUR BEST WORK

READ: Nehemiah 3:28–32

KEY VERSE: 'the priests made repairs, each in front of his own house' (v28)

Nehemiah had a strategy for deciding which section of the wall each worker would repair. Those living near the wall were asked to repair the damage nearest to them. Travelling to work in the morning was easy – you opened the front door and you were at the office!

No one wanted to mess up the part of the wall nearest their house or business, so this was a great strategy from Nehemiah and guaranteed to get everyone doing their best. Teams of priests, businessmen and families all worked hard to clear the site and build.

Think of your Christian life as a city wall – where are the weak points in your defences? What temptations sometimes take over you? What are you likely to cave in to? We have to work at guarding our hearts and minds from attacks. The things we watch on TV or see online might try to make us do things that don't please God, things that are no good for us. So tell God what pressure you are under, and ask Him to help you. He loves you and wants to help.

PRAY

Father God, I believe that You know me more than I know myself. Show me what my 'weak spots' are and help me to repair them. Amen.

CONCRETE FAITH

MAKING A MOCKERY

READ: Nehemiah 4:1–6

KEY VERSE: 'Hear us, our God, for we are despised. Turn their insults back on their own heads.' (v4)

As the walls went up, Sanballat and his gang tried to bring the people down – by some non-stop mick-taking.

It's quite common for people to act big in front of their mates by making sneering comments about others – and making fun of God's people has always been a thing. Look at how Sanballat and Tobiah only got mouthy when they were with the army of Syria. And what a bunch of one-liners they came up with to look smart in front of the troops!

How did Nehemiah react? He didn't throw a couple of insults back at them. And neither did Jesus when He was being mocked. The temptation to get revenge can be overwhelming – but holding yourself back is always the better way. Nehemiah took the problem straight to God. After all, it was Him they were really insulting – and He's big enough to look after Himself.

Nehemiah and his workers refused to let hurtful comments ruin their enthusiasm to live for God. The more they were put down, the more bricks they put up.

THINK Have you ever got into a war of insults with someone? These only ever make arguments worse and worse. What could you do differently?

IS THAT A THREAT?

READ: Nehemiah 4:7–9

KEY VERSE: 'But we prayed to our God and posted a guard day and night to meet this threat.' (v9)

The wall had been built. When Sanballat and his gang saw that their insults were ignored, they started to lose their cool. The insults became threats – and it got pretty messy.

The enemies were ganging up and threatening to do some serious damage. This was a serious problem for Nehemiah. He was outnumbered by well-armed troops and about to be caught with his defences down. So he and his workers tackled the threat with prayer. Together they told God what was happening and asked for help. After that, they posted a guard outside to be a look out.

Following insults, threats are often the next mode of attack.

So how should a Christian handle things when they get nasty? Nehemiah took the problem upwards, then outwards. He took the problem to God first, but also got together with other believers to talk through what was happening. What a great way of dealing with problems!

THINK If you're having a hard time, you don't need to face it alone. You have God and His people to give you support. Pray and try talking to your youth group or a Christian friend about it.

CONCRETE FAITH

WATCH THIS SPACE

READ: Nehemiah 4:10–13

KEY VERSE: 'Therefore I stationed some of the people behind the lowest points of the wall... with their swords, spears and bows.' (v13)

Some sections of the wall needed more work than others. There were still big gaps to be filled. Without mechanical diggers and cranes to move the huge blocks of stone, the work was beyond exhausting. The workers were drained. Each block might as well have been a mountain – and adding to their physical weakness was the constant fear of an attack. They were spread out across a wall that had big gaps in it. They were an easy target.

Nehemiah knew he had to do something so he stationed armed guards by all the low points. The plan? 'Watch this space.' Literally.

Nehemiah was strong because he knew where he was weak. He guarded the low points so the enemy couldn't burst in. We also have low points. Tiredness, difficulties and being tempted to sin can bring us down. But turning to God lifts our defences and makes us strong. Praying and reading the Bible strengthens our faith, and ultimately strengthens us. So it's important to always keep building our relationship with Him.

PRAY Lord Jesus, thank You that You have no weaknesses at all. Help me to become stronger in You today. Amen.

GOT YOUR BACK

READ: Nehemiah 4:14–18

KEY VERSE: 'Remember the Lord, who is great and awesome' (v14)

Nehemiah's team of builders needed a reminder that GOD IS AWESOME! He's bigger than any tough situation we face. And that simple fact transformed the way they worked on the building site.

Nehemiah's tactics were to 'mind the gaps' and 'mind your backs'. So the people both worked and kept guard. Half of the men became guards, while half carried on building. But the builders now carried weapons with them. As for those working on the outside of the walls, they knew they could be attacked from behind, so armed officers were placed to protect them.

Difficulties can creep up on us too. We can be caught off guard, out of contact with God, the Bible and other Christians – and realise that we're starting to mess up quite a lot. But, like Nehemiah's builders, we can carry a sword around with us: the Bible. Read God's words and carry them around in your head wherever you go. Remind yourself of how awesome God is. And remember, He's always got your back.

THINK Is there a difficulty in your faith that keeps sneaking up on you? Why not look up some Bible verses to help you fight it off in future?

CONCRETE FAITH

WHEN YOU'VE HIT A WALL...

READ: Nehemiah 4:19–23

KEY VERSE: 'Our God will fight for us!' (v20)

Sometimes, God calls us to some pretty interesting challenges. Sometimes, you feel like you've hit a wall.

The builders could have used the following as excuses to quit God's work....

POSSIBLE EXCUSE 1: 'God's work is taking up too much of my time. I can't commit to it.'

The building work went on from the crack of dawn until the stars came out – all day, every day. But that was God's plan. Some people only serve God when they can fit Him into their busy lives. Has God got first dibs on your time, or does He get the leftovers?

POSSIBLE EXCUSE 2: 'This work is lonely and boring!'

The project was so big that the workers had to be spread out along the wall. The work was hard and was the same every day. Some felt lonely and fed up. Have you ever felt like that? Nehemiah kept up the team spirit by reminding them that God would fight for them.

Doing God's work can be hard, but we can be sure of one thing: 'Our God will fight for us!' (v20).

PRAY **Father God, when my energy levels are low, instead of walking away from You, help me to run to You. Amen.**

RIPPED OFF

READ: Nehemiah 5:1–13

KEY VERSE: 'Shouldn't you walk in the fear of our God...?' (v9)

Have you ever lent something to a friend and not had it back? Things can take an awkward turn when that happens...

Years of famine and the requirement to pay tax to the king left many people in Jerusalem in poverty. Before Nehemiah rocked up to the scene, some of the richer folk had lent money to those in trouble. The problem was, when the people paid it back, they had to pay a whole load more. When the builders couldn't do this, their houses got taken away from them. Some parents were so swamped in debt that they even felt they needed to sell their children as slaves!

Nehemiah had to step in pretty quickly to stop things from getting even worse. He called a meeting and called out the people who had lent the money, showing how greedy they were being. The money lenders were told to give back everything they had taken from the rest of the people – and they did. They were all part of the same community, and they needed to live well together.

THINK Do you find it hard to get along with someone at your church? If you do, start praying for them – ask God to change how you see them.

ALRIGHT, GUV'NAH!

READ: Nehemiah 5:14–19

KEY VERSE: 'But out of reverence for God I did not act like that.' (v15)

Nehemiah had the position of Governor – and that came with perks that could make him stinking rich. But he decided to put God first. He didn't use his position to line his pockets. That wasn't the way God expected him to behave.

So Nehemiah didn't demand money or land, instead he shared his food around. He didn't pose in the palace, instead he was out supervising the building work every day. And he didn't let his assistants opt for the easy life either when there was work to be done. They all had to muck in.

When the builders saw how the 'Guv' behaved, they were impressed. And they liked working for him. 'Alright, Guv, I'll do that,' they said.

Nehemiah was a good Governor because he respected *his* Governor – God. One of the most powerful ways we can show respect to God is by doing things His way, not in a way that makes life easy for us – and sometimes that means saying, 'No, because I love God I won't do that'.

PRAY God, I don't want to be selfish, I want to always put You first. Thank You for always knowing the best way to live. Amen.

A BIG ONO-NO

READ: Nehemiah 6:1–4

KEY VERSE: 'I am carrying on a great project and cannot go down. Why should the work stop...?' (v3)

The troublemakers were still making trouble for Nehemiah. The wall had gone up but the gates and doors had not gone in yet. At the news of that, Nehemiah received an invitation.

The enemies had invited Nehemiah to a meeting in a village called Ono. (It already sounds suspicious doesn't it?!) They didn't want witnesses around when Nehemiah had a 'nasty fall'... onto a sword. If it were today, they'd have kindly invited him to meet them down a dark alley for a friendly chat.

But Nehemiah was a wise guy and saw right through them – plus, he had more important things to do like getting on with God's work. And besides, why wouldn't such an important 'meeting' be held in Jerusalem? The troublemakers wouldn't take no for an answer though. They 'invited' Nehemiah *four times* – but each time, with God's help, Nehemiah gave them a big, fat 'O-NO'.

When we receive an invitation to go somewhere that we're not sure about, it's always a good idea to chat with God and others about it.

THINK Have you ever been invited out with friends but thought it might end in trouble?

CONCRETE FAITH

LIAR, LIAR (PANTS ON FIRE)

READ: Nehemiah 6:5–9

KEY VERSE: 'But I prayed, 'Now strengthen my hands.' (v9)

Rumours are an easy way to cause a massive amount of damage to someone. And it's scarily easy to get caught up in all the rambling.

Sanballat and his gang were not the least bit impressed that Nehemiah had said 'no' *four times* to the 'friendly chat'. So they hatched a plan to ruin his reputation. Sanballat spread a rumour that Nehemiah was planning to set himself up as king.

How did Nehemiah react to this when he heard all the lies being spread about him? He knew it could ruin everything, maybe even meaning the Persians would be able to knock the walls down again. But look at his reply to Sanballat: 'you are making it up out of your head' (v8). He totally called him out for his lies! Next, He prayed for the more strength to get God's work done.

Do you speak up for others when you hear something about them that isn't true? As Christians, we can ask God for the guts to do this.

PRAY Lord Jesus, I know that You hate rumours and gossip. Give me strength to not get caught up in it, and to stand strong when things are said about me. Amen.

CHECK IT OUT

READ: Nehemiah 6:10–14

KEY VERSE: 'I realised that God had not sent him' (v12)

The rumours hadn't brought down Nehemiah, so the troublemakers had to come up with yet *another* plan. (These guys had way too much free time!) Along comes Shemaiah the prophet claiming that God has warned him and his mates that there was a plot to kill Nehemiah. He told Nehemiah, 'Don't worry, you'll be OK if you hide in the inner Temple and lock the doors.'

Alarm bells rang in Nehemiah's head. He knew that this part of the Temple was out of bounds to everyone but the high priest, and even he only went in once a year! If the builders heard that Nehemiah was hiding, they'd stop work. And if they found out *where* he was hiding, they would lose all respect for him. So Nehemiah didn't fall for the trick.

Just because someone says that God has spoken to them or said that something's OK, it doesn't mean He has. Nehemiah knew that God doesn't say one thing in the Bible and then tell you to do something else. He trusted the Bible rather than the con men.

THINK
There will always be people who go against what the Bible says. That's why it's so important to read the Bible first-hand!

CONCRETE FAITH

HATE MAIL

READ: Nehemiah 6:15–19

KEY VERSE: 'they realised that this work had been done with the help of our God' (v16)

Nehemiah kept obeying God. Incredibly, the project was finished in just 52 days! The walls were up and the last gate was put in place. The workers in their overalls stood back to admire their work. Good job, people!

Panic struck in the enemy's camp. They had lost, not just against the Jews but against God. They knew that God had been the mastermind – how else would they have finished it in such a short space of time? The walls were finished but the enemy wasn't. Nehemiah said that even afterwards, he was still receiving hate mail from Tobiah the troublemaker – the definition of a sore loser.

God's enemies like to have a go at those who succeed for God. We see it all throughout the Bible. Some people just take every opportunity to have a go, making unfair comments. If these comments are aimed at you, it can be really hard to keep on living for God. But with God's help, Nehemiah did it – and so can you!

PRAY Lord Jesus, I know that You have had people treat You unfairly. Help me to ignore it when people try to bring me down. Amen.

GUARD YOUR GATES

READ: Nehemiah 7:1–5

KEY VERSE: 'he was a man of integrity and feared God more than most people do' (v2)

Just because the walls were up, it didn't mean Nehemiah could sit back with an easy life. He suspected the troublemakers would try to sneak their men into the city. So he got the place on full alert.

Nehemiah personally hired the gatekeepers and delivery men who would carry items in and out of the city. He suspected the troublemakers would try to bribe people into letting them into the city, so he wanted to make sure the gatekeepers were top-notch.

The next guy he hired was Hananiah who was an honest man. His job was to be commander of the city defences, and that was a very important role. Then, Nehemiah made rules about how the gates should be kept at night, and even made a neighbourhood watch scheme to keep the troublemakers away! That's how much he wanted to guard those gates.

God has given us gates to guard too – the gates to our mind. These are our eye and ears. There's lots of stuff that wants to sneak its way through those gates and harm us, so we have to be on guard.

THINK Have you ever noticed yourself changing because of something you've seen or heard? If it's a bad change, ask God for His help.

CONCRETE FAITH

HANDS UP

READ: Nehemiah 8:1–6

KEY VERSE: 'Ezra praised the LORD, the great God; and all the people lifted their hands and responded, "Amen! Amen!"' (v6)

The people living in Jerusalem were protected, but what about their hearts and minds? Now the wall was built, it was time to rebuild their lives for God. Jewish tradition meant that they all gathered together on the first day of the seventh month to hear God's commands.

Ezra was the preacher who opened up God's Word. As he started reading, the people stood up. Then they raised their arms in the air and cheered on what was being said. Repeating 'Amen!' and 'Amen!' was their way of saying 'Sure thing! We want to obey God!' It was an atmosphere that would make the World Cup finals look tame! Next thing, they all dropped to the floor – bowing down to worship God.

God's Word is powerful – just look what happened when Ezra started reading! The Bible changes us and it leads us to worship God. Do you sometimes find it hard to get excited about God? Ask Him to show you what He's really like – He's far from boring!

PRAY Dear Lord, You are totally awesome and deserve endless praise from me! I want to worship You always, even in the times when I might not feel like it. Amen.

UNDERSTAND?

READ: Nehemiah 8:7–12

> **KEY VERSE:** 'so that the people understood what was being read' (v8)

As Ezra read from the Scriptures, some of the workers started getting brain ache. There were lots of fancy, long words. Some of the old Jewish lingo was kind of confusing. And the children listening just didn't know where to start.

Have you ever looked at a sum in maths that just totally fries your brain? We can switch off at school if we don't understand stuff. But a good teacher who can make things easy to understand makes all the difference.

Rather than bore everyone to sleep, Ezra sent out teachers to help everyone get their heads around what he was saying and how it all worked in real life. It worked. They understood where they had been going wrong in following God, but they also found out that they were forgiven and could live with joy and celebration. It was time to get the party poppers out!

We've got someone helping us to understand the Bible too – the Holy Spirit. He's a great teacher who helps us to get to grips with what the Bible says and means.

THINK Do you struggle to figure out what the Bible is actually saying? Here's two things that help: asking the Holy Spirit to make things clear, and talking with other Christians.

CONCRETE FAITH

DON'T MISS OUT!

READ: Nehemiah 8:13–18

KEY VERSE: 'And their joy was very great.' (v17)

Teachers have a hard job don't they? Those lessons where no one listens to them must be horrible! But Ezra's teaching experience was really quite different to this. The workers were all keen to listen to him and learn. And when they discovered what God wanted them to do that day, well... they got on and did it!

It was the week that they should have been celebrating how God led them to the Promised Land. It was written that they were to camp out in shelters for a week just as they had done in the wilderness. And while they camped, they were to remember God's goodness is setting them free from slavery. Did the workers do a quick check of the weather before agreeing? No they didn't. They said, 'If that's what God wants, let's get to it!'

In a matter of hours, Jerusalem turned into a campsite. Everyone slept in shelters, ate together, and spent time hearing from God and celebrating how good He is. It was great!

PRAY Lord, it's such a great adventure having You in my life! Even when I'm really busy, I want to set time aside to hang out with You. Amen.

GET RIGHT

READ: Nehemiah 9:1–5

KEY VERSE: 'Stand up and praise the LORD your God, who is from everlasting to everlasting.' (v5)

Have you ever avoided a person because you've felt guilty about something you've done? Perhaps it's a teacher at school because you haven't done your homework, or maybe a parent because you've been helping yourself to the food you're not meant to!

A couple of weeks after their week-long celebration, the workers met up again. They came to admit their sin and ask for forgiveness. Before the meeting, they sorted out any issues between themselves. Then they started the long service. Three whole hours of listening to God's Word, then three whole hours of admitting their sin and praising God. And guess what? Not one person was bored.

Sometimes we can avoid God because we know He's got something to say to us that might be tough to hear. But that only means that we lose out. When we become Christians, God forgives us for all our sin, every single little bit. Nehemiah learnt to be honest with God and encouraged others to do the same. Let's admit when we've made a mistake, and go back to God.

THINK God already knows everything there is to know about us — so why keep things from Him? Get it all out in the open and get close to Him again.

CONCRETE FAITH

READ: Nehemiah 12:27–43

KEY VERSE: 'rejoicing because God had given them great joy' (v43)

The walls were up, the people were strong and Nehemiah called for a praise march to celebrate God's goodness.

When the Babylonians destroyed Jerusalem, it seemed impossible that the Jews would ever live there again. But God promised to bring His people back to control the city. Not because they deserved it, but because Jerusalem is special to Him. Nehemiah knew that God had carried out His promise and it was time to celebrate. Jews rushed to the city to give God the credit.

First they confessed where they'd messed up. Then they declared their loyalty to God. Then two parades were organised, both meeting up in the Temple for a massive praise party after. This all-age worship service was one that went down in history. The praise could be heard from miles away!

The people got right with God, put Him first and offered big-time praise. And God gave them great — seriously great — joy! When we are right with God and living for Him, we can experience that joy in our lives too.

PRAY Father, I praise You for all You do. I want to live to please You and experience that awesome joy that only You give out. Amen.

TEMPLE TAKEOVER

READ: Nehemiah 13:1–9

KEY VERSE: 'I gave orders to purify the rooms, and then I put back into them the equipment of the house of God' (v9)

After the enormous praise party, Nehemiah returned to his day job In Persia. But while he was away, the troublemakers move in on Jerusalem.

Just because you have been jumping at a big praise event, getting excited about what God has done, that doesn't mean life will be smooth sailing from now on. God's enemies look for ways to try and trip us up. And while Nehemiah's back was turned, Tobiah shows up again. Using his family connections with the high priest, he got one of the largest storerooms in the Temple and kitted it out as his new pad. The high priest should have known better. The Temple storerooms were dedicated to God, not a wrong'un like Tobiah.

Nehemiah realised the danger of turning away from God so there was no way he was going to let this slide. He immediately raided Tobiah's pad, throwing all his gear out in the street. Then he gave orders for the room to be handed back over to God.

THINK Our bodies are temples too – temples of the Holy Spirit. With that in mind, let's do our best to not let anything into our lives that God doesn't want there.

CONCRETE FAITH

COME BACK

READ: Nehemiah 13:10–14

KEY VERSE: 'Why is the house of God neglected?' (v11)

Today's the last time we will hear from our mate Nehemiah for a while. As always, he has another problem to sort out.

Have you ever gone a long time without talking to God, without even realising it? God's people had promised to bring 10% of their top quality grain, wine, oil and fruit to the Temple storerooms. These supplies were to feed the priests, making them free to lead worship and teach God's commands. But the giving had gone down, so the priests had to get jobs instead of completing their duties. Nehemiah came back from Persia to find the priests working in the fields instead of singing psalms.

Straight away he reminded everyone of what they should have been doing. God's work was being ignored. Why? No excuses were given. The priests went back to their duties and rest of the people put their money in the offering baskets to support them.

It can be scarily easy to forget about God. Despite wanting to put Him first, we so often just don't. Sometimes God needs to ask us, 'Why?' – and then it's time to go for it again.

PRAY Lord God, thank You that You always give us second chances. I never want to give up on my faith in You. Amen.

HE'S WITH US

READ: Psalm 121:1–8

KEY VERSE: 'My help comes from the LORD, the Maker of heaven and earth.' (v2)

Life can feel pretty scary sometimes. Worries and fears can come rushing in – even as soon as we wake up! But God doesn't want us to worry about or be afraid of anything. Have a read of today's psalm...

The writer asks a very important question: 'where does my help come from?' Notice what the writer was looking at when he said this: 'I lift up my eyes to the mountains' (v1). Some things can feel like mountains in life – a really tricky piece of homework, an illness or a family problem. Where is our help?

That's when the writer realises it. The maker of all is our helper! And what a helper God is! For one thing, He is not uncaring or blind to our situations. He sees *everything, all* the time. And more than that, God is *with* us. He stands by us, guiding, protecting and equipping us.

Those 'mountains' are nothing compared to the greatness of our God. And He is with us, always.

THINK What worries or scares you today? Read this promise out loud (based on today's reading): God will keep me from harm. He will watch over my life, wherever I go, now and forever.

PSALM

DON'T HOLD BACK

READ: Psalm 62:1–12

KEY VERSE: 'pour out your hearts to him' (v8)

There are loads of great songs in the world that are actually about some really deep topics. You can tell a lot about a musician by the music they produce. Sometimes their song lyrics even tell you exactly what's going on their lives right now. The psalms can be a bit like that – the writers are telling God exactly how they feel.

Look at how this psalm tells us to share what's going on in our hearts with God. There's no filter needed, He can handle it all. In fact, the psalmist advises his listeners to 'Trust in him at all times' (v8). In good times, sad times and bad times, we can trust God.

Sometimes we believe that we have to always be polite to God. But the truth is, God already knows how we feel and it's so much better for us to be completely honest with Him. When we talk to Him, it's like we're opening the door for Him to come in and help us with what we're facing. Remember, He has the ability to take away anything weighing us down and instead fill us with peace.

PRAY Lord, I want to be honest and open with You, no matter what kind of emotion I'm feeling. Thank You for always being there to talk to. Amen.

PSALM

LESSON ONE

READ: Matthew 5:1–10

KEY VERSE: 'His disciples came to him, and he began to teach them.' (vv1–2)

The guys that Jesus chose to be His disciples were a funny crew. None of them were particularly clever, rich or cool... just 12 young guys who found themselves quitting their day jobs to be trained by Jesus in the art of living differently. And they changed the world.

But what were they like then? Well, James and John kept getting into fights, Simon had been part of the zealot gang, Peter kept losing his cool, and Matthew had done well at school but no one liked him. This lot had quite a few issues!

So, how would Jesus go about getting this motley crew ship-shape? Jesus' first lesson to the disciples was not a great big list of 'don'ts', but instead some very different instructions:

Be happy with God, don't be arrogant, learn and do what's right, be kind, be good, be a peacemaker, be prepared to be hated because of Him.

This stuff was world-changing...

THINK What do you see as the most challenging part of Jesus' list? With God, nothing is impossible. Make it your mission to live differently in that area – asking Jesus for help to do this!

DELIBERATELY DIFFERENT

MAKING AN IMPRESSION

READ: Matthew 5:11–12

KEY VERSE: 'Blessed are you when people insult you, persecute you and falsely say all kinds of evil against you because of me.' (v11)

It seems to be a pretty strong pattern throughout human history: Christians don't tend to be popular. When Jesus was a hit with the crowds, the disciples wanted to be seen with Him. They were having the time of their lives. But when they got to Jerusalem and the locals moved in to hurt Jesus, they ran away.

Are we any different? At big Christian events where Jesus is the headline act, we want to be part of the action – but back in the classroom, we just want to blend in. Fear of rejection is very real. Worries about what others might think, say or do can influence us to change our behaviour. What does Jesus say about this?

When being real for God means you're on the receiving end of insults, you're blessed! What?! Yep, you're blessed because you are being noticed for Jesus, which is amazing! Fear forces us to follow the crowd. But faith encourages us to follow Jesus.

PRAY Lord, give me the courage to live differently for You. Help me not to be upset when people tease me for my faith. Let it motivate me to live for You even more! Amen.

PASS THE SALT

READ: Matthew 5:13–16

KEY VERSE: 'You are the salt of the earth. But if the salt loses its saltiness, how can it be made salty again?' (v13)

What's with all the talk about seasoning? Well, in Bible times there were no fridges or freezers. So the only way to keep meat fresh was to pack it in salt. Salt was also rubbed into wounds to stop the becoming infected. It would sting like mad, but it kept the wound clean.

So what did Jesus mean when He called His disciples the 'salt of the earth'? He wanted them to be His agents, stopping the rot (bad stuff) and cleaning things up. Their job was to feed the hungry, look after the poor, and be friends with outsiders. Doing so would be very different. People would notice this.

But what happens when salt loses its flavour? Damp salt was useless. This second-rate salt was chucked around to make the Temple courtyard less slippery during wet weather. People walked all over it.

Don't be the useless salt that people walk all over. Sort out your priorities, and be a light in the darkness.

THINK Do you speak up when someone else is being given a hard time? How could you be like salt in that situation?

DELIBERATELY DIFFERENT

A REBEL WITH A CAUSE

READ: Matthew 5:17–20

KEY VERSE: 'not the smallest letter, not the least stroke of a pen, will by any means disappear from the Law until everything is accomplished' (v18)

The Pharisees were ruled by rules. It wasn't the Ten Commandments that were the problem, but the 600 do's and don'ts they added to the list.

God made the Sabbath a rest day. Great idea! But the Pharisees made it a drag by saying you couldn't even swat a fly on the Sabbath – that was hunting, not resting! If you did something that looked even slightly like work, you were in the wrong. The Pharisees were hypocrites, looking down on others.

Jesus stood up to that. He didn't break any of God's rules – not once – but if He needed to break any silly tradition so that He could help those in need, He did. The Pharisees watched to see if Jesus would heal of the Sabbath – He did! That's because Jesus did things God's way.

We can't get right with God just by keeping a bunch of rules, but by trusting in Jesus.

THINK Do you ever feel like you have to reach a certain level of 'good' to be accepted by God? Anyone who trusts in Jesus is accepted as God's child – that's great news!

POTTY MOUTH

READ: Matthew 5:21–26

KEY VERSE: 'First go and be reconciled to them; then come and offer your gift.' (v24)

If words could kill, how many people would you have assassinated recently? Words spoken in anger can do a lot of damage. Jesus gave His team two examples of insults dished out at that time. 'Raca' meaning 'you empty fellow' was a really offensive swear word that could land you in court! 'You fool' seems tamer, but this was a savage thing to say to someone back then.

As Christians, we might not use swear words, but we might use other words to put people down. Jesus was saying that it's not just the words, but it's the way we say them. It's all well and good not using the 'F' word, but if we use other insults is there really that much difference?

The challenge for us here isn't just to clean up our *language* but our *lives*. If our attitude changes, the way we speak to others will too. Let's try to think about what we are saying, and realise that our words can affect people. Do we need to ask for forgiveness from anyone today?

PRAY Father, give me a good attitude that uses words to be kind to people and not put them down. Amen.

DELIBERATELY DIFFERENT

GET RID OF IT

READ: Matthew 5:29–30

KEY VERSE: 'if your right hand causes you to stumble, cut it off and throw it away' (v30)

Sorry, what?! No – we're not supposed to go around literally chopping off bits of ourselves. What today's passage means is that sin is serious and if there's something in our lives that causes us to keep on messing up, we need to turn our backs on it.

If spending all day playing a violent computer game makes you want to hit your brother, the game is probably the problem. If the TV shows you watch make you speak rudely to people, it's probably best to avoid them. That's what Jesus means by 'cut it off and throw it away' – walk away from these things and don't give them a chance to influence you.

But sometimes it takes a longer look at ourselves to realise what causes us to mess up. There's a whole bunch of reasons why we end up sinning, so ask Jesus to show you what it is that sets you off. He's in the business of turning lives around – so He's up to the challenge!

THINK Is there something you do that you know isn't helpful? How can you avoid doing those things?

PROMISES, PROMISES

READ: Matthew 5:33–37

KEY VERSE: 'All you need to say is simply "Yes," or "No"' (v37)

Have you made any promises lately? Maybe to tidy your room, work harder at school, or get on better with your sister? How are you doing with those?

Sometimes we promise to do something and get one of those looks – *I'll believe it when I see it* – in return. We've all broken promises at some point, and unfortunately this can mean that we lose people's trust. When we can tell that someone doesn't believe us, we might say things like, 'I swear I'll do it' or 'cross my heart'.

In Jesus' time, people would make promises and swear to keep them in 'heaven's name' or 'by Jerusalem'. Jesus wanted His followers to be different – to be *honest* and not make promises they wouldn't keep. If we're honest people, then a 'Yes' or a 'No' is enough.

There are lots of con-artists in the word who are out to get their own way, but Jesus wants us to be deliberately different: say what we mean and mean what we say. It represents Jesus really well when people know that they can trust us to be honest.

PRAY

Lord God, You are always so real with me. Help me to make good choices. I want to be trustworthy and honest like You. Amen.

DELIBERATELY DIFFERENT

DEFIANT GRACE

READ: Matthew 5:38–48

KEY VERSE: 'But I tell you... If anyone slaps you on the right cheek, turn to them the other cheek also.' (v39)

In Old Testament days, if someone punched out your front teeth you had the right to knock out theirs. However, Jesus had a radically different approach: turn the other cheek.

You might have heard this saying before, but what does it actually mean? Well, Jesus specifies the right cheek. Back then, you'd use your right hand for pleasant business, and your left hand for... other things. To hit someone on their right cheek, you need to use your left hand. It was the king of insults.

But the 'turn the other attitude cheek' is a brave response not to strike back. By presenting the left cheek, you allow them to hit you again with their 'good' hand.

The secret is learning to forgive those who drive you mad. Which means praying for them too. Nobody was treated as badly as Jesus, but He prayed from the cross, 'Father, forgive them...' He never hit back. He met their hatred with grace and love.

THINK
People will notice how we react to hurtful words or behaviour. Have you hit back at someone recently? How could you sort this out now?

JUST DO IT

READ: Matthew 6:1–4

KEY VERSE: 'But when you give to the needy, do not let your left hand know what your right hand is doing' (v3)

Giving can be selfish. Yep, you read that right. The Pharisees, who were pretty well-off anyway, made a big show of giving money away. They would announce what they were doing and make sure everyone knew about it and clapped them on.

They gave selfishly – their motive wasn't to help the poor, but to help themselves in gaining a Mr Nice-Guy image.

Jesus had a completely different way of helping those in need: just do it – and don't show off about it. This raises a question: how much do we do for others when no one is watching to give us a pat on the back? That's not just about our money but about our time and talents too.

Jesus went out of His way to meet and help the poor, sick and hated people. He never made it about Him. There wasn't a huge show, He didn't tell people how much He gave, and most of the people He gave to could do nothing for Him in return.

Why was He so different? His motive was love.

PRAY
Dear Lord, I'm sorry for when I've made giving about me. Help me to do good out of love. Amen.

DELIBERATELY DIFFERENT

HOW TO PRAY

READ: Matthew 6:5–18

KEY VERSE: 'But when you pray, go into your room, close the door and pray to your Father, who is unseen.' (v6)

The Pharisees liked to pray seven times a day – in public, where everyone could see and admire them. But Jesus revealed to His disciples a powerful secret weapon – private, personal prayer.

For Jesus, praying wasn't about posing, but was about power. He would often walk off to a quiet place to spend some quality time with God, just Him and His Father. It was in these times that Jesus made decisions about what He should do next. Lots of us will know the prayer that Jesus prayed. It gives us these helpful tips as to how to pray:

- Show God respect; Tell Him you want to fit into His plans;
- Ask for help where you need it; Admit you've messed up and ask for His forgiveness;
- Be open with Him about actions you take to forgive others;
- Ask God to help you not give up on doing good or give in to doing bad.

That's some pretty good advice!

THINK Write down something you want to say to God for each tip that Jesus has given you, and then pray – go for it!

TREASURE

READ: Matthew 6:19–21

KEY VERSE: 'For where your treasure is, there your heart will be also' (v21)

The 'big cheeses' in Israel had land, servants, big houses, fields full of animals, and the top seats in the synagogue. And some of the disciples wanted that life, especially if Jesus were to become king of Israel. But Jesus had other ideas.

If you want to be better off, don't put all your effort into spending money to make you feel important, put your effort into God's plans. Looks fade, metal rusts and even the latest, greatest gadgets won't fit the sockets in heaven.

Jesus didn't care much about owning a house, driving a fast car or dressing in designer labels. He lived simply and was able to meet people and help them. Jesus went where God wanted Him – doing what God asked of Him. He was deliberately different – out to give, not out to get.

Those who are all-out givers show God's love to those around them. In the eyes of our Father in heaven, that's what really makes someone rich.

PRAY Father God, I don't want my life to just be about stuff. You're way more important to me than things. Help me to value what You value and use what I have to help other people. Amen.

DELIBERATELY DIFFERENT

WHAT YOU LOOKING AT?

READ: Matthew 6:22–23

KEY VERSE: 'The eye is the lamp of the body. If your eyes are healthy, your whole body will be full of light.' (v22)

It's a good idea to be careful with what stuff we put into our brains – once it's in there, it's hard to get it out. Once you've seen something, you can't un-see it. Our world today seems obsessed with seeing it all, doing it all, experiencing it all – but that's not always a good thing.

Have a think about the sorts of TV programmes and movies you watch. If Jesus sat down beside you on the sofa, would you quickly reach for the remote and change the channel? Jesus doesn't want to be a kill-joy, but He is interested in keeping you full of light, not darkness. So, when we do see things that are not good for us, we need to save our eyes and look the other way.

We read in verse 22 that by keeping our eyes clean, we take care of our whole body. That's how much what we see can affect us! Knowing that, what are you more interested in looking at – the light stuff, or the dark stuff?

PRAY Lord God, please protect my eyes from seeing things that would cause me harm. Help my life to be full of Your light. Amen.

MONEY TALKS

READ: Matthew 6:24

KEY VERSE: 'You cannot serve both God and Money.' (v24)

Take a look at that verse again. Notice anything weird? God has a capital 'G', and money has a capital 'M'. Is this a mistake? Is someone going to get fired for this? Actually, no. Money has a capital 'M' because we give it far too much importance in our lives.

Money is important – we use it to buy the things we need. Jesus wasn't saying money is evil, but it's how we see money that is the problem. Money is at the centre of the world for many people.

Jesus warned that you can't give money the big 'M' treatment and still give God the big 'G' in your life. Only one can be boss. You can't be ruled by both.

Big 'M' shouts, 'Get, get, get!' God says, 'Give, give, give!' Who do you listen to?

Those who follow God give money a small 'm'. It's for their needs, but it's not what they dream of. Being generous is God's way. When He is in control, we become givers, not grabbers. So don't aim to get noticed by the change in your pocket but the change in your life!

THINK **Have you ever given money, even a small amount, to your church or a charity? Is this something you might consider doing?**

DELIBERATELY DIFFERENT

NO WORRIES

READ: Matthew 6:25–34

KEY VERSE: 'But seek first his kingdom and his righteousness, and all these things will be given to you as well.' (v33)

Do you worry about the future? You're not the only one who has felt a bit wobbly about this – even the disciples were worried about what would happen to them.

But Jesus has got it all under control! To fear about our future is a waste of time and energy. It's all in God's hands and He has promised to provide for all our needs. He's got 10/10 marks in keeping His promises – so what's there to get wound up about?

Today's reading is a great reminder of this if we're ever freaking out about the things the future holds. Birds don't get stressed over all they've got to do. They wake up singing, knowing their creator will give them what they need. Of course make plans, but ask God His opinion too. Work hard and have motivation, but don't panic about the small things. Look after your money, but don't love it. Jesus said it Himself – 'do not worry about your life' (v25). A good challenge, right?

PRAY

Lord Jesus, I know that I can trust You with my future. Thank You that You have a plan for my life. Help me to make my plans with You. Amen.

DON'T BE A PLANK

READ: Matthew 7:1–12

KEY VERSE: 'Do not judge, or you too will be judged.' (v1)

We have all messed up. All of us. But Jesus was very clear on something: we're all in the same boat, but we're loved.

As Christians, we want to be good. But sometimes, being 'good' becomes more important to us than loving other people. We start to compare ourselves to other people and look down our noses on people who are 'worse' than we are. We've all done it, and sometimes we might even enjoy watching something go wrong for someone because of what they've done.

But this attitude was never something that Jesus wanted for us. Our job isn't to pick out the bad things that other have done, but to sort out the bad things that we do. This is what Jesus is on about when He tells us not to point out specks of dust in other people's eyes where we have a gigantic plank in our own! It's not a good idea to embarrass people, but it's a great idea to show them Jesus. So leave the judging up to God, and get on with your job – loving.

THINK Is there something that one of your friends does that really bothers you? Could God be using this to show you how your attitude should change?

DELIBERATELY DIFFERENT

THE SCENIC ROUTE

READ: Matthew 7:13–14

KEY VERSE: 'But small is the gate and narrow the road that leads to life' (v14)

Living life for Jesus is all about *not* taking the easy option. It can be tough, but it's totally worth it.

Jesus uses the analogy of the wide road and the narrow road. The world will tell you that the best way to have an easy life will be to have pretty much nothing to do with God or His rules, or His ideas about loving people, sharing our money, etc. That's the wide road. Looking out for number one. Everyone is going in the same direction, so you'll fit right in. But where does that road lead? Nowhere good.

As Christians, we're told to take the off-road track – the slightly less appealing road that might offer a bumpier ride. The narrow way isn't for the narrow-minded but is for the brave – those prepared to trust Jesus, not the crowd. This road leads to life to the full with God, now and forever!

Don't be tempted to go along with the crowd, just because it's popular. Go Jesus' way instead.

PRAY Lord Jesus, I know that following You isn't always easy, but I know that You are with me every step of the way. Help me not to take the easy way in life, but to go Your way, always. Amen.

FIVE A DAY

READ: Matthew 7:15–23

KEY VERSE: 'by their fruit you will recognise them' (v20)

When Jesus talks about producing 'fruit', He's talking about what we produce in our lives; what grows as a result of how we live.

Think of yourself as a tree. If your roots are selfish, you'll branch out into all kinds of selfish behaviour. A tree like that might look nice, but the fruit it produces will taste gross. But those who know Jesus grow like Jesus – when they listen to Him and do what He says. Good fruit only grows when we allow the Holy Spirit to influence our lives. Becoming a Christian doesn't turn us into super saints overnight. But the more we allow God to get rid of the old and bring in the new, the more we'll notice we're different.

Later on in the Bible, we're given a list of what good 'fruit' looks like: love, joy, peace, patience, kindness, goodness, faithfulness, gentleness and self-control (see Gal. 5:22–23). We can't grow all of that on our own – that's why it's called fruit of the Spirit. Why not ask God to plant those seeds in you today?

PRAY Father God, You are so kind and generous. Please grow Your good fruit in me. I want to be more like You! Amen.

DELIBERATELY DIFFERENT

FOUNDATIONS

READ: Matthew 7:24–28

KEY VERSE: 'everyone who hears these words of mine and puts them into practice is like a wise man who built his house on the rock' (v24)

Jesus finished off His incredible mountaintop talk with a pretty important point about foundations. Remember this one? If you want your house to be built to last, you've got to dig deep for a strong foundation. The quality of the foundation is what decides if the house will stay up in stormy weather or not.

Jesus described two builders. One built his home on the sand that got washed away with the tide. The other guy chose a rock-solid foundation. We can choose what we build our lives upon. It can be on things that change and don't last, or on God's Word. And if we choose God's Word, we've got something that will last.

God calls us to live differently to the rest of the world. This isn't easy! But if the Bible is our foundation for life, with God's help we can go for it! Spending time with God and getting to know who He is will inspire us to live differently.

THINK How much time do you spend with Jesus every day? Are you happy with that amount, or do you want longer?

HE IS!

READ: Psalm 100:1-5

KEY VERSE: 'Know that the LORD is God.' (v3)

How do you do in quizzes? Are you good with your facts? The questions that get asked in quizzes can be on absolutely anything! But it's when we're challenged that we realise we know quite a lot more than we thought we did – including quite a lot of random stuff!

Here's a fact that isn't random at all – it's really important for us to know: 'The LORD is God.' He's the one who made us, and so 'we are his' (v3). Wow! We *belong* to God. Have you ever thought about it like that?

There is no one higher than God. Not one person. No one can measure up to Him. He's over everything, and we belong to Him! God is king, you are His son. That changes everything.

When you go through a difficult time, knowing who God is makes such a difference. He's in charge, He's the highest, greatest, most-powerful, and He absolutely adores YOU! With that in mind, bad times don't seem as overwhelming – we've got God on our side!

So be confident in who God is, and what that means for you today.

PRAY Father, I praise You and recognise You as my God. Thank You for making me Your son, it is such a privilege! Amen.

PSALM

FOREVER

READ: Psalm 110:1–7

KEY VERSE: 'The LORD has sworn and will not change his mind: "You are a priest for ever, in the order of Melchizedek."' (v4)

Psalm 110 may have been sung when a new king of Israel was crowned. These kings were in the family line of King David, who God had promised a special relationship with. They would be known as His sons and He would be known as their Father.

The ordinary kings never had the kind of power that this psalm sings about. When people realised that God had brought Jesus back to life, they knew that this psalm was actually about Him.

Jesus is called the Son of God in the New Testament. He is the King. Of course, once Jesus rose from the dead everyone realised that He was no ordinary king of Israel – He is the King who rules forever!

As Christians, we need to remember that it's important for us to enjoy Jesus and celebrating who He is, just like this psalm did. Enjoy singing songs to, and about, Jesus. Enjoy trusting Him. Enjoy letting Him use your life to change the world!

THINK
Could you make a little change today to enjoy some time with Jesus, your King?

PSALM

I'LL BE BACK!

READ: Acts 1:1–11

KEY VERSE: 'This same Jesus, who has been taken from you into heaven, will come back in the same way you have seen him go into heaven.' (v11)

Have you ever had to say goodbye to a friend or family member, knowing you won't see them again for a very long time? It can be really tough to do this, and we might wonder if we will still have a close relationship with that person. Forty days after Jesus had risen from the dead, He left the disciples to return to heaven. The disciples were keen to know what was going to happen next. Was He leaving for good? What would they do without Him?

As the disciples watched Jesus lift off to heaven, they were told by two angels that Jesus would come back one day. Wow! The angels couldn't say when (they didn't know), but a date and time had been set. And in the meantime, the Holy Spirit was going to be with them, actually living in them.

THINK **Did you know that Jesus will come back to earth one day? Every day we get one day closer to His return. What would your reaction be like if Jesus came back today?**

FAST FORWARD

WHAT A DIFFERENCE

READ: Revelation 1:12–18

> **KEY VERSE:** 'Do not be afraid. I am the First and the Last. I am the Living One; I was dead, and now look, I am alive for ever and ever!' (vv17–18)

John was the only disciple who stuck around to see Jesus being crucified. Years later, God gave him an amazing glimpse of Jesus in heaven. Just look at the difference between Jesus our crucified Saviour, and Jesus our risen Lord...

At the cross, Jesus' face was bruised, He wore a crown of thorns on top of His bloodstained hair, His eyes were swollen, He was silent. His clothes were taken and shared among the soldiers, He was stabbed in His side with a spear, He was given a staff so that people would laugh at Him, His feet were nailed to the cross.

Now in heaven, His face is shining like the sun, His hair is white like wool and snow, His eyes are like blazing fire, He speaks loudly, He wears a royal robe and a gold sash worn by high priests. He is the King of power and is pictured with a sword coming out of His mouth, He holds stars in His hands, His feet are now like bronze.

Our future is safe with Him.

PRAY Jesus, You really are amazing. I put my trust and my future in Your hands. Amen.

ON THE THRONE

READ: Revelation 4:1–11

KEY VERSE: 'You are worthy, our Lord and God, to receive glory and honour and power' (v11)

What's the nicest house you've ever seen? Maybe it has a pool? A massive TV? A fridge filled to the brim? Well, it's got nothing on what we're about to see...

Let's look into the future with another of John's visions. This time it's a guided tour of God's headquarters.

This is some throne room. There's every colour you've ever seen. Then – thunder! Lightning! This is awesome! As we look closer, we see someone there – almighty God! He appears to glisten light like a diamond. Wow! Just wow! This whole scene is fantastically majestic.

Around the throne, representatives from the 12 ancient tribes of Israel, and the 12 apostles take off their golden crowns and worship God. They've been awarded crowns because of how they've stuck by God, but they know that it is only God that deserves to be worshipped.

One thing's for sure, God reigns and always will do! He sits on the throne of heaven and is absolutely glorious.

THINK Imagine there's a throne in your heart. Does God have the top spot? Or do you need to knock something or someone else off that seat so God can sit at His rightful place?

FAST FORWARD

LION AND LAMB

READ: Revelation 5:1–14

KEY VERSE: 'Worthy is the Lamb, who was slain, to receive power and wealth and wisdom and strength and honour and glory and praise!'

So why all this fuss about a scroll? We're not told what it is – but John was crying was because there didn't appear to be anyone in heaven worthy enough to open it. And that wasn't good.

Just at that moment, Jesus breaks into the scene. As a lion – powerful and strong – He has won and is able to carry out the task. How is this possible?

The clue was right before John's eyes. Jesus had been introduced as a lion, but appeared as a lamb. In Old Testament times, God's agreement with humans was that a lamb could be sacrificed to take the punishment for their sin. Jesus came to earth as 'the Lamb of God' to offer Himself as a once-and-for-all-time sacrifice. No one else could do that.

The 24 elders then got the harps out and started singing about Jesus. Then a ginormous choir of angels burst in to join the praise party. Following that, they were joined by every creature in heaven and on earth. Who's worthy of such worship? Only Jesus!

PRAY Jesus, lion and lamb, thank You so much for making me part of God's family. You are worthy of my worship – forever. Amen.

LOUD

READ: 1 Thessalonians 4:13–18

KEY VERSE: 'the Lord himself will come down from heaven… and the dead in Christ will rise' (v16)

Let's fast forward to a great event still to take place – Jesus returning to earth. A secret date and time is set. Some people claim to know when this will happen but the truth is that no one knows when Jesus will arrive.

Here's what we do know: it won't be a small event, it's going to be massive. We'll hear Him first. There'll be a loud sound. Loud enough to raise the dead, which is just what will happen!

That was great news for the people receiving this letter. They'd been wondering what will happen to Christians who die before Jesus comes back. Paul reminded them that God has the power over death! And when Jesus returns, God's people who are dead will be the first to go and join Him. No, we're not going to be running away from real-life zombies, the people will be made alive and given new bodies – instantly!

Even the Christians living when Jesus returns will also be transformed with new bodies. And they will join the others with Jesus, forever!

THINK Are you a loud Christian? Loud doesn't need to mean that you're a shouter, but that you're happy to let people know what you believe.

FAST FORWARD

SURPRISE

READ: Matthew 24:36–44

> **KEY VERSE:** 'So you also must be ready, because the Son of Man will come at an hour when you do not expect him.' (v44)

How mad is it that Jesus could return at any time? Technically, He could come back before you even finish reading this! So it's best we get prepared for it.

When God said that He would be sending a flood, bad enough to drown the entire earth, no one listened. They carried on their ways of ignoring God. Noah, however, spent his life getting ready for the flood, and managed to escape it in the ark.

Although Jesus has promised to return and is giving the world time to turn to Him and ask for His forgiveness, most people live their lives not caring about God. As Christians, we have the exciting, scary, brilliant and important task of telling people about Jesus. People will be shocked when He returns and it may be too late for them to join Him. So let's make it our job to 'ruin the surprise' and give people a chance to get to know Jesus and be saved!

THINK Think of one person you know who doesn't know Jesus. Pray for them, asking God to show Himself to them. Then try and bring up the topic of Jesus with them this week. Go for it!

TIME

READ: 2 Peter 3:3–10

> **KEY VERSE:** 'The Lord is not slow in keeping his promise... Instead he is patient with you, not wanting anyone to perish, but everyone to come to repentance.' (v9)

Peter says that our planet has a sell-by date. It won't last forever, it's on its way out. And Peter wasn't the first to learn this. God told Isaiah, 700 years earlier, that He would create new heavens and a new earth. The new earth will be so absolutely awesome that we won't even think about our current earth. You might be thinking about all the unlimited food there may be, but on this new earth, there's an even better feature: no tears or sadness, only joy.

God's plan is to put an end to death. Yes — death itself will be destroyed. God will raise us from the dead and we will live with Him on a new and awesome earth forever.

But Jesus is taking His time returning to earth for a very good reason (v9). He wants to give people the chance to turn to Him for forgiveness. The seconds are ticking away, and in every moment we have before the big event, Jesus is desperate for people to meet Him.

PRAY

God, thank You for being patient with us. Please help me to tell the people around me about You and Your forgiveness. Amen.

FAST FORWARD

WRITTEN IN THE BOOK

READ: Revelation 20:11–15

KEY VERSE: 'Another book was opened, which is the book of life.' (v12)

Do 'good' people go to heaven, and 'bad' people go to hell? Lots of people think that. But the truth is it's all down to Jesus and His book.

You see, there are two books that we're told about. Daniel had a vision of the Book of Judgment (Dan. 7:10). This books records all the things that anyone who has ever lived has done, and is the 'guilty' book. That's a scary thought, isn't it? The incredible news is that anyone who trusts in Jesus has their record rubbed out! It's like it was never there. But those who haven't trusted Jesus still have their records and face spending eternity without Him.

Then there's the Book of Life. Anyone listed in this is seen as 'not guilty'. How does a person get their name written in this book? By choosing to follow Jesus. Those in this book get a free pass to heaven to spend eternity with their Saviour, Jesus. Have you decided to follow Jesus? If you want to, pray the prayer below:

PRAY
Lord Jesus, I'm sorry for the things I've done wrong. I choose to turn away from living selfishly and follow You instead. Thank You for dying for me and rising again. Be welcome in my heart. Amen.

STAMP OUT

READ: 1 Corinthians 15:24–28

KEY VERSE: 'For he "has put everything under his feet".' (v27)

Have you ever supported or been a part of a team that's losing? It's rubbish, isn't it? Some people seem to react OK to this, while some throw tantrums that could rival a toddler's!

Here's a fact: Jesus will have the ultimate victory in the end, and we are on His team. To show how Jesus is 'on top' of everything, we're given a picture of Jesus having everything 'under His feet'. Jesus will stamp out His enemies. They will be flattened. But who are they?

Enemy number one is the devil. He's the main one. He tempts us, lies to us and tries to get us to ignore God. He's a defeated evil loser who's still causing trouble. But he'll be put to an end completely one day, and all the evil that he's caused will be squashed to pulp then too. The second and last enemy to be flattened is death. Jesus will do away with death, pain, sadness and grief – that's amazing news!

Jesus is the ultimate winner. Isn't it great to know you're on the ultimate winning side forever?

THINK **Do you sometimes let things get on top of you? Remember whose side you're on. With Jesus you're on top! There's nothing too big for Him to handle.**

FAST FORWARD

NEW EVERYTHING

READ: Revelation 21:1–7

KEY VERSE: 'He who was seated on the throne said, "I am making everything new!"' (v5)

Heaven. What will it be like? Well… new, new and more new. As sin damaged and diseased all of God's creation, it will be binned and replaced with a new creation. Just listen to this: if anyone is in Christ, the new creation has come: the old has gone, the new is here!' (2 Cor. 5:17).

Jesus became a real human being — the kind of human being that God wants us to be. We can't be like that by just working hard, but by allowing God to work in us. And one day, if we believe and trust in Jesus as King, God will completely recreate us to be like Him.

In God's new heaven, we will be His people and He will be our God. He'll care for us in every way. All the hurt and pain of our old lives will be history. We'll never experience sadness, pain, fear, anger or death again. And the great thing is that God isn't offering us this five-star accommodation for a weekend getaway. We'll enjoy it forever!

THINK **Write down a list of things you think might be included in the new creation, both for you personally and for the world, eg no more arguments, everyone has enough to eat…**

WHEN?

READ: Mark 13:1–8

KEY VERSE: 'Tell us, when will these things happen? And what will be the sign that they are all about to be fulfilled?' (v4)

No one but God knows the date and time when Jesus will return. If anyone ever claims to know the date, they're lying. But Jesus did gave some clues.

There have been wars throughout history, but from what Jesus said it appears that the world He surprises will be a very unfriendly place. Because of greed, wars and natural disasters, many will starve or become ill.

Jesus also warned that people would pretend to be Him and that many would believe them. Today, there have already been con men trying to fool people into believing they are Jesus, persuading people to become their followers.

Things on earth will get tough before Jesus returns, but remember, there's new life on the way! In fact, Jesus describes it as a woman being in labour – the pain is worthwhile because something amazing is about to happen. Difficulties won't last forever. God is in control and our future is safe with Him.

PRAY
God, however tough things get, I believe that You're still in charge. Thank You for having the future planned out. Please help me with the tough situations I face today. Amen.

FAST FORWARD

POPULARITY

READ: Mark 13:9–13

KEY VERSE: 'Everyone will hate you because of me, but the one who stands firm to the end will be saved.' (v13)

Do you ever feel like you put on a bit of an act to make people like you more? We all need to be loved, and sometimes we can see being popular as a way of getting a kind of love. No one wants to be hated, and no one wants to be hated by everyone!

The problem is that following Jesus won't always make us popular. That's because we do what God wants. Sometimes that makes people like us – eg helping people or being kind – and that's great. But other times it could make us very unpopular – eg standing up for people who are being picked on, or refusing to lie about something.

Jesus became so unpopular that He was crucified. He knows what it's like for the crowd to turn against someone. But here's the thing: some people crave popularity because they don't know that they are already loved. If we know we're loved by God, the creator of the entire world, then other people's opinions don't matter as much. God loves you more than you can imagine and He thinks you're brilliant!

THINK Do you need some help from God to not let the opinions of others get to you? Talk with Him today about this.

SPRING CLEAN

READ: 2 Peter 3:10–18

KEY VERSE: 'make every effort to be found spotless, blameless and at peace with him' (v14)

Does your family like to make sure that the house is spotless when visitors are coming around? That's what Jesus wants our lives to be like when He suddenly shows up. That's why it's important to have a catch-up with God every day for a little spring cleaning.

It's so important to be good friends with God. Living His way is the best way, and part of that means saying sorry if we go off on the wrong track. 'Hiding' from God because we know we've done something He wouldn't be pleased with doesn't do any good – and actually means we'll miss out on loads of fun with Him. Instead, let's own up to our mistakes, ask for His forgiveness and move on. That way, if Jesus does surprise the world in our lifetimes, we won't be embarrassed – we'll be over the moon!

PRAY Jesus, thank You that You are the way to God and heaven, and You forgive me. Help me to come to You, not hide from You, when I mess up. I want to always be open with You. Amen.

FAST FORWARD

COMING SOON

READ: Revelation 22:12–21

KEY VERSE: 'Yes, I am coming soon.' (v20)

Coming soon to a cloud near you – Jesus! He's coming back to earth and it could be any moment now...! Or now! Or... even now!

What we do today is important. Our choices affect our future in one way or another. If we choose to put things off like going to bed on time, we might feel very tired the next day.

So how do we live the best life we can? With Jesus, of course! As we read today, Jesus offers us 'the free gift of the water of life' (v17). The Holy Spirit living in us gives us all we need. Without God, we are 'thirsty'. That's not to say that our friends who aren't Christians are all at risk of dying from dehydration. What it means is that something is missing. People try to quench that thirst for God with things like friends, fame, money, popularity – but nothing works. Because we need God, who is the 'living water', to quench that thirst forever.

True, life-changing happiness is being made clean by Jesus and having Him in our lives now and forever.

THINK **Are you excited about the day that Jesus comes back to earth? If you are a follower of Jesus, this is something to look forward to.**

EVERYBODY NOW!

READ: Psalm 150:1–6

KEY VERSE: 'Let everything that has breath praise the LORD.' (v6)

We've reached our last day of *One You, One Year*! What an awesome time it's been! Well done for sticking it out. It's time to celebrate all that God's done in your life, and today's psalm is a party starter!

It's good to be quiet to listen to God. It's very good to read the Bible and find out about Him. It's also great to talk straight to God about your life.

BUT... sometimes the very best thing we can do – and the thing we need to do the most – is join in with the rest of the universe and praise God with everything we've got.

You can jump around, shout your head off, laugh, sing, beat the life out of a drum kit, wave your arms around, rip up a guitar solo, spit some bars or even blow a trumpet! God will be praised, and if we don't do it, someone else will.

It's a MASSIVE privilege to praise God. It brings us closer to Him, and it makes the problems we face seem tiny compared to Him.

God's the greatest! Make the most of every opportunity to praise Him.

THINK Think about what you are grateful to God for doing in your journey through *One You, One Year*. Now give Him all the praise!

PSALM

GET EXCITED ABOUT THE BIBLE, EVERY DAY!

Want to understand the Bible more?

The reading curriculum for *One You, One Year* is adapted from various issues of *YP's*, daily Bible reading notes for ages 11–14.

YP's is packed full of amazing insights into what the Bible actually says, and what it means to live every day for God. Stay in the daily rhythm you're in and order your *YP's* today. It couldn't be easier!

Published every two months.
Available as individual copies or a one-year subscription.

Check it out and buy at cwr.org.uk/youth
Also available from Christian bookshops.

YOUR FRIENDS AND FAMILY ARE UNIQUE AND IMPORTANT TOO!

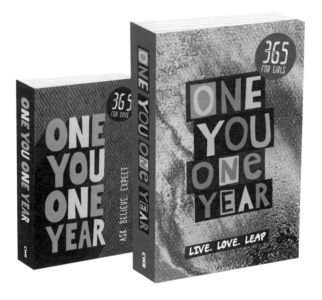

The Bible has got so much to say about who God is and who we are, and this is the stuff we all really need to hear. To help your friends and family, we've picked out a year's worth of great topics for both boys and girls your age.

Check them out and buy at cwr.org.uk/youth
Also available from Christian bookshops.

MORE GREAT STUFF TO READ...

YP's Guide to the Bible

Want to get stuck into the Bible but don't know where to start? Well, this one's for you! Helpful definitions, timelines, guides to every book in the Bible, and much more.

Guide to Knowing God

See how what you believe about God really does affect your life. This guide will help you to think bigger than ever before – and you'll have fun along the way!

YP's Guide to Starting Secondary School

Starting secondary school can be a bit overwhelming... but help is at hand. This little book is full of useful advice, puzzles, questionnaires and reminders that God is always with you.

YP's for New Christians

Being a Christian sounds great, but what exactly does it involve? In just 30 days you can find out how completely mind-blowing life with God can be.

Check these all out and buy at **cwr.org.uk/youth**
Also available from Christian bookshops.